RECONSTRUCTING POP/SUBCULTURE

RECONSTRUCTING POP/SUBCULTURE

ART, ROCK, AND ANDY WARHOL

VAN M. CAGLE

SAGE Publications
International Educational and Professional Publisher
Thousand Oaks London New Delhi

For information address:

SAGE Publications, Inc.
2455 Teller Road
Thousand Oaks, California 91320

SAGE Publications Ltd.
6 Bonhill Street
London EC2A 4PU
United Kingdom

SAGE Publications India Pvt. Ltd.
M-32 Market
Greater Kailash I
New Delhi 110 048 India

Printed in the United States of America

Library of Congress Cataloging-in-Publication Data

Cagle, Van M.
Reconstructing pop/subculture : Art, rock, and Andy Warhol / Van M. Cagle.
p. cm.
Includes bibliographical references and index.
ISBN 0-8039-5743-2 (alk. paper) — ISBN 0-8039-5744-0 (alk. paper : pbk.)
1. Art and music. 2. Rock music—History and criticism.
3. Warhol, Andy, 1928– . I. Title.
ML85.C34 1995
306.4′7—dc20 94-48049

This book is printed on acid-free paper.

95 96 97 98 99 10 9 8 7 6 5 4 3 2 1

Production Editor: Yvonne Könneker
Copy Editor: Linda Gray
Typesetter: Christina Hill

Contents

Acknowledgments

The author gratefully acknowledges the following for permission to reprint within this book:

Creem Magazine, for extracts from the following: "Get Down and Get With It—Or the White Meanies Will Get You," "Iggy in Exile: Love in the Fire Zone," "New York Dolls: Luv 'Em or Leave 'Em," "1969 . . . the Stooges," "Purging the Zombatized Void With Alice Cooper," "What's the Ugliest Part of Your Body?"; "Alice Cooper: Punch and Judy Play the Toilets," "Alice Cooper All American," "Dead Lie the Velvets Underground" by Lester Bangs; "The Dolls Greatest Hits Vol. I" by Ben Edmunds; "The New York Dolls in L.A." and "Alice Cooper Did Not Invent Glitter" by Lisa Robinson.

EMI Music Publishing, for lyrics from "All the Young Dudes" by David Bowie.

Fiz, for extracts from "Glitter Goddess of the Sunset Strip" by Fran Miller, March/April 1993.

Harcourt Brace & Company, for extracts from *Popism: The Warhol '60's* by Andy Warhol and Pat Hackett, copyright © 1980 by Andy Warhol, reprinted by permission of Harcourt Brace & Company.

Lance Loud, for extracts from his article "Rock Autopsy" in *Rock Sane,* March 1975.

LWT, for material from "The Snow Bank Show," produced and directed by Kim Evans, 1987.

Melody Maker, for extracts from the following: "Caught in the Act" by Chris Charlesworth; "American Music," "Can David Bowie Save New York From Boredom?", "The Pop Establishment," and "You Wanna Play House With the Dolls?" by Roy Hollingsworth; "Horizon" and "Roxy Music: Sound of Surprise" by Richard Williams; "A Star is Born" by Ray Coleman; "Oh You Pretty Thing" and "Meet Rodney Bingenheimer, Friend of the Stars" by Michael Watts; "Alice's Moving Performance" by Chris Welch.

Methuen, for extracts from *Subculture: The Meaning of Style,* by Dicl Hebdige, 1979.

Polygram Records, for material from the Mercury/Polygram album *New York Dolls Double Reissue.*

Straight Arrow Publishers, for extracts from the following: "Alice Cooper" in the *Alice Cooper Scrapbook,* by Robert Christgau; "Ground Control to Davy Jones" in *Rolling Stone,* by Cameron Crowe; "Inside Alice" in the *Alice Cooper Scrapbook,* by Harry Swift; "Introduction" in the *Alice Cooper Scrapbook,* by David Marsh; "Lou Reed" in *Rolling Stone,* by Stephen Holden, "Random Notes" in *Rolling Stone;* and "Where Are the Chickens Alice?" in *Rolling Stone,* by Elaine Gross.

Introduction

During the month of January 1966, pop artist Andy Warhol was invited to lecture at the annual banquet of the New York Society for Clinical Psychiatry. In an unconventional gesture, Warhol suggested that several of his movies should provide the "speech," and he would simply be on hand to offer explanations and answer questions.[1] The banquet director agreed that such an informal approach might interest the psychiatrists—just the encouragement Warhol craved to willfully take advantage of those attending the black-tie event.

On the evening of the dinner, just as the second course was in progress, the lectern curtain slowly parted. There on center stage stood Andy's newly acquired rock and roll protégés, the leather-clad Velvet Underground, who proceeded to break decibel levels with amplified guitar feedback and droning as well as monotonous vocals. Directly on the fringe of stage left, Warhol's assistant, Gerard Malanga, engaged in his notorious "whip dance" while, nearby, participant Edie Sedgwick flailed her arms frenetically as her hips "fruged" go-go style. As the proceedings continued, Warhol dispensed with the idea of projecting his films; instead, he had decided to transform the event into a film project. Thus, in an act of further disruption, avant-gardists Barbara Rubin and Jonas Mekas shuffled lights and handheld movie cameras into the room and, moving from table to table, posed blatant sexual questions to both the doctors and their spouses and dates. Within minutes, the once calmly orchestrated "banquet" had erupted into a chaotic media psycho-event. As if the hotel's fire alarm had just sounded, the attendees pushed one another through exit doors, completely baffled by what they perceived to be a profane confrontation. Amid the confusion stood the quiet yet omnipresent Warhol, keenly aware that he had instigated a multimedia pop art/shock rock spectacle. Of the evening's proceedings, Warhol stated:

> The next day there were long write-ups about the banquet in the *Tribune* and the *Times*: "Shock Treatment for Psychiatrists" and "Syndromes Pop at Delmonicos." It couldn't have happened to a better group of people. (Warhol and Hackett 147-48)

Precisely six years later, a rising young London singer and musician had become philosophically enveloped in Warhol's approach to media manipulation and montage. On January 19, 1972, David Jones, aka David Bowie, was on the verge of customizing his own alter ego "Ziggy Stardust," a bisexual "alien invader" with a message that would guide the barometers of glitter rock and punk in the 1970s: apocalyptic nihilism. In an unprecedented attempt to guarantee the attention of the rock press, Bowie/Ziggy arrived for an interview with *Melody Maker's* Michael Watts in what was to become postmortem 1960s attire: a blinding crimson satin jacket, tight polka-dot pants, red plastic shoes, bracelets, space makeup, and hair cropped short and dyed orange. During the course of the interview—originally intended to result in a brief mid-section story—Bowie first described his sexual orientation as "gay," then, "bisexual . . . if you really want to know." Consequently in the January 22, 1972 issue of *Melody Maker*, Bowie, as "Ziggy," was presented as front-page news. The effect was immediate, and within months "Ziggy Stardust and the Spiders from Mars" had cast their spell on unsuspecting audiences in both the United States and Great Britain. By the end of the year, the most familiar catchphrase among Bowie's newly found fans was proudly proclaimed across promotional T-shirts: "David Bowie Is Ziggy Stardust / Ziggy Stardust Is God."

These anecdotes are cited because each represent—on a number of interrelated levels—specific forms of dissent and "disruption" within normative structures of communication and mass mediation. In both cases, we find a double-edged sense of irony, metaphorical quotes within quotes, and riddle-like dilemmas that are amusing on the surface yet, underneath, decidedly (and deadly) serious.

At the broadest level, we can begin to comprehend the most striking of these ironies and inlaid quotes by considering one fundamental idea that was apparent in the majority of work produced by Andy Warhol and David Bowie. Both artists selected and used "raw materials" from a variety of popular sources, and in so doing, they transformed the contextual meanings commonly associated with those sources. Specifically, Warhol's pop art projects—at different times and in varying degrees—"raided" the world of consumer culture (Coke bottles, Brillo boxes), thereby provoking critical debates that focused on the *reasons* we should (or should not) contemplate the aesthetics of popular commercial objects. Likewise, many of Warhol's films translated the boredom of everyday life (sleeping, getting a haircut) into something worthy of our critical observation. In a similar manner, the Warhol/Velvet Underground collaborations both celebrated and attacked the aural and visual structures of meaning that had come to define the boundaries of popular rock and roll in the mid-1960s, thus offering a series of projects in which rock and roll materiality provided a resource for the recontextualization of some of rock's most common tenets.

In a comparable manner, David Bowie altered the very nature of rock and roll representation in the early 1970s by swirling together certain aesthetic premises from Warhol's Factory "underground" with lessons he had learned from Antonin Artaud and Lindsay Kemp. Like Warhol and his collaborators, Bowie laid to waste many preordained assumptions concerning the relation between music and visual presentation while (re)constructing methods by which to fuse a whole series of popular forms: Broadway theater, rock and roll (as art and artifice), and the more avant-garde formats associated with experimental literature and theatricality. At the same time, he integrated into popular music unorthodox claims regarding sexuality, ones that eventually became central to the entirety of "glitter rock." In all of the ways indicated above, Bowie disrupted what it meant to perform in a rock and roll context during the early 1970s, what it meant to be gay or bisexual[2] and in the disharmonious "center field" of popular culture, and what it meant to coil discordant images together while recasting the essence of these images into a new and dramatic youth symbol: glitter rock.

What becomes particularly significant is the manner in which Warhol and Bowie repeatedly applied their aesthetic ideas to a number of taken-for-granted situations, such as the lecture and the interview. As the opening anecdotes suggest, such situations served as integral sites through which the chaotic aesthetics of pop (as art and as lifestyle) could receive an inordinate amount of public attention through mass media. Thus, in Bowie and Warhol's terms, the media were *never* to be taken at face value; the media's most revered forms (the interview, the gossip column, the feature story) were points for strategic intervention. These were the passageways that both Bowie and Warhol fully exploited: playing up the notion of a "speaker" by not being one, suggesting the "stupidity" of pop art by never commenting on it, undermining the formality of the interview itself by professing one's sexual "secrets," arriving at an interview as Ziggy Stardust. In all of these cases, and in many more to be presented in this book, the artists under consideration represented a new breed of aesthetic arbiters of the 1960s and 1970s, using the media directly as a channel for expressing their most "insidious," and subsequently, their most lethal, artistic ideas and arguments. In turn, those audiences who were attuned to the intonations of Bowie and Warhol, became keenly aware of the orderly relation between the aesthetics of pop art/glitter rock and the "manipulative" methods these artists used in "translating" their aesthetic principles. In this sense, the media became yet another canvas, one that had to be watched closely by the adherents of pop art and glitter rock, for they were indeed the ones most likely to get the punch line. They were the ones who celebrated the very notion of double entendres. In this sense, pop art and glitter rock were underlined with the notion that popular culture did not always consist of totally accessible forms of leisure entertainment. The surfaces may have seemed easy, but the foundations were constructed from the perspectives of two rather crafty cultural politicians. Locating and illuminating the "easy" yet contradictorily "difficult" nature of the surfaces and foundations of pop art and glitter rock is the primary goal of this book.

Pop as "Pop": Some Anecdotal Elaborations

To return specifically to my original anecdotes, let's evaluate Warhol's interventionist tactics at the Delmonico, and ask, Why was he invited to present *his* films within the context of an "intellectual" event? The majority of such films consisted of simply made, grainy black and white pseudodocumentaries in which Warhol's Factory "superstars" and friends posed before a static camera for lengthy durations. Add to the thematic tone of the films one of Warhol's most repeated maxims concerning pop art: "It doesn't *mean* anything." Therefore, the assumption that Warhol's films could "speak for him" seems ludicrous at best.

This assumption becomes doubly amusing when set against the background of Warhol's highly publicized television, radio, and magazine interviews. Typically, his responses to any number of questions veered between "no," "yes," and "I don't know." In fact, in an infamous live interview with Henry Geldzahler, Warhol answered "no," even if the response was inappropriate. So, the notion that Warhol would provide explanations (or answer questions) is without basis.

Presuming that the psychiatrists had knowledge of Warhol's interactional resistance, one can only speculate that, at least in some sense, the doctors must have been willing to "buy into" Warhol's pop practices. After all, much of New York had already surrendered. By January 1966, Warhol's pop art paintings and silk screens had achieved the status of "haute kitsch," even in the prestigious circles dominated by curators such as Eleanor Ward. In addition, his monomorphic underground films, with all of their lack of intention, had received serious attention at the Cinematheque, where Jonas Mekas awaited each new release with marked anticipation. At the same time, Warhol's "decadent/chic" Factory entourage governed New York party lists and international fashion columns alike. All the while, Warhol quietly professed that the pop mentality was something one must earnestly acquire. In fact, "getting" pop was akin to gaining membership in a secret society. In Warhol's terms, "Once you 'got' pop, you could never see a sign the same way again. And once you *thought* pop you could never see America in the same way again" (Warhol and Hackett 39-40). Along similar lines, during a trip to Los Angeles in 1963, Warhol claimed, "Vacant, vacuous Hollywood was everything I wanted to mold my life into. Plastic. White on white. I wanted to live my life at the level of the script of *The Carpetbaggers*" (Warhol and Hackett 40).

Given these comments, it seems likely that the intellectuals at the Delmonico banquet did not have the same satiric, critical, "insiders" take on pop as Warhol did. Presumably, they desired to simply observe pop in whatever form(s) Warhol offered, thus hoping to come to a clearer understanding of a phenomenon that was rapidly permeating American cultural taste at all levels. At the same time, the psychiatrists probably realized that their perceived "appreciation" of Warhol's pop would confirm their status in the public eye as hipsters, of the intellectual variety, certainly, but hipsters nonetheless. As Andrew Ross suggests,

> This *cordon sanitaire* is evident in categories of intellectual taste like "hip," "camp," "bad," or "sick" taste, and most recently, postmodernist "fun," each of which are described . . . as secure opportunities for intellectuals to sample the emotional charge of popular culture while guaranteeing their immunity

> from its power to constitute social identities that are in some way marked as subordinate. (5)

If the intellectuals at the psychiatric banquet were in fact involved in the time-honored convention of "slumming" as they attempted to assess pop's vitality, the joke was ultimately on them. The punch line involved an apparent inability to conceptualize the often discrete relations between the Velvet's avant-performance rock, Warhol's pop art/films, and the subcultural behaviors that fueled Warhol's 24-hour Factory studio. By January 1966, however, these forms *had* become institutionalized to some degree, as art critics, fashion columnists, and film critics were attempting to locate Warhol's projects within a hierarchy that had theretofore been neatly demarcated by popular art at one end and high art at the other, with experimental art often residing somewhere in between, its placement often depending on a critic's ideological, as well as aesthetic, criteria. At this time, some of the most widely circulated "analyses" of Warhol's art were ones that "appreciated" its "commentary" on (or from within) American culture. Thus a critic like Rainer Crone was prompted to write, "Warhol portrays the condition of society rather than his own aesthetics" (23).

At the same time, there was an implied acknowledgment among both creators at the Factory and some of its close adherents that the authentic marginal aspects of their productions actually required an ironic, shared, and specialized understanding of how pop was often capable of signaling a sense of *refusal.* In this case, Warhol and the Factory participants often appeared to blatantly disregard any accounts that tended toward serious critical appraisal. Such self-effacing approaches seem to make clearer the notion that the most important feature of the Delmonico assault was the forthright suggestion that to acquire a pop mentality, one must be culturally predisposed to the (in)visible, sometimes indecipherable, and always loaded fringes of pop taste. And such taste was not simply consumed with gratuitous pleasure, easily observable and understood as entertainment. Warhol's pop taste had to be "earned" from a particular cultural vantage point. In fact, Warhol's pop practitioners were quick to demarcate the "insiders" from the "outsiders," and in so doing arrive at their own negatively inspired version of bourgeois culture. As Ellen Willis claimed of Warhol's protégés, the Velvet Underground, "Like pop art, which was very much a part of the Velvet's world, it [their music] was anti-art art made by anti-elite elitists" ("Velvet Underground" 74).

Given the disruptive repercussions of the Delmonico offensive, the approach of Warhol's Factory-based subcultural practitioners becomes more understandable. Here, Dick Hebdige's assessment of the power of subcultural pronouncements is particularly relevant, and, even though he was focusing on British youth subcultures, his claim serves as one explanation of the Factory's "assault":

> Spectacular subcultures express forbidden contents (consciousness of class, consciousness of difference) in forbidden forms (transgressions of sartorial and behavioral codes, law breaking, etc.). They are profane articulations and they are often significantly defined as "unnatural." (*Subculture* 91-92)

As Hebdige suggests in *Subculture: The Meaning of Style,* such unnatural and profane representations typically evoke querulous responses.[3] But given the specificity of our Warhol anecdote, one might think that of all mental health professionals, the New York psychiatrists should have—at least in practice—been open-minded when confronted with such self-conscious forms of "irreverent" and "unrefined behavior." Instead, the doctors found themselves in the disconcerting state of maladaptation. The scenario created by Warhol defiantly excluded authoritarian/intellectual rationalizations that might have regarded pop as an ambitious strategy that was laden with pleasurable contradictions. A cultural divide became apparent that night at the Delmonico, and it had to be very evocative and powerful if 300 psychiatrists became fearful of the Factory's superficial yet somber implications.

By way of comparison, we should consider that the "success" of the Delmonico assault subsequently prompted Warhol to produce similar pop media scenarios at East Coast and Midwestern college concert halls, in experimental film theaters, and in New York nightclubs. But entrance into these multimedia "Exploding Plastic Inevitable" experiments had one requirement. Unlike the psychiatrists, audiences had to *really* get pop. And the fabricated, decadent codes of Warhol's multimedia exhibitions implied that participants approach them with a knowing discourse that was satirical and definitely against the grain of austere sensibilities. In other words, at such events, audiences maintained the status of a veritable insiders' club that both applauded and condoned the Factory's subterranean subcultural media montages.

If we compare, then, the psychiatrists' reactions with those of the insiders' clubs, we may begin to see more clearly the often dichotomous relation between the textual nature of Warhol's Factory-based media/art projects and the contextual frameworks that guided the acceptance/rejection of such projects. To reiterate what should now be apparent: Warhol's media montages professed that pop as art had the ability to represent both blatant and hidden contradictions, ones that forthrightly blasphemed the dominant intellectual conception that all of "pop culture" could be securely framed within the confines of 1960s leisure/consumer society. In the case of Andy Warhol, something else was going on, something else indeed.

Warhol, Pop, and the Intellectual Vanguard

Up to this point, I have been discussing the manner in which Warhol's pop practices were represented and interpreted within the framework of several specific locales. Here, I will consider the related question of how Warhol "fit" into a larger, more regimented discussion: the mass culture debate that was taken up by intellectuals just prior to and during Warhol's emergence as a pop painter and filmmaker. Considering this debate will further determine how Warhol's complicated and celebratory pop spectacles might be clarified as cultural reference points that intertwined within a larger academic concern: how to confront the "invasion" of popular culture, and subsequently, how to "explain" Andy Warhol.

To suggest that Warhol's pop art and media spectacles represented contradictory constructs of the popular as art is to dismiss many of the academic claims leveled against popular culture, especially during the middle years of the 20th century. The principal intellectual assertions concerning the popular culture of this time are collected in Rosenberg and White's 1957 anthology *Mass Culture,* which for the most part repudiated all popular artisans and expressions. Although the editors attempted to include "neutralist" arguments (Gilbert Seldes, Max Lerner, David Reisman), it was the (ultraleftist) radicals and archconservatives who constructed the most compelling positions, ones suggesting the conspiratorial nature of mass culture and/or kitsch.

Given the contexts created by the Great War, World War II, and the cold war, it is understandable why conspiracy theories linked popular culture with totalitarianism. Forms of popular culture were treated both literally and metaphorically as invading forces that dominated and homogenized the passive "masses." In this view, high ("correct") culture and the intellectual avant-garde were being replaced by seemingly vulgar, crass representations of the human condition. As Bernard Rosenberg writes,

> There can be no doubt that the mass media present a major threat to man's autonomy. To know that they might also contain some small seeds of freedom only makes a bad situation nearly desperate. No art form, no body of knowledge, no system of ethics is strong enough to withstand vulgarization. (9)

Likewise, one of the most referenced articles in the collection was written by Dwight MacDonald, the socialist scholar who once claimed that Elvis Presley should have no rights in American culture because he was a "common thug" (Greil Marcus lecture). In "A Theory of Mass Culture," MacDonald sarcastically reinforced the classic radical perspective:

> Like nineteenth century capitalism, Mass Culture is a dynamic, revolutionary force, breaking down the old barriers of class, tradition, taste, and dissolving all cultural distinctions. . . . Mass culture is very, very democratic: It absolutely refuses to discriminate against or between anything or anybody. All is grist to its mill and all comes out finely ground indeed. (62)

The general tone of this elitist and class-based position is assessed by Andrew Ross: "The debate about mass culture was conducted in a discursive climate that linked social, cultural, and political difference to disease" (43). And Rosenberg helped inform this opinion when in 1957 he wrote, "A genuine esthetic (or religious or love) experience becomes difficult, if not impossible, whenever kitsch pervades the atmosphere" (9).

To accept such positions, as many critics did, was to acknowledge that popular culture's representations were to be viewed as intentionally obtrusive formations that forced mass-mediated fodder on wholly noncritical publics. In these terms, the popular thus epitomized homogeneity and an insensitivity to purist artistic intentions. Popular culture was nonreflexive; it had no ability to develop a critical attitude toward itself. In accordance with such principles, the high-culture proponents in *Mass Culture* were engaging in preservationist tactics. Their claims suggested that heterogeneity, pure intentionality, meaning, and culture must remain as absolutes that would continue to guide both the creation and representation of (all) cultural products. This meant ensuring the perpetuation of a "naturalized" aesthetic order, mainly for the sake of circumventing the disintegration of cultural hegemony.

There are certain parallels here between my introductory stories and the opinions of these pop culture detractors. On the one hand, Andy Warhol and his projects implied a metaphorical attack on such paternal demands. For Warhol simplified art to the point of absurdity by insinuating that there were no "proper" painterly techniques. Unlike Dadaists or Surrealists, Warhol (and other pop artists) didn't offer specific manifestos or alternatives. Likewise, Warhol was not engaged in the credible procedure of working on a critical "problem" in contemporary art. Pop art was to be accepted instead as a platform for acknowledging artistic enterprises that produced mass-mediated iconography. As Dick Hebdige points out,

> In other words pop formed up at the interface between the analysis of "popular culture" and the production of "art," on the turning point between these two opposing definitions of culture: culture as a standard of excellence, culture as descriptive category. (*Hiding* 125)

These contradictions were represented during the post-World War II years as pop art avoided serious reflection through its depiction of the obvious while also managing to insinuate its way into the high critical regions that had once vehemently denounced it. In turn, Warhol's leap to prominence as pop's most enigmatic artist/celebrity fueled the debates examined so directly in Rosenberg and White's anthology. Indeed, the former commercial artist succeeded in persuading much of the New York contingent of serious, contemporary art critics to accept simple reproductions of mass-produced objects as iconographic images worthy of observation. In a similar vein, Warhol's films inspired austere clarifications by highly credible observers who focused explicitly on the filmmaker's *lack* of authorial intent. For example, film archivist and critic Jonas Mekas offered the opinion, "That's the story of Warhol's art: it's always so unbelievably simple a thing that makes it work" (139).

Mekas was on the right track, because the combination of the banal, commercial content of Warhol's pop art with the underlying philosophy of the Factory (pop art as pop life) began to suggest a rather radical notion: The seeming simplicity of pop, the lack of commitment involved in creating it, its obvious anti-intellectual posturing—all of these elements simultaneously created the conditions for pop's "devious" play on *populism.* As Frith and Horne (120) point out, pop art was democratizing in practice and theory ("everyone is an artist," "you don't need an education to understand it."). In addition, pop art ironically exposed the commodity nature of *all* art. But even more important, pop reversed the traditional role of the contemplative viewer who ponders the intentionality of the artistic process. In essence, the viewer becomes the "artist of perception," no longer requiring the guidance of the art historian and the critic. A stark, reproduced image, such as a Coke bottle, could indeed lend itself to a number of "personalized" interpretations.

In adding to the observations above, I believe that part of the radical nature of Warhol's pop also lay in the artist's ability to demonstrably transform the calm flow of everyday life into the appearance of a pointless joke, as with the Delmonico intervention. Warhol *was* the tycoon of passivity (Koch). At the same time, he had the ability to instigate a crisis at the level of the natural. His interviews, films, media assaults, and often his mere presence, always raised the same series of questions: What is really going on? Are we being challenged? Is this a mockery of art and of us as participants? Is Warhol vandalizing the already popular or recontextualizing it? In attempting to find answers to these often frustrating questions we are once again forced to recognize the complexity of Andy Warhol's artistic productions, the subculture that emerged at his Factory studio, and the widespread influence of Warhol and the Factory on musicians and artists.

Bowie, the Factory, Glitter Rock, and Gay Culture

One such artist/musician who took most of his aesthetic and philosophical cues from Warhol was David Bowie, particularly as the self-invented, media-manipulating Ziggy Stardust. Today, it is almost tempting to dismiss Bowie as a charlatan; after all, in the 1980s he repeatedly insisted on setting the record "straight" in relation to his Ziggy period. Here, however, we must remember that Warhol, Bowie's mentor, courted the Reagans in the 1980s, but that didn't necessarily qualify him as a patriot for the right wing. Likewise, with Bowie we must take several steps backward and reconsider his agenda in the early 1970s. Within such a framework, we will recognize that Bowie, like Warhol, was in effect a cultural politician who was responsible for "opening up questions of sexual identity which had previously been repressed, ignored, or merely hinted at in rock and youth culture" (Hebdige, *Subculture* 61).

This assessment is in no way meant to imply that politically pure motives operated behind the construction of Bowie's bisexual/gay persona(s). Instead, his flamboyant characterization of Ziggy embodied contradictory sexual features that informed an entire genre (glitter rock) whose raison d'être was gender bending. Often referred to as "costuming" and "creating a persona," Bowie and other glitter rockers *implied* that one could "try on lifestyles" within the framework of rock and roll and not always "take on the consequences."[4] Although such gestures might seem slightly conservative on the surface, they were informed by potentially subversive notions of how to construct a wonderfully *artful* signification of androgynous, nonstraight style and attitude.

In many ways, this style and attitude can be traced back to David Bowie's preoccupation with Warhol's Factory. At the Factory, one could enter as an everyday dullard and create one's "self," the act suggesting an aesthetic decision to stomp on the mundane and suddenly emerge as a superstar. This is in effect a crafty proposition in the sense that hoodwinking the mass media became the desired goal and the price for acceptance into the Factory's underworld. Indeed, the perpetrator didn't have to be famous for doing anything *except* reinventing his or her self; thereby, one could easily acquire "fifteen minutes of fame" by simply engaging in a performance-art-based sense of trickery, pure and simple. It was in fact possible to enter the Factory as a street criminal, nonactor, or disinherited Catholic society girl and emerge within days as a flamboyant "Ultra Violet," "Paul America," or "International Velvet." Thus acquiring fame did not mean working one's way up the ranks, so to speak (although the Factory had an impeccable pecking order), but instead, the acclamation was, "whatever you perceive yourself to be; you are." And in the process, the more one's newly acquired identity rested on the laurels of cultural transgressions, the better.

In considering Bowie's incorporation of the Factory's ideas, it becomes profitable to also evaluate how Bowie's sexual pronouncement to *Melody Maker* fit within the gay cultural milieu of the early 1970s. By January 1972, gay culture had not yet emerged with an overtly consistent and culturally acknowledged iconography, even among white male homosexuals.[5] Gay liberation, the demand for gay rights, and gay activism in general, were in their formative stages. Consider that just three years prior to Bowie's *Melody Maker* interview, the Stonewall riots had helped to spark a nationwide grassroots liberation effort (D'Emilio 233). By 1972, gay protests, direct political organizing, and a spreading national movement to "come out" were considered important strategies in building a radical front that viewed gays as victims of homophobic oppression. As D'Emilio points out, coming out became a prolific political statement:

> The open avowal of one's sexual identity, whether at work, at school, at home, or before television cameras, symbolized the shedding of the self-hatred that gay

> men and women internalized and consequently it promised an immediate improvement in one's life. To come out of the "closet" was a quintessential expression of the fusion of the personal and the political that the radicalism of the late 1960s exalted. (235)

Given this claim, what are we to make of David Bowie, the "king" of glitter rock, who obviously gained credence as a popular musician by advancing his own unconventional propositions concerning sexual orientation? We could acknowledge that Bowie was playing the role of a rock and roll Warhol, and in some senses, this is the case. Bowie postured for the media and went to great lengths to exaggerate his image as a bisexual/gay Ziggy-like messiah.[6] But Bowie's 1972 image wasn't interpreted by followers as parody located solely within quotes. The Ziggy hype was not a matter of great concern for the hordes of fans/glitter rockers in that in the early 1970s Bowie never led followers to believe that he wasn't bisexual. In fact, as his former wife Angela has claimed, she and David became role models in 1972 for many gay and bisexual followers (74). In this sense then, Bowie's gay and bisexual posturings were thus filtered through a Warholian projection of fame as ironic yet based on certain experiential realities. Thus Bowie's "ironically serious" demeanor made possible fans' considering positive models of sexual identity outside the strict confines of heterosexist models. Along these lines, music historian Boze Hadleigh points out, "His 1972 incarnation as Ziggy Stardust was cited by *Esquire* as No. 3 of the Top Ten events which helped 'homosexualize' American pop culture. On stage Bowie carried out a virtual revolution" (19).

Suddenly, "playing with" sexual identity and/or openly exposing one's (alternative) sexuality, and/or exploring gender politics at the level of posing and posturing all became ways for glitter participants to express radical premises within the context of rock and roll (both on- and offstage). At the same time, we must keep in mind that such activities were constructed within the subcultural, aesthetic, and ideological confines of the year marked as *1972.*

"Anti-Anthems for an Anti-Time" (Duncan 95)

In a sense, it is unnecessary to suggest that Bowie, Warhol, and the Factory should have acted directly to produce powerful forms of confrontational politics. Simon Frith argues:

> As a star Bowie never pretended to represent his fans, but he did make available to those fans a way of being a star. Bowie's pop masterpiece from the early 1970s, "All the Young Dudes" (the record he wrote and produced for Mott the Hoople) was about this, about the way in which youths, by dressing up, construct their own stage, write their own parts, set up their own audience. Glam-rock dissolved the star/fan division not by the stars becoming one of the lads, but by the lads becoming one of the stars. ("Only Dancing" 137)

Accordingly, Robert Duncan credits "All the Young Dudes" with anthem status, professing that it was a statement of something noble within the contextual construction of sexual difference in the early 1970s. In Duncan's terms, the song explicitly pronounced

> the goodness of the bad, the morality of the immoral, the dignity of the undignified, and the humanity—shared on a sweaty dance floor as well as any place—of us all. Thus did David Bowie put forth a decadence that was in fact healing. (97)

In this manner, Bowie's pleasure-ridden and aesthetically informed "transformation of identity" represents a radical pose that characterizes him as a subversive cultural figure in the era of glitter rock. As Frith has claimed, "Bowie's career is interesting not because of anything he has stood for specifically but because of what it reveals about the making of pop meaning" ("Only Dancing" 133). This notion of making meaning is doubly important in the case of Bowie's Ziggy period. For it can never be known whether Bowie had pure intentions or not. Nonetheless, he and others like him (Lou Reed, Iggy Pop, Mott the Hoople, etc.) suggested to fans that sexual identity needn't be framed within dominant discourses and that sometimes the disruption of such discourses—even at the level of pop practice—can reveal something potent, something that goes beyond "trivial" costuming. An additional strength of Bowie's glitter image was revealed not only in the cultural boundaries he crossed but also in his ability to transform the diatribes about pop consumerism common in the 1950s and 1960s, which were rooted in notions of the "passive masses." In both the United States and abroad, Bowie and his glitter rock followers helped usher in a new post-1960s moment—a "revolt into style" as a social practice in which commercialization and consumerism were the means to a radical end.[7] As I will claim, glitter rock "lifted" sexual and artistic premises from the under-underground world of the Factory and transformed them into styles that left their original ideological intentions intact. Bowie's glitter rock then, for all of its self-conscious posturing, was the first absolutely forthright form of rock and roll to move queerness from subtext to text and make it unashamed, playful, and still very much "decoded" for mass consumption by a public that was largely unaccustomed to homosexuality or bisexuality as orientations that they were encouraged to admire and unabashedly celebrate. In this sense, we can begin to understand how glitter rockers came to represent a resistant subcultural form. As I will argue, they may not have maintained an allegiance to many of the qualities (class unity, territoriality) that are typically associated with "unified" youth subcultures of the 1950s through the 1970s, yet they most certainly took on many of the more spectacular features (style/attitude) that were associated with such groups. For these reasons, I want to examine the art, songs, musicians, and events that helped give rise to the genre of glitter rock. In turn, I want to analyze the manner in which glitter rock fans maintained a resistant stance toward the heterosexual hegemony of the early 1970s.

Conclusion

In tracing the lineage of Andy Warhol's impact on rock and roll style, this book advances a number of interrelated positions and claims that are presented through complementary yet often paradoxical accounts of pop art, underground rock, and glitter rock. Such accounts offer particular kinds of counterexamples to contemporary theories and critiques of popular music and art, as well as of youth subcultures and style. In considering the range of ideas examined within this broad framework, I believe that the book can thus be comprehended on a number of associated levels.

At the most fundamental level, the book provides a series of integrated case studies that examine the interactional foundations that gave rise to the genre of glitter rock. In this sense, the book is as much about *how* this genre emerged through aesthetic networks and social/interactional milieus as it is an analysis of the genre's conventions. In revealing the interactional networks, I have attempted to account for the productivity of pop art and rock and roll genres that laid the foundation for glitter and/or merged with its stylistic forms. Thus I am focusing on, first, the ways that a number of genres (leading up to and through) glitter were actually composed within the course of certain interactional practices and moments and, second, the ways that these genres came to be represented: on stage, on the screen, in the press, and among youth whose identificatory relationships with pop art and glitter rock created certain spectacular subcultural practices in the late 1960s and early 1970s. On yet another level, the book can be interpreted as a particular kind of historical account, one that traces the tensions that arose in culture both among and between various factions that were forced to engage in explicit confrontations, especially in regard to the "lived" stylistic parameters that characterized distinct artistic/musical genres and their audiences. Some of these confrontations are examined in subsequent discussions with reference to the following pairings: the counterculture/underground rock, glitter rock/mainstream rock, pop art/high art, youth subcultures/subcultural youth. At each conjunctural moment, one glaring similarity becomes apparent: no matter the particular artistic and/or musical formation, it was forced (usually without provocation) to confront a related artistic and/or musical formation that was perceived as "the enemy." The aesthetic and ideological tensions that developed from these confrontations then splintered into further conflicts. In the process, allegiances formed within the ranks that defined themselves against the enemy. Thus, for example, glitter rock was at first a genre that expressed collective animosity toward much contemporaneous rock. In turn, glitter rock emerged with its own privatized forms and rituals, ones that excluded outsiders but that also demarcated insiders as part of this or that club. Within the span of a year, glitter had broken off into various subsets and strands (Roxy Music fans, New York Dolls fans), each with a primary devotion to the imagery and attitudes provoked by Bowie, yet each with its own particular (subcultural) boundaries and practices. The intersecting points where numerous subcultural peripheries connected *and* split apart interest me the most.

Finally, the book can be read, not as a way "to do" cultural studies per se but as a way in which cultural studies provides theoretical configurations and avenues for the interrogation of already interrogative cultural practices. Although I will examine some of the major theoretical concerns of British cultural studies, my concentration will be more specifically directed toward Birmingham subculture theory and its applicability to this study. This focus will provide a new way to conceptualize and reevaluate many of the theoretical claims of subculture theory, subsequently attempting to revitalize its most central interests and premises. In this manner, the book provides a conceptual reexamination of the critical relationships between style, youth culture, incorporation, hegemony, and resistance. Along these lines, I am particularly concerned with the ways fans take up trends presented through mass media and adopt them through highly disingenuous practices.

In this final sense, however, what will matter are the ways that both the popular art and music under consideration produced representations that deviated from the dominant cultural milieu of the 1960s and 1970s. Most important, I am concerned with how these representations were transmitted, taken up, lived out, and how they came to restructure the lives of fans. Here, I will argue that glitter fans, through sub*cultural* practices, positioned themselves within lines of representation that reflected their own active determination in how they were to be "marked" and thus (re)"inserted" within the lineages of glitter rock. Given these claims, then, the book addresses notions of production in relation to reception, as the case studies examine the ways that particular genres came into being as well as how such genres were interpreted and "used" by audiences (subcultural participants).

Subculture theory provides us with an exemplary model for understanding these relationships; thus, through using and extending the premises of subcultural analysis, the following questions will serve as guideposts: If subculture theory is recognized as a contextually specific body of work that was in fact "working through" a number of related theoretical terrains, then what does it offer for an analysis of Warhol, pop art, and glitter rock? Likewise, what methods does subculture theory provide for an analysis of *kinds* of youth groups that identified with these genres? Indeed, as I will posit, this question raises a related one: What features of subculture theory are appropriate, transformable, or dismissable when studying phenomena that were, on the one hand, not indicative of subcultures (but instead functioned as subcultural forms) and, on the other hand, while operating parallel to the overall model developed by the Centre for Contemporary Cultural Studies (CCCS) were in some places resistant to it. Next, in transforming the original applications of particular concepts taken from subculture theory, and through appropriating others more directly, how does the new model apply to Andy Warhol's Factory, which was not a subculture in the British sense; to glitter rock, which was a widespread, mass-mediated subcultural *form,* and, finally, to a broader range of popular culture? Given the complex nature of these questions it will be necessary in Chapter 2 to outline some of the central preoccupations of British cultural studies. I will then provide an overview of Stuart Hall and Tony Jefferson's *Resistance through Rituals,* focusing on the major concepts concerning subcultures that were developed at the CCCS during the late 1960s and early 1970s. Next, I will link this document to Dick Hebdige's widely read *Subculture: The Meaning of Style,* and in so doing, I will focus on the "grammar" that Hebdige developed in his analysis of post-World War II youth subcultures and punk. After providing a short critique of subculture theory, I will contribute a framework for analyzing the case studies in Chapters 3 through 10. In Chapter 11, I will then return more directly to my analysis of subculture theory and will examine in detail the questions outlined earlier.

Notes

1. In *Popism,* Warhol and Hackett indicate that by the time of the banquet Warhol may not have actually shown the films. Still, the fact remains that he was invited to show them.

2. In the context of 1972, it was widely assumed that Bowie was bisexual, and during the Ziggy Stardust period he presented himself as a bisexual performer.

3. See "Style as Intentional Communication" in *Subculture: The Meaning of Style* 100-02.

4. In the final chapter, I will explain why this implication was double sided. In some cases, it was interpreted as a way to experiment with subordinate sexual premises. In other ways, however, this suggestion was interpreted in a more literal manner.

5. This is not meant to suggest that the members of gay culture had no "identity." Instead, I am claiming that urban gay culture was in the process of developing a public identity that would eventually revolve around a set of culturally acknowledged themes and icons.

6. My intention is not to merge the qualities/orientations of gay and bisexual people. Instead, I am using the term *gay/bisexual* because Bowie often used this dichotomy to describe both himself and his Ziggy character. For an example, note the Michael Watts interview in the January 1972 issue of *Melody Maker.*

7. I am not claiming that glitter rockers were the first group to "revolt into style" via consumerism/commercialism (see Hebdige, *Subculture*; Hall and Jefferson, *Resistance*).

British Cultural Studies

CONJUNCTURAL ANALYSIS AND THE CONCEPTUALIZATION OF SUBCULTURAL "DIFFERENCE"

Cultural Studies and the Practice of Critique

In "Cultural Studies and Its Theoretical Origins," Stuart Hall poses the following self-referential (and highly cynical) question, "Didn't cultural studies emerge somewhere at that moment when I first met Raymond Williams, or in the glance I exchanged with Richard Hoggart? In that moment cultural studies was born; it emerged full grown from the head!" (277). In raising some rather ardent questions about the politics of theory, Hall begins his chapter by denouncing any account that characterizes cultural studies as a "pure" discipline. Hall stresses that cultural studies is often the result of awkward projects, and he points out that common perceptions of cultural studies as a grand patriarchal narrative are deeply misguided. Along these same lines, in both recent lectures and articles, Hall continues to reinforce the notion that "cultural studies is not one thing, it has never been one thing" (Nelson, Grossberg, and Treichler 3). In a similarly succinct manner, John Clarke explains that "the practice of theoretical critique within the CCCS [Centre for Contemporary Cultural Studies] resisted the instillation of any one theoretical hegemony: appropriations of new theoretical directions were woven alongside (sometimes with the seams still showing), rather than displacing, previous models" (*New Times* 9-10).

The accounts given by Hall and Clarke are of particular significance because they address the complex, interdisciplinary, and multidimensional concerns of British cultural studies. Such concerns have been and remain a major preoccupation of cultural studies; it consistently grows out of analyses that demand an engagement with a number of theoretical traditions and models. Thus the method of critique suggests that negotiations with theoretical frameworks and (accompanying) methodologies serve both positive as well as negative missions: theories are thoroughly interrogated and challenged at the same time that they are used for inspiration and guidance. As Cary Nelson, Lawrence Grossberg, and Paula Treichler claim, "British cultural theory is not, and never was, a homogeneous body of work; it has always been characterized by disagreements, often contentious ones, by divergences of direction and concern, by conflict among theoretical commitments and political agendas" (11). In *We Gotta Get Out of This Place,* Grossberg continues this line of thinking by stressing that "at every moment, every practice of cultural studies is somewhat of a hybrid, with multiple influences" (19). In addition, he suggests that "cultural studies is not a thousand points of light, and not every project labelled 'culture studies' is cultural studies" (18).

If the practice of cultural studies can be described in these terms, then one necessarily needs to give consideration to the foundational literature in the field (Richard Hoggart, Raymond Williams, E. P. Thompson, Stuart Hall). Unfamiliar readers, in particular, should examine the theoretical guideposts of cultural studies as well as the principal motivations and concerns of cultural studies scholars.[1] Indeed, the guiding principles provided by the early work in cultural studies, as well as the achievements of international scholars in the field, *must* be examined if one is determined to understand where cultural studies has been and where it is heading.[2] However, the history of cultural studies and its preoccupations have been thoroughly examined in a number of sources.[3] Therefore, I will not rehearse the most commonly cited arguments here. At the same time, I will present some general claims concerning British cultural studies, noting in particular the manner in which the "subculture project" arose in relation to a specific series of social conditions in postwar British culture. Further, I will consider the usefulness of certain theoretical precepts and methods as seen by the Birmingham "subculture group." I will then describe and analyze Dick Hebdige's work on youth subcultures and follow that with a consideration of how subculture theory may be reevaluated and reconsidered in relation to my analysis of Andy Warhol and glitter rock.

British Cultural Studies: The Context of British Subculture Theory

In his 1964 inaugural lecture at the Birmingham CCCS, Richard Hoggart "indexed Cultural Studies as primarily concerned with 'neglected' materials drawn from popular culture and the mass media, which he suggested, provided important evidence of the new stresses and directions of contemporary culture" (Hall, "The Centre" 21). As Stuart Hall explains, however, this seemingly plausible statement on the emerging field of cultural studies was enough to cause consternation among traditional sociologists and conservative humanists. Accordingly, the point Hall makes is quite simple: "Spending time analyzing modern cultural forms was a positive collusion with the 'modern disease' " ("The Centre" 22). By way of clarification, Hall suggests that "cultural studies was then [considered to be] either hopelessly unscientific or a product of the very disease it sought to diagnose—either way, a treason of the intellectuals" ("The Centre" 22).

Over the past 30 years, what has perhaps made cultural studies so additionally "threatening" is its ability to interweave diverse theoretical positions and problems into a series of broadly complementary projects (the subculture project and media and ideology).[4] In considering the general features of these projects, I believe that the unique emphasis of (British) cultural studies is that it stresses an understanding of the "raw materials" of contemporary (and often popular) culture while examining these materials (in varying ways and to varying degrees) through a critical engagement with semiotics, economic and political theories, structuralism and poststructuralism, continental philosophy, deconstruction, phenomenology, feminism, psychoanalysis, Marxism, post-Marxist analyses, "queer" theory, and postmodernism. At the same time, cultural studies does *not* require that one have the exceptional ability to denote each and every point within the field where these (as well as numerous other) theoretical terrains have cross-pollinated. The particularity of the question being asked is what matters most; all questions must be guided first by context, second by theory.[5] One cannot, for example, apply a theoretical model in advance, as if all the answers will unfold. One cannot merely employ textual analysis, resistance theory, or singular models of gender, race, sexuality, class, or ethnicity. Accordingly, because theory is always fundamentally related to context,[6] cultural studies finds itself positioned outside the autonomous "space" where cultural forms and representations are automatically assumed to be "loaded down" with meaning. Consequently, the intellectual work of cultural studies demands that the questions being asked really do *matter.* They are driven by the political, social, and historical dimensions of everyday life. They make a difference[7] because they examine and reflect the concerns and strategies of a number of social groups that have often been delegated to marginal positions in the cultural milieu (women, sexual minorities, racial minorities, youth, the working class). Therefore, the kinds of questions that cultural studies scholars ask are as important as the kinds of answers they seek.

I will now consider how the early work of British subculture theorists fits within the broad field that I have been describing as cultural studies. A useful starting point is provided by *Resistance through Rituals* (Hall and Jefferson), an edited collection of research studies conducted by the Birmingham CCCS during the late 1960s and early 1970s. Although the book contains a series of projects, the first chapter (Clarke et al.) presents the central theoretical strategies and contextual aims that guide the entire body of work. In focusing on this chapter, I will stress the thematic unity[8] that makes *Resistance through Rituals* a distinctive document on subcultural style.

In "Subcultures, Cultures and Class" (Clarke et al.), the authors use a combination of theories and traditions that demonstrate a concentrated critique of seminal works by Marx, Gramsci, Althusser, Levi-Strauss, and Barthes. Consequently, the authors elaborate on a number of associated premises that are influenced heavily by Phil Cohen's thesis that working-class youth subcultures "magically resolve" the contradictions of the parent class (Cohen 23). In adopting a Cohenite framework, the authors suggest that through rituals involving fashion, music, language, and territory, working-class youth subcultures attempt to win cultural space as a way of resisting the dominant order. In this manner, youth subcultures are identified as being structurally relational to their working-class parent culture. The difference is that whereas working-class parents often use direct strategies when confronting dominant institutions,[9] working-class youth subcultures engage in ritualistic, symbolic forms of resistance. Thus, in considering the tactics used by both the adult culture and youth subcultures, the authors privilege a view that suggests a subordinate (class/culture) "push" against the dominant culture. At the same time, however, the Birmingham scholars note that the dominant culture usually attempts to incorporate all symbolic victories that are exposed by youth subcultures.

To further understand how these ideas evolved out of critical, theoretical practices it is necessary to consider that the Birmingham scholars were extremely attentive to the contextual framework of postwar British capitalism (with special attention paid to the period from the early 1950s to the mid-1960s). A main part of the analysis focuses on two terms—*affluence* and *consensus*—which were central to the debate concerning postwar social change in Great Britain (Clarke et al. 21). According to the authors, these terms were "woven together" in the form of a social myth ("embourgeoisement") that suggested that "working class life and culture was ceasing to be a distinct formation in the society and everyone was assimilating rapidly towards middle class patterns, aspirations, and values" (Clarke et al. 21). A large part of the analysis, then, is devoted to the "deconstruction" of this myth. This process requires that the authors draw a number of distinctions between the mythological/ideological scenarios constructed during this period and the "real" relations of class cultures.

Such distinctions are significant because they inform the explanatory scheme in which the Birmingham scholars deciphered the *particular* lived conditions of the working class during the 1950s and early 1960s. Of primary interest was the repertoire used by the working-class adult culture in its attempt to negotiate solutions to the problems posed by class subordination. According to Clarke et al., such solutions took on a number of forms and were manifested through a number of methods: the working-class adult culture at times adapted to, struggled with, or resisted the dominant institutions. As the authors point out, the particular type of response varied, depending on the specificity of the problem being addressed (labor union struggles, party politics, the redistribution of neighborhoods). In all cases, however, the subordinate class culture maintains an "us versus them" stance in its attempt to win particular victories against and/or within the forces of hegemonic domination. Therefore, the working class has always been positioned in a structurally oppositional formation.

Drawing on the theoretical work of Antonio Gramsci (*Selections from the Prison Notebooks*), the Birmingham scholars claim that the dominant culture represents itself as the prevailing culture, and in so doing, it attempts to frame competing definitions (from) within its own range. In this sense, as suggested in the preceding section, the parent culture often addresses problematic aspects of class subordination through a series of struggles with the "hegemonic bloc" (39). Indeed, the parent culture may attempt to modify, resist, change, or even overthrow the hegemonic cultural order (12). But the dominant culture stands as the most "natural" social order, the hegemony, which, according to Clarke et al.,

> involves the exercise of a special kind of power—the power to frame alternatives and contain opportunities, to *win and shape consent,* so that the granting of legitimacy to the dominant classes appears not only "spontaneous" but natural and normal. (38)

Here, Clarke et al. point out that dominant culture is never represented by a homogeneous ideology or social structure. It may in fact reflect a number of different interests that emerge from *within* the dominant class. Likewise, the subordinate class/culture, by the nature of its subordination, is not always in direct conflict with the dominant class/culture. The subordinate class may at times feel aligned with dominant class interests, especially when dominant belief systems help to influence the subordinate group in such a way so as to position it within acceptable peripheries of dominant culture. Still, regardless of the perceived set of conditions or the real affiliations, "cultures always stand in relations of domination—and subordination—to one another, [and] are always, in some sense, in struggle with one another" (Clarke et al. 12-13).

At this point, we can consider the relation between the Birmingham authors' analysis of hegemony/class subordination and the premises that they developed in regard to postwar working-class youth subcultures. Most important, the authors arrive at a series of associated theses that propose that youth subcultures be viewed as formations that occurred across three intersecting axes. First, youth subcultures were considered to be "subsets" of the subordinate (working) class (i.e., "parent culture") into which they were born. Second, youth subcultures were recognized not only as being integrated within their particular parent culture, but they were also understood as a formation that arose at the intersection between the subordinate class culture and the dominant culture. Youth subcultures not only retained some of the elemental features of the working-class parent culture, but they also (in varying ways) maintained a strong sense of autonomy as well. Accordingly, as the authors explain, the autonomy of working-class subcultures was manifested through subcultural style that expressed the distinctiveness of the youth/parent dichotomy as well as the subculture's symbolic contention with the dominant culture. Third, according to the Birmingham scholars, class-based determinations were also blended within the broader formation commonly referred to as 1950s and 1960s "youth culture." Thus the authors scrutinize prevalent/dominant social myths concerning the postwar youth while taking account of the institutions and familial contexts that had most affected postwar working-class youth subcultures. To provide an example, postwar working-class youth subcultures were part of a "new consumer culture" that had arisen during this period. At the same time, they were subject to a number of social myths ("youth culture as incipiently 'classless' ") that proved nonrelational to their particular class-based experiences. In other words, the authors forthrightly propose that—given the contextual framework of the period—an analysis of subordinate British youth subcultures had to recognize that *class*—"that tired, 'worn out' category—refused to disappear as a major dimension and dynamic of the social structure" (Clarke et al. 25).[10]

Drawing broadly on Cohen's analysis of London's East End, the subculture scholars analyze the conditions that led to the restructuring of British urban working-class communities after World War II. In so doing, attention is called to the reorganization of the economic mode of production, the redevelopment of housing in working-class neighborhoods, and the disintegration of many traditions common to working-class family life. Most important, the authors suggest that

> the 1950s seem to us a period of true "hegemonic domination," it being precisely the role of "affluence" as an ideology, to dismantle working-class resistance and to deliver the "spontaneous consent" of the class to the authority of the dominant classes. (40)

At the same time, however, it is stressed that hegemony is culturally and historically specific; it "is not universal and 'given' to the continuing rule of a particular class. It has to be *won,* worked for, reproduced, sustained" (40).

The main reason that hegemony constantly has to be asserted and reasserted is that the working class does not in all cases react to domination in passive terms. There are numerous solutions to the problems posed by subordination, and, according to Clarke et al., these often "occur on a spectrum" between negotiation, resistance, and struggle. The principal point to be considered is that the analysis of the strategies used by the working-class (adult) culture brings the Birmingham scholars to a clearer understanding of the kinds of strategies that are most commonly employed by youth subcultures.

In comparing the youth subcultures to the parent culture, the authors propose that subordinate youth "win cultural space" through the appropriation of fashions, objects (such as scooters), music, territorial space, and "languages" (i.e., "distinctive argot"). In particular, through the "reorganization" of meanings implicit in particular fashions and material objects, as well as through the development of specialized linguistic terms, youth subcultures engage in "resistant rituals" that "symbolically announce" their contention with the hegemonic forces that attempt to "structure" the lives of (all) working-class youth. However, as the authors point out, these strategies—although resistant—are always "symbolic" in that the problems posed by class structure are consistently addressed solely through stylistic mediums. Thus the subcultural response has an ideological dimension in that the problematics of class cannot be resolved at the level where the youth subculture lives its subordination (47).[11] Youth subcultures may (in rare cases) "negotiate" with the dominant culture (for example, by claiming the right to a particular territorial space) or they may resist it (by completely dismantling "proper notions" of public appearance). They can do little, however, to circumvent hegemony except through the sphere of ideological/symbolic resolutions. The combined efforts behind style/language/territory thus "mark the subculture's struggle" with dominant culture. As Clarke et al. suggest:

> There is no "subcultural career" for the working class lad, no "solution" in the subcultural milieu for problems posed by the key structuring positions of the class. . . . There is no "subcultural solution" to working class youth unemployment, educational disadvantage, compulsory miseducation, dead-end jobs, the routinization and specialization of labour, low pay, and the loss of job skills. Subcultural strategies cannot match, meet, or answer the structuring dimensions emerging in this period for the class as a whole. (47)

However, the Birmingham scholars were not willing to dismiss the stance of youth subcultures simply because their strategies were not explicitly confrontational. Instead, the authors find extraordinary (and particular) significance in the *process* of style construction for it represents the moment when subcultures attempt to resist the dominant order. Seen in this manner, youth subcultures use the "tools" that are most readily at their disposal, and in so doing, they "rearrange" inscribed meanings, thereby creating a momentary yet dramatic challenge to the dominant cultural order.

Although stressing the importance of this process, the authors are also interested in the relation of style to other aspects of group life. Thus visual styles must be examined in relation to the "outlooks and activities" of subcultural members. The appropriation and "resignification" of objects and fashions are homologous with the subculture's focal concerns, activities, group structure, and collective self-image (56). According to the authors, then, the symbolic aspects of the subculture cannot be separated from "the structure, experiences, activities and outlook" that give shape to the group's identity (56).

To conclude this analysis of *Resistance through Rituals,* by looking at the first chapter (Clarke et al.), it should be stressed that the authors focus on the notion that working-class youth subcultures engage in resistant rituals that signify a symbolic attempt to win space from the dominant culture. In taking this idea several steps further, Dick Hebdige, who was also a member of this "working group," began a project to examine the more intricate features of subcultural style. And as we will see, he advances a conceptually sophisticated account of the ways in which style operates in a resistant manner.

Dick Hebdige: Semiology and Ideology

Although *Subculture: The Meaning of Style* does provide an original theoretical focus, the main concepts therein also bear some similarity to those found in *Resistance through Rituals.* In particular, Hebdige does not dismiss class as a structural dimension of British youth subcultures; at the same time, he shifts the focus of the analysis to race, thereby offering a more elaborate examination of the complex social relations in youth subcultures. In addition, Hebdige's work addresses what Tony Jefferson cites in *Resistance through Rituals* ("Cultural Responses") as a "missing component" of subcultural analysis.[12] Here, Jefferson claims that "there is no grammar for decoding symbols like dress" ("Cultural Responses" 86). One of Hebdige's central goals is to demonstrate a methodology whereby Barthesian semiology can be merged with Althusserian Marxism; in the process, he sets out to develop a "grammar" that will reveal "the hidden messages inscribed on the glossy surfaces of style" (*Subculture* 18). Hebdige proceeds to link this grammar with Gramsci's theory of hegemony, and in so doing, he provides an interpretation that has both structural and cultural inflections.

Finally, although Hebdige focuses on many of the same subcultures as were examined in *Resistance through Rituals,* his principal concern is punk. Thus the contextual features of British society during the rise of punk are often related to the stylistic manifestations of punk style. In the latter half of the book, however, Hebdige privileges a poststructuralist interrogation of style over the contextualist dimensions that are explored. In this manner, the production of style is explained but not elaborated, and as I will determine, Hebdige concludes his book with an acknowledgment of the limits posed by his own particular poststructural approach to subcultural style.

In the introduction to *Subculture* (1-19) Hebdige explains the theoretical strategy offered in Roland Barthes's *Mythologies.* The strategy permits an examination of the "normally hidden set of rules and conventions through which meanings particular to specific social groups (i.e., those in power) are rendered universal and 'given' for the whole of society" (*Subculture* 9). In phenomena as disparate as wrestling matches, soap advertisements, and striptease, Barthes finds the same kind of "ideological work" occurring. Common, everyday social events and conditions can thus be viewed as analogous in that they are infiltrated with dominantly inscribed "mythologies." Accordingly, the social world that people inhabit actually "supersedes" them in that the most "natural" forms and representations are framed by myths that operate as sign systems. Seen in this manner, the dominant social order "converts," "distorts," and in the process, "organizes" the meaning systems that come to "inhabit" the "whole" of society. Barthes argues then that society is "steeped in anonymous ideology," and his goal is to "decode" the mythological frameworks whereby cultural representations are "naturalized."

In analyzing Barthes's semiology, Hebdige relates the notion of "ideological anonymity" to Althusser's conceptualization of ideology as a "system of representation" that "acts functionally" on people in a manner that "escapes them" (Althusser). Arguably, all representations have an ideological dimension, and as Althusser suggests, even though people "live in the world," they also "live *within* ideological structures." Hebdige argues accordingly that ideology achieves its sense of "naturalness" through the world of signs.[13] Consequently, Hebdige proposes that if there is an ideological dimension to every signification (*Subculture* 13), then the connotative "codes" through which meanings are organized must be disentangled (14). For, as Hall suggests, these connotative codes are in essence "maps of meaning," which "cover the face of social life and render it classifiable, intelligible, meaningful" (qtd. in Hebdige 15). In summarizing Hall's argument, Hebdige claims that "we tend to live inside these maps as surely as we live in the 'real' world: they 'think' us as much as we 'think' them, and this in itself is quite 'natural' " (14). Disentangling these maps of meaning, however, is no simple task. As Hebdige maintains, ideologies shift, alliances form and reform, and contexts are interrelated to the ideologies that prevail at any given moment. At the same time, particular questions remain central, regardless of context: Which groups organize the power? Which groups have the most say? Which ideas gain dominance and which remain marginal (Hebdige 14-15)? As Marx argued, the ideas of the ruling class are the ruling ideas (qtd. in Hebdige 15). But as seen in arguments of the Birmingham subculture group, social/cultural change is built into the system. Hebdige acknowledges this concept of human agency, and in so doing, he finds that Gramsci's theory of hegemony provides for a clearer understanding of the ways mythologies perform their vital functions (16).

Hebdige explains that hegemony refers to the notion that consent must be won and shaped so that the power of the dominant classes *appears* to be legitimate and natural (Hall, cited in Hebdige, *Subculture* 16). Of utmost importance is not only the framing of competing definitions but also the containment of subordinate groups within an ideological space that does not "seem ideological" but seems "natural" (16). In other words, ideology operates in such a way so as to convert the cultural into the natural. As Hebdige states:

> This is how, according to Barthes, "mythology" performs its vital function of naturalization and normalization and it is in his book *Mythologies* that Barthes demonstrates most forcefully the full extension of these normalized meanings. However, Gramsci adds the important proviso that hegemonic power, precisely *because* it requires the consent of the dominated majority, can never be permanently exercised by the same alliance of "class fractions." (16)

The connections between Barthes and Gramsci are important for two related reasons. First, Hebdige suggests that if cultural forms are never rigidly in place, then they can be disentangled, stripped of their coded "layers," bleached through for their hidden connotations. Second, if commodities are endowed with dominant meanings but never set into place permanently, then they can be "lifted" from dominant discourses and reorganized so as to have oppositional meanings. Thus hegemony "has gaps," and as Hebdige states, "The consensus can be fractured, challenged, over-ruled, and resistance to groups in dominance cannot be lightly dismissed or automatically incorporated" (17).

Hebdige views youth subcultures as representing both a broad and a narrow gap in the hegemonic process. On the one hand, postwar youth subcultures "signalled in a spectacular fashion the breakdown of consensus in the post war period" (*Subculture* 17). In a more oblique manner, however, these subcultures challenged the hegemonic dominion through the medium of style. As Hebdige sees it, youth subcultures act as everyday semioticians who disrupt dominant codes through the process of recontextualization (style construction). Accordingly, this central feature of subcultural groups suggests that style represents a struggle over the possession and interpretation of signs. Although signs may be coded with dominant meanings and although they "read us as much as we read them," the real importance of signs, in Hebdige's terms, lies in the use made of them in the subversive sphere of everyday life:

> Style in subculture is, then, pregnant with significance. Its transformations go "against nature," interrupting the process of "normalization." As such, they are gestures, movements towards a speech which offends the "silent majority," which challenges the principle of unity and cohesion, which contradicts the myth of consensus. (18)

Throughout *Subculture,* Hebdige reflects on the contradictions posed by subcultural style and its functioning as a form of provocation in the naturalized world. Style provides a key into the ways that subcultures detach themselves from the laws of common sense; it is the material that contains the hidden codes of subcultures. For Hebdige, the process of disentangling these codes involves, first, an interpretation of postwar British youth subcultures that positioned them in relation to a series of black and white social dichotomies. Second, in the major theoretical portion of the book, Hebdige explicitly examines the precept that style operates as a form of refusal (2). Here, I should point out that I will deal only briefly with Hebdige's analysis of race, because it is analyzed through a series of case studies that can easily be referenced by the reader in Hebdige's *Subculture: The Meaning of Style.* More specifically, however, I will present a description of Hebdige's major points on style, because these have to do with my analysis of Warhol and glitter rock.

Youth Subcultures and Race Relations

In the case studies presented in *Subculture,* Hebdige analyzes the dominant black musical forms in Britain (ska in the early 1960s, reggae in the early 1970s) as well as the presence of Rastafarian and other West Indian cultures and styles. His perspective suggests that the music, the physical presence (immigrant communities), and the styles of West Indians all became a point of reference for many postwar white youth subcultures. However, Hebdige's central theoretical argument is that black and white relations are not often directly negotiated; the interplay between black and white languages is typically represented through symbolic dialogues. For example, Hebdige specifies the positive, almost "psychic," identification between Mods and West Indians, the ambiguous relations between skinheads and blacks, the avoidance of black cultural elements in glitter, and the overt, yet contradictory racial connotations of punk. This list by no means exhausts the subcultures dealt with in the book, but at the same time these brief examples still allow for the consideration of another main tenant of Hebdige's analysis.

He suggests a strong correlation between the structural dimensions of race relations and the class-cultural dimensions that so concerned Clarke et al.: As Hebdige sees it, British youth subcultures symbolically resolved racial tensions and the tensions of class through borrowing (to varying degrees) elements from an already doubly alienated black population. In theorizing these tensions, Hebdige offers a semiotic interpretation of the cultural languages that interacted on the surfaces of subordinate subcultural styles. This allows for an analysis of the equal social condemnation that was given to both black and white youth subcultures, leading Hebdige to the assertion that *all* subcultural refusal "begins with a movement away from consensus (and in Western democracies, the consensus is sacred). It is the unwelcome revelation of difference which draws down upon the members of a subculture hostility, derision, 'white and dumb rages' " (132).

Subcultural Analysis: Contentions and New Directions

Hebdige enters into a specific analysis of style with many of the same concerns and criticisms that were put forth in *Resistance through Rituals.* Accordingly, Hebdige criticizes accounts of youth that essentialize notions of generational identity, and he argues for an approach that examines the historical specificity of subcultural youth groups. In addressing Phil Cohen's work, Hebdige acknowledges that there *are* certain similarities between working-class parents and youth subcultures, but Cohen's emphasis on integration and coherence denies the specificity of the subcultural form (*Subculture* 79). In addition, to overstate the fit between parents and youth lends itself to a view in which so-called respectable youth subcultures are seen to be similar to ones that are "marginalized" (78-79).

Even more important, the theorization of the youth-parent dichotomy does not account for media representations that operate so as to provide dominantly encoded interpretations of subcultures.[14] For example, Hebdige suggests that subcultures are, in general, often dismissed, denounced, and canonized—and nowhere are these actions more apparent than in media reports, documentaries, and fashion exposés. In these sources, we find the discordant "noise" of subcultures examined through a number of contradictory methods: the media often celebrate the subculture's "outrageous styles" while alternately locating such styles within the parameters of a "social problem." In both senses, the media often present a somewhat distorted picture.

Relative to this picture are the results produced within the subculture. For as images of subcultures are found on the pages of the *Observer* and on nightly news reports, subcultures face the simultaneous process of diffusion and defusion (*Subculture* 93). In this sense, the media are involved in effectively incorporating the subculture from within the domain of dominant social relations. In turn, the inhabitants of a spectacular youth subculture are "returned to the place where common sense would have them fit," as " 'folk devil,' as Other, as Enemy" (94).

Hebdige analyzes two related forms of incorporation: the ideological form and the commodity form. The ideological form has many varieties, but some of the more generalizable features are presented here.[15] In this form, the media typically exploit the subculture by making it seem more *and* less bizarre than it really is. The task may involve a simple reinforcement of the images already assumed by those unaccustomed to subcultures. These may include definitional frameworks that represent the subculture as a collection of "animals," "hooligans," "indecent people," and so on. On the other hand, the subculture may be located within the realm of the family; the media may "domesticate" the subculture, for example, through vivid presentations of "punks who also have kids," "punks who *have jobs* [emphasis added]," punks who are indeed "people just like 'us.' " Hebdige examines other methods as well, but his point is that all forms of ideological incorporation work coherently so as to complement one another. They warn the "straight world" of the dangers posed by the subculture while also defining the subculture through a series of normalized terms that have no relation to the actual lived relations of the subculture. In summation, then, ideological incorporation returns the subculture to the social order that it has so adamantly rejected: The subculture therefore becomes acceptable because within this order it can be perceived through commonsensical categorizations.

Although the ideological and commodity forms are treated separately in *Subculture,* Hebdige claims that they are not completely distinct. Nonetheless, the methods of each form are most typically different, because commodity incorporation involves the exploitation of subcultural style in the marketplace. This process, however, is not as unidimensional as one might assume. First, as Hebdige and the Birmingham scholars point out, subcultures maintain an ambiguous relation to consumption. Subcultural members are often rabid consumers who appropriate objects that are then recontextualized so as to subvert the original meanings connected with such objects. But because subcultures are often consumed with the process of consumption, the exploitative process whereby the subculture faces its own commercialization is not something that is easily examined as an absolute category. Still, as Hebdige wants to suggest, the original members of the subculture are well aware of the differences between their own creative consumption and the commercial exploitation of their styles.

How, then, does commercial incorporation typically occur? Styles often "feed back" into the fashion industries and what was once "punk clothing," is marketed as a "fashion statement," usually with little regard to the creativity implied in the original design or usage of the apparel:

> Once removed from their private contexts by the small entrepreneurs and big fashion interests who produce them on a mass scale they become codified, made comprehensible, rendered at once public property, and profitable merchandise. In this way, the two forms of incorporation (the semantic/ideological and the "real"/commercial) can be said to converge on the commodity form. (*Subculture* 96)

In particular, this process was made overtly apparent to the punk subculture of the late 1970s, as it witnessed the rise of mail order houses, the creation of couture lines of punk styles, and the commercial production of items such as preripped T-shirts. In such cases, as Hebdige argues, commodity incorporation was both ideological and "real." The meanings manifested through subcultural styles were "devitalized," and the real relations of commercialism fed back into the broader context of culture. In other words, if punk style could be bought off the racks, simply to shock, then who were the real punks and what of their very real social conditions?

The implications of these questions are discussed as Hebdige sets out to examine how subcultural style makes sense to the members themselves.[16] Here, Hebdige distinguishes between the "intentional style" of the subculture and the more conventional styles of the surrounding culture. What marks subcultural style as different, or even deviant, is its obvious fabrication and the manner in which the subculture's codes are displayed (*Subculture* 101). Both acts suggest the subversive force behind subcultural style: subcultural participants act as *bricoleurs*; they subvert the straight meanings that are associated with commodities (in a normalized social context) and at times they recontextualize the original purposes of such commodities. A case in point can be seen in the Mod subculture, which turned the "ultra-respectable scooter" into a "menacing symbol of group solidarity":

> In the same improvisatory manner, metal combs, honed to a razor-like sharpness, turned narcissism into an offensive weapon. Union jacks were emblazoned on the backs of grubby parka anoraks or cut up and converted into smartly tailored jackets. More subtly, the conventional insignia of the business world—the suit, collar and tie, short hair, etc.—were stripped of their original connotations—efficiency, ambition, compliance with authority—and transformed into "empty" fetishes, objects to be desired, fondled, and valued in their own right. (104-05)

In a practice similar to that of the Mods, punks "cut up" traditional codes, and they juxtaposed meanings in a number of ways. For example, traditional objects such as safety pins (innocence) and garbage bags (dirt) were worn in a contemptible manner. Likewise, makeup was worn to be *seen*, not applied to fabricate a natural look. In addition, clothes lifted from pornography were worn openly, an act that publicly announced the most "depraved" of private desires. Similarly, punk music, which contained minimal chords and relentless antimelodies, reacted against traditional forms of rock and roll. In a corresponding manner, punk album covers used paste-on type, thereby taking on the look of tabloids (for example, the Sex Pistols used such type in covering the eyes and mouth of the Queen).

On the surface, an outsider might very well consider such chaotic elements to represent the internal chaos of the subculture itself. But as Hebdige suggests, even though punk "broke codes" through a number of methods, its "disorderliness" cohered on every level. Each method of punk "cut-up" meshed consistently with the other, thus establishing a homological relation—an "internal order"—whereby the forms and rituals of the subculture were bonded in a socially cohesive manner. Yet even though punk's chaotic elements were homologous, Hebdige argues that this particular subculture problematizes any attempt toward a (traditional) semiological analysis. According to Hebdige, to "read" the "chaotic elements" of punk style from such a perspective would only result in an analysis that is too literal and conjectural (*Subculture* 115). For even as there may be a correspondence between garbage bags and trash, the objects used by punks were self-consciously emptied of their meaning.

Hebdige's prime example is the swastika, which, in one sense referenced punk's "interest in a decadent and evil Germany—a Germany which had 'no future' " (*Subculture* 116). In this specific instance, however, the swastika was recontextualized in such a way that it did *not* reference its natural meaning (fascism); so, we are led to ask, why was it worn and what did it signify (116)? As Hebdige suggests, the swastika was worn simply "because it was guaranteed to shock" (116). He states, "Its primary value and appeal derived precisely from its lack of meaning: from its potential for deceit" (117). Hebdige continues by claiming:

> Ultimately the symbol was as "dumb" as the rage it provoked. The key to punk style [thus] remains elusive. Instead of arriving at the point where we can begin to make sense of the style, we have reached the very place where meaning itself evaporates. (117)

In working through the problematic issues raised by a semiological interpretation of punk, Hebdige references the work of the Tel Quel scholars. In essence, this group rejected the conceptual notion of "fixed messages," and replaced it with the idea of polysemy, thereby suggesting that texts themselves may generate "infinite ranges of meaning" (*Subculture* 117-18):

> This approach sees language as an active, transitive force which shapes and positions the "subject" (as speaker, writer, reader) while always itself remaining "in process" capable of infinite adaptation. This emphasis on signifying practice is accompanied by a polemical insistence that art represents the triumph of process over fixity, disruption over unity, "collision" over "linkage"—the triumph, that is, of the signifier over the signified. (119)

Hebdige concludes that punk could only be read as signifying *practice.* In Hebdige's terms punk was "bereft of the necessary details—a name, a home, a history—it refused to make sense, to be grounded, 'read back' to its origins" (121). Consequently, Hebdige finds that punk represents a "radical text" in that its signification subverted the process of meaning construction for the "reader." Hebdige states, "It invites the reader to 'slip into' 'significance' to lose the sense of direction, the direction of sense" (126). Hebdige thus views this quality of "absence" as one of the defining features that displaced punk from the tradition of subcultures that had maintained a symbolic or imaginary relation to the conditions of their parent class. Punk, with its ruptures and contradictions, did not form an allegiance with its class community but, instead, worked to define itself apart from the parent class while "dressing up" its more explicit class connotations with exaggerated yet meaningless significations.

Hebdige's conclusions further explicate the problematic position posed by a semiotic analysis of punk style. On the one hand, Hebdige formulates a positive assertion about the general nature of all youth subcultures. They act as "lay semioticians" who disturb the orderly flow of everyday life. They recontextualize the "raw materials" given to them by dominant and parent cultures, and they announce a spectacular presence that disavows the hegemonic attempt toward total social control. Although their subcultural behaviors are attacked and their styles are usurped, the members still manage to pose a discomfiting identity; they "play" with signs as much as they subvert them. Yet, as Hebdige suggests, an analysis of these ruptures only leads the semiotician to a rather bleak position. In fact, in the conclusion he bemoans the nature of his own work by suggesting that it did not accomplish its intended goals:

> The study of subcultural style which seemed at the outset to draw us back towards the real world, to reunite us with "the people," ends by merely confirming the distance between the reader and the "text," between everyday life and the "mythologist" whom it surrounds, fascinates and finally excludes. It would seem that we are still, like Barthes, "condemned for some time yet to speak *excessively* about reality." (*Subculture* 140)

Regardless of Hebdige's discouraging conclusion, *Subculture* remains a convincing document. In making possible the consolidation of past approaches and in providing important paradigm shifts within the framework of semiotic analysis, Hebdige established important theoretical precedents for cultural studies. In the process, *Subculture* has had a significant impact in that it has encouraged further analyses of subcultural style. For all the perceived shortcomings in his analysis, Hebdige's *Subculture* still serves as the guiding model for those interested in the tension and power posed by subordinate youth subcultures.

The Limits of Subculture Theory

Although I have dealt separately with *Resistance through Rituals* and *Subculture,* my intention was to demonstrate the links between the two, thereby focusing on the strategies employed by Hebdige in light of the former text. Having laid out the major premises of both the CCCS's subculture project and Hebdige's study of subcultural style, I will briefly examine some of the limitations posed by these studies. I will then argue that subculture theory provides a valuable framework for discerning the intricate connections between Warhol's pop-oriented Factory subculture and the musicians and fans who embraced glitter rock. In this sense my reading of *Resistance through Rituals* and *Subculture* is paired with an attentiveness to theoretical shortcomings and a belief that these texts contain important ideas that allow for extended applications beyond those that were originally produced.

Subculture theory (Clarke et al.; Hebdige) has been thoroughly critiqued from within the CCCS[17] as well as by theoreticians who were not directly involved in CCCS'S work on subcultures.[18] Interested readers should examine these critiques; here, I will provide only a brief summary of the most frequently cited arguments. As a starting point, let us consider Simon Frith's claim that subculture theory, in general, is too pessimistic in its assertion that "the moment of refusal is the act of symbolic creation itself" (*Sound Effects* 219). According to Frith, this unilateral viewpoint lends itself to a more problematic issue: how to account for the uses of leisure *within* and between various subcultures, especially given that a number of youth subcultures are *not* composed of "full-time" stylists (*Sound Effects* 220). Frith suggests, then, that subculture theory doesn't account for the complex social conditions that are also relevant to the emergence of particular subcultural styles (*Sound Effects* 220).

In a critique directed specifically toward Hebdige's version of subculture theory, Frith and Horne point to the limitations of an approach that concentrates too stringently on "brief moments" of subcultural defiance (*Art into Pop* 2). Frith and Horne once again underscore the pessimism of subculture theory, because, in Hebdige's view, youth subcultures ultimately undergo the process of marketplace incorporation (2). In addition, the authors suggest that Hebdige does not make clear the conditions under which resistance becomes possible (2). Thus the relations between subcultural resistance and incorporation need to be further explicated in *Subculture: The Meaning of Style.*

In a much more scathing critique, Gary Clarke addresses what he perceives to be numerous problems with the theoretical approaches taken by both the CCCS subculture group (*Resistance through Rituals*) and Dick Hebdige (*Subculture*). Clarke argues that the subculture group's Cohenite strategy does not provide for an explanation "as to how and why class experiences of youth crystallize into a distinct subculture" (82). As he sees it, the Birmingham scholars assume that all flamboyant working-class subcultures proceed with quite similar agendas. This parallel configuration across subcultures, in turn, characterizes them as highly static social formations that are "essentialist and noncontradictory" (82).

In addressing Hebdige's *Subculture,* Clarke makes clear the problems involved in focusing only on the innovations of "original subcultures"; this approach dismisses youth who may adopt subcultural trends by way of stylistic co-optation. In Clarke's terms, Hebdige pits subcultural "innovators" against "mainstream" youth, thereby intimating that mainstream youth are always deceived by commercial incorporation. Clarke's counterargument is that those who embrace subcultural trends *after* the moment of incorporation should not be neglected (in subcultural analyses) because very few young people have the privilege of joining an authentic subculture. Clarke argues that "we ought to focus on the moment when style becomes available—either as a commodity or as an idea to be copied. . . . Any future analysis of youth should take the breakthrough of style as its starting point" (92). In addressing this same issue, Lawrence Grossberg claims that subculture theory

> continues to read the mainstream and its signs as if they could be read in isolation, as if one could know that the simple fact of a sign's entrance into that anonymous space of the masses guaranteed that it had been coopted. ("Politics" 149)

Angela McRobbie provides another dimension to the critique of subculture theory. Specifically, in relation to Hebdige's *Subculture,* she argues that while he "extrapolates race as a signifier *par excellence,*" he seems "oblivious to sex and sexism" (71-72). Although McRobbie's arguments are quite intricate and should not be underestimated, I would suggest that although Hebdige does focus solely on *male* youth subcultures in the case studies, the majority of his analysis of punk does not necessarily privilege boys over girls. As we have noted in the preceding section on signifying practice, Hebdige finds that punk problematized a semiotic attempt to decode the surfaces of subcultural style. It is therefore plausible that gender is not addressed in the *final* analysis because punk's signifiers were emptied of their meaning. Thus, although Hebdige could have focused on gender-related issues in other sections of his study, it is conceivable that his poststructuralist analysis of punk does not lend itself to an explicit account of girls and subcultures. Indeed, as Anne Beezer points out, the emergence of punk may have allowed for the more visible presence of girls, yet this emergence may or may not have been reflected in the surface forms of subcultural style (107).

Here, I will focus briefly on a few of the preceding criticisms while also providing additional critical remarks that will prove relevant to my study of glitter rock. Given this agenda, let me point out that although McRobbie concentrates on problematic theoretical issues relating to Hebdige's analysis, she also secondarily critiques the subculture group's seeming inability to make explicit the relations between popular culture and youth subcultures. Of course, here we must keep in mind that popular culture is possibly underrated by Clarke et al. as a result of the authors' central focus on the symbolic refusal of youth subcultures. This point in mind, whereas McRobbie doesn't offer an expanded argument concerning the authors' oversight, I would offer an augmentation of her point concerning popular culture and youth subcultures.

It is important to stress that even as most youth subcultures have not been consistently involved in radical political movements, at specific moments the distinctive class-based experiences of the subcultures under consideration (in *Resistance through Rituals*) *were* addressed explicitly from within the popular arena. And as youth subcultures intersected with the popular arena, it provided them with authentic meanings that were affectively aligned with their group experiences. For example, the rock and roll bands appropriated by the Mods (the Who, the Animals) often presented politically charged anthems concerning the problems posed by class subordination.[19] In the case of the Teds, American musicians such as Elvis and Jerry Lee Lewis were well received in part because they effectively translated into song the contradictions of their own working-class backgrounds. These points in mind, although Clarke et al., in *Resistance through Rituals* view music as integral to the homology of the subculture, very little is said about how and why the music plays a significant role in the identity-making process of the subculture (54-56).

Given these claims, I now turn specifically to a further examination of Dick Hebdige's *Subculture.* Here, I believe that his analysis reveals the operational procedures of incorporation while ignoring the contradictory features that may be intertwined within the commercial and ideological forms. Hebdige's theoretical approach, as Gary Clarke suggests, assumes a "pure" moment of subcultural resistance, which is ultimately rendered powerless in that subculture's styles are inevitably translated into "fashion statements." However, the moment of incorporation itself remains untheorized, which is problematic in that it is difficult to determine how the mainstream is being contextualized. Consequently, the question arises as to the manner in which one moment is determined as pure and the other as co-opted when the *stylistic form* is the most significant feature that is misrepresented. Of course, any reader with a knowledge of subcultural practices is aware that the incorporation of style has detrimental effects on the subculture's sense of group cohesion. Hebdige addresses this issue in his description of ideological incorporation, proposing that media representations tend to posit the subculture's values of otherness within the ideological boundaries of common sense. In addition, he briefly suggests that commercial incorporation often leads to subcultural defusion; the subculture's style becomes "frozen" and is thus open to multiple interpretations in the marketplace. However, the problem with these suggestions is that not enough is said about *what it is specifically* that is being taken away.

In relation to the preceding claims, one may intuitively want to believe that dominant institutions are "hard-set" on usurping subcultural difference for the sake of maintaining cultural order and social control. But a more specific analysis might reveal the complex processes of incorporation that often occur on both sides of the pure-impure dichotomy. In the case of punk, Hebdige virtually ignores the fact that it was also partially produced by both art school graduates and fashion maverick entrepreneurs.[20] For example, in *Art into Pop* Frith and Horne claim that art schools in Britain played a seminal role in the development of punk, and integral to this formation were entrepreneurial fashion artists, such as Malcom McLaren. Of course, McLaren had somewhat different intentions than those of a Macy's designer, yet the point made by Frith and Horne is one I find intriguing: punk was *never* a pure subculture with noncommercial intentions (*Art into Pop*). In all areas, it exposed its own contradictions, ones that indeed made for a more difficult process of cooptation.

Finally, along these lines, I argue that Hebdige's theorization of the cycle leading from opposition to defusion is totalizing; the subculture is always rendered powerless as a result of the omnipotent process of conversion. In taking a more optimistic stance, I believe that in some instances subcultures fight real battles; they secure real spaces; they issue real threats—ones that actually make a difference. In the search for such instances, we need to examine more closely the perceived intentions of the subculture, thereby asking, What is going on beneath the surface? Thus we need to come to a clearer understanding about how the subculture makes sense to its own members.[21] Most important, we need to determine the kinds of results that occur as the subculture's style splinters out into mainstream culture. In focusing particularly on this last issue, I believe that the incorporation process deserves more scrutiny, given Hebdige's view that ideological/commercial incorporation *always* operates in such a manner so as to usurp the power of subcultural style.

Subculture Studies, Pop Art, and Glitter Rock

In considering the limitations of subculture theory, we should note that the scholars were attempting to describe particular contexts, and in so doing, they were not striving to arrive at a generalizable model. This in mind, I want to make clear the reasons that subculture theory is relevant to an analysis of Warhol's pop art practices, the Factory's subcultural endeavors, and glitter rock. Let me stress that I am not attempting to take the premises presented in *Resistance through Rituals* and *Subculture* and simply write them onto an analysis that takes no account of the contextualism of cultural studies. Clearly, just as subculture theorists justified the contextualism of their own studies, I will also be concerned with the justification of certain contextual practices and moments, ones that gave rise to the genre of glitter rock. In each conjunctural case, both the applicability and the limitations of subcultural analysis will therefore become apparent.

In noting the contextuality of the studies herein, and in considering the contextualism of British subculture theory, I am neither challenging head on the class cultural model in *Resistance through Rituals* nor directly confronting the poststructuralist paradigm that informs Hebdige's studies. My argument is that subculture theory—particularly as it was developed by Hebdige—provides an effective framework for grounding pertinent questions concerning pop art and glitter rock. My reasoning is based on the observation that aside from subculture theory, no theoretical tradition in cultural studies provides an adequate account of nonmainstream youth (thus, in case of this book, certain aspects of subculture theory become pertinent to an analysis of glitter rock participants). At the same time, subculture theory inadvertently maintains that mainstream youth are duped by media/commercial incorporation. Mainstream youth are thus conceptualized[22] as being inauthentic because they are the ones most likely to provide the economic fuel that helps to ignite the defusion of original subcultures.

As my analysis will illustrate, through the medium of glitter rock, young people adopted "incorporated versions" of Warhol's pop ethos and the Factory's subcultural attitude and style; yet these young people were certainly not victims of a commercial industry, nor did the medium of glitter rock victimize Warhol or the Factory. Accordingly, I propose that, in certain cases, youth who adopt commercialized/incorporated versions of subcultural style may also take on a sense of otherness; they may also engage in "style wars" that represent resistance movements. These points in mind, my intention is not to *conclude* with subculture theory as a model but to *begin* my analysis by employing it as a substantive guide for theorizing conceptions of what it means to be subversive within the framework of popular culture. Thus I want to discern the features of subculture theory that are appropriate, transformable, or dismissable when studying groups that do not qualify as subcultures but, instead, function as subcultural forms. In analyzing these forms, I am also interested in determining the ways in which they warrant a comparison to subcultures such as Teds, Mods, and punks. In this sense, some of the central questions I am asking are similar to those raised by Hebdige and Clarke et al., although the cases I am analyzing provide different kinds of answers.

Some Definitions

In both *Resistance through Rituals* and *Subculture,* the authors imply that a distinction may be drawn between two broad categories of youth: mainstream youth, who are typically implicated in the analysis by default, and youth subcultures, which possess certain qualities that mark them as non-mainstream. Clarke et al. state:

> Generally, we deal in this volume *only* with "sub-cultures" . . . which have reasonably tight boundaries, distinctive shapes, which have cohered around particular activities, focal concerns and territorial spaces. When these tightly defined groups are also distinguished by age and generation, we call them "youth sub-cultures." (14)

Hebdige provides a similar definition, although, as we have noted, his study is more specialized in that his main focus is on the "tensions between dominant and subordinate groups," which are "reflected in the surfaces of the subculture—in the styles made up of mundane objects which have a double meaning" (*Subculture* 2). He goes on to suggest that such objects

> warn the "straight" world in advance of a sinister presence—the presence of difference—and draw down upon themselves vague suspicions, uneasy laughter, "white and dumb rages." On the other hand, for those who erect them into icons, who use them as words or curses, these objects become signs of forbidden idennity, sources of value. (2-3)

In light of these definitions, what can we suggest in relation to the types of youth groups that receive treatment in this book? I will focus on two particular groups: (a) those who gathered at Warhol's Factory studio and defined themselves as a subculture and (b) glitter rock fans, who corresponded to British youth subcultures in a number of ways (even though these fans did not qualify as a youth subculture). Thus I am not focusing on youth subcultures, because they have been formally defined by the British scholars; at the same time, I am concentrating on youth groups that *looked* like and *behaved* like subcultures, and in so doing, these groups possessed the essential qualities of otherness that were operational in the Teddy Boy, Mod, and punk subcultures. This shift in focus therefore requires the constitution of a new definitional framework.

As a way of constructing this framework, let us briefly consider that the Factory studio provided the literal space where Warhol developed his artistic ideas, and it was the ideological space where many of his aesthetic notions about pop art were translated into a lifestyle. This translation occurred as Factory regulars and participants assimilated pop aestheticism into their everyday lives. In so doing, they formed a subcultural unit that consisted of a network of groups: young, upper-class women, bohemian artists, Harvard students, working-class gay men, transvestites, street people, rock musicians, and speed addicts (as well as numerous other social types), with the categories often overlapping. This network as unit provides an example of a particular type of chaotic/harmonious subcultural formation that typically develops at the local level; it evolves within a specific contextual boundary, and its practices intermesh with particular aesthetic principles. These principles provide the subculture with the core framework through which it establishes an identity: the subcultural members unite around shared visions concerning the relation between art and everyday life. In the case of the Factory, what is most significant is the fact that a number of subordinate as well as "dominantly encoded" groups converged, and in so doing, these groups formed a unified subculture that established its own language, desires, projects, and styles.

At this point it is profitable to distinguish between "in-there" and "out-there" subcultures—a distinction that suggests a slight contrast between subcultures and subcultural forms. In the cases examined in this book, the reader may consider that Factory participants constituted an in-there subculture, whereas glitter rockers constituted an out-there subculture. In the first case, the in-there subculture has many (but not all) of the characteristics of subcultures as described by Clarke et al. The term *in-there* refers to a subcultural youth group that has a coherent sense of style and this stylistic sensibility reveals a symbolic resistance toward dominant culture. In addition, subcultural members are bound together due to a number of structural determinations, and they cohere around particular activities, focal concerns, and territorial spaces.[23] At the same time, the term in-there implies only a loose comparison to the kinds of subcultures studied by the Birmingham authors (see Hall and Jefferson). Indeed, the Factory may be seen to correspond only in a broad manner to subcultures such as the Mods or the Teds. One difference is that the Factory did not represent one specific kind of response to subordinate-dominant class relations. Whereas the authors represented in *Resistance through Ritual* (Hall and Jefferson) saw the determining level as being the relations between the dominant and working classes, the Factory can be viewed as a social formation wherein a number of working-class, middle-class, and upper-class groups willfully intertwined. These groups, however fractious, converged and formed a network that operated as a subcultural unit. This unit functioned in such a manner so as to *refuse* the precepts of the American class system as a whole. In other words, the Factory's strategies represented solutions to particular problems faced by members of all economic classes during the mid- to late 1960s.[24]

Thus we can consider that the Factory attempted to win space from the dominant culture, not through the uniform act of bricolage as it was described in relation to groups such as the Mods but, instead, through individualized applications of recontextualization. To explain, many members of the Factory's in-there subculture resignified fashions and objects in their own individualized manner, and in so doing, they subverted the original meanings of such objects. In these instances, then, the Factory's subcultural members cohered through *collective* notions concerning individual stylistic bricolage as well as through collective notions concerning methods for undermining traditional class-based American cultural standards. Hence, in many ways, the

Factory as network maintained an agenda similar to that which was relative to British youth subcultures. In the case of the Factory, however, a number of networks merged—first, due to a correspondence with particular aesthetic ideas and, second, through a realization that these ideas allowed for the establishment of a collective (subversive) identity.

By way of comparison, I want to examine the notion of out-there subcultures, especially because the main focus of this book is on the development of out-there style. *Out-there* subcultures consist of young people who possess most of the stylistic characteristics that Hebdige attributes to subcultures, although out-there subcultures are not necessarily confined to one local area, nor are they necessarily determined by class or race relations. Unlike Hebdige's subcultural innovators, out-there subcultures take styles from mass-mediated sources (out-there) and appropriate them in a subcultural manner. Thus the out-there subculture is not pure in that it takes particular images given to it by commercial sources that have already incorporated innovative subcultural styles. Out-there subcultures, however, may engage in the recontextualization of an already commercialized (incorporated) style, but in so doing, they also engage in an act that symbolically resists the supremacy of dominant/mainstream culture.

In the case under analysis, glitter rock fans actually arrived at subcultural notions of queerness and style due to the pop practices of certain musicians who were originally established in Ann Arbor/Detroit, New York, and London. During the late 1960s, these musicians had their own subcultural followings in these cities; then, as they began to incorporate ideas from Warhol and the Factory, they began to hypothesize about an out-there genre that would eventually be labeled glitter rock. In other words, as Warhol and members of the Factory entourage began to interact with rock and roll musicians such as Lou Reed, David Bowie, and Iggy Pop, the concepts that would guide glitter rock began to surface. By the time that David Bowie was critically acclaimed as the king of glitter rock, an interesting phenomenon had occurred, particularly in light of the ways most British youth subcultures originate (i.e., as a result of class-race relations). Interestingly enough, glitter rock as subcultural practice was not grounded in class or race conditions in Britain or in America. Instead, glitter was instigated via media seduction; the rock press—looking for a new trend—heavily promoted glitter in the early 1970s. In turn, fans took the raw materials given to them by the rock media (i.e., both performers and journalists), and in the process, they created a spectacular version of out-there subcultural style.

In giving further consideration to the out-there glitter rock subculture, I suggest that even though it did not problematize the structural dynamics of class or race, it did operate so as to discomfit the heterosexual hegemony that had gone largely unchallenged in both the United States and Great Britain during the late 1960s and early 1970s. In the terms proposed by glitter rock, queerness suggested a way of being that was assimilated in such a manner so as to express ideological contradictions between dominant and subordinate sexual prescripts. Among some youth, such expressions "magically resolved" the dilemmas posed by dominant constructions of sexuality in the early 1970s. In more specific cases, however, these expressions were far less symbolic in that they actually represented concrete responses to real social conditions (concerning sexual oppression). And as the case study points out, glitter rock's conversion of Warholian/Factory premises for a mass audience meant that young people had access to the materials that provided the foundation for glitter rock style. Finally, this foundation was provided not only by the direct sources of glitter rock (the musicians, albums, performances) but also by certain rock journals (*Creem, Rock Scene*), which presented fans with forums as well as with information concerning glitter music and style. Thus glitter rockers had as their basis media-induced images of bands, commercial fashion marketing, and journalistic impressions of style. Consequently, although these elements represented incorporated versions of the Warholian pop ethos and the Factory's in-there style and attitude, such elements still provided powerful tools that were used by youth in a subversive/subcultural manner.

Production of Subculture

Clearly, the case studies provide for an extension of many of the main claims made by the British subculture theorists. At the same time that these claims are extended and often reworked, however, this study's methodological focus differs from that employed by Clarke et al. and Hebdige. Whereas Clarke et al. and Hebdige tend to analyze subcultures that are essentially composed of anonymous groups and whereas they render few accounts of the aesthetic forms and conditions that gave rise to subcultures, my analysis attempts to expose the artistic and musical processes that led to subcultural production. Thus the route I take toward arriving at a subcultural analysis may initially seem quite odd, especially to those who are overly familiar with the work of the CCCS. Throughout the book, I emphasize the artists and musicians who were integral to the Factory's emergence as an in-there subculture. Concurrently, because Andy Warhol and the Factory intermittently influenced glitter rock, I provide accounts of the musicians and artists who produced methods for effectively translating the Factory/Warholian ethos for a mass public. The case studies, then, often maintain a sense of "author centeredness," and this intentional focus is provided so that the reader can understand the conditions under which particular people met and exchanged ideas about pop practices. As we will see, these ideas were significant in that they resulted in genres (pop art, glitter rock) that were used in a subcultural manner.

In this sense, I am suggesting an unconventional method for arriving at an analysis of particular kinds of subcultural groups. For even though I examine cultural conditions, I am stressing the aesthetic forms and practices that determined the specificity of the glitter rock subculture. The reader will therefore gain a sense as to how and why pop art was produced within particular artistic and musical contexts and how and why glitter rock drew on particular aesthetic forms (such as pop art).

My analysis will therefore suggest that *incorporation* will take on a different meaning than that given to it by Hebdige. In the cases I examine, incorporation did occur, yet it was a particular kind of incorporation that cannot be described in such a way so as to suggest that the form destroyed the intentions of authentic subcultural participants. Instead, as I will demonstrate, incorporation took place through the medium of glitter rock itself. As mentioned earlier, the main proponents of glitter lifted ideas from Warhol and his Factory subculture, and in so doing, they transformed the essence of these ideas into a commercial genre. But the transformation did little to destroy the original precepts established by Warhol or the Factory subculture. Warhol's social world thus provided the materials through which commercial appropriation could take place; the incorporation process, however, provided for the formation of a subversive out-there subculture: glitter rockers.

Therefore, in examining the foundation of glitter rock, we must begin with a description of the pop practices of Andy Warhol. And although his influence is not always directly related to praxis, all indications point to the fact that his ideas, and his general artistic presence can be explicitly mapped out within the areas of popular culture that the case studies address—namely, certain genres of rock and roll music (both written and performed) and the subcultural networks and forms that took these genres as their rallying point. I will begin assessing Warhol's influence on rock and roll through an examination of the ways pop art emerged as a cultural force in the 1950s and 1960s. By examining the origins of pop art, we will gain insight into the leading premises that inspired both the musicians and fans of glitter. In addition, we will determine how glitter rock became the most opulent form to emerge from the fusion of pop art and rock and roll.

Notes

1. In particular, see Turner 1-84; Bratlinger; Nelson, Grossberg, and Treichler; John Clarke, *New Times* 1-19; and Grossberg, *We Gotta* 16-32.
2. See Grossberg, Nelson, and Treichler, *Cultural Studies.*
3. See notes 1 and 2.
4. See Nelson, Grossberg, and Treichler 9; Hall and Jefferson; Hebdige, *Subculture*; Hall, "Encoding/Decoding," "Culture, Media"; Turner 87-130, 195-225; Barker and Beezer.
5. See Nelson, Grossberg, and Treichler 8; Grossberg, *We Gotta* 21-22.
6. See Nelson, Grossberg, and Treichler 2; Grossberg, *We Gotta* 16-22.
7. See Nelson, Grossberg, and Treichler 6.
8. See Beezer 101-02.
9. Yet, as the authors point out, the strategies may or may not be direct.
10. Here, I would point out that this claim was made in regard to the embourgeoisement myth that had come to define all of working-class culture. Thus the authors did not use this particular definition in direct correspondence to youth subcultures; yet they applied the terms used in the definition to their detailed description of the class-based structure of such subcultures.
11. In this sense, Gramsci's theory of hegemony was combined with an Althusserian notion of ideology. For elaboration, see Brake 3-15; Beezer 102.
12. See also Beezer 102-03.
13. See also Beezer 109.
14. Hebdige provides an extensive account of the relation between mass media and youth subcultures. Here, the reader should refer to Chapter 5 in *Subculture.* The following section on media in my analysis deals with Chapter 6.
15. Note: This paragraph is, in effect, a summary of pages 92-99 in *Subculture: The Meaning of Style.*
16. See "Defending Ski Jumpers" (Gary Clarke 87).
17. See Hebdige, *Hiding* 7-41; John Clarke, *New Times* 8, 82-83, 110-11; Grossberg, "Politics"; McRobbie, "Settling Accounts."
18. I refer to authors such as Simon Frith and Lawrence Grossberg (who studied at the CCCS but was not involved directly in the subculture project).
19. See "We Gotta Get Out of This Place" by the Animals, and "Substitute" by the Who. In addition, see "My Generation" as it is used in the film *Quadrophenia.*
20. See Frith and Horne's *Art into Pop.*
21. Hebdige points out that he is attempting to analyze, in part, the ways that subcultural styles and behaviors make sense to members of the subculture. But this aspect of subcultural practice does not receive an inordinate amount of attention in his text.
22. Again, this "conceptualization" is inadvertent.
23. See Clarke et al., "Subcultures, Cultures and Class" 56.
24. This point will be examined in greater detail in the final chapter.

Andy Warhol and the Rise of Pop Art in the 1960s

Although pop art arose independently in London and New York in the late 1950s and 1960s, British critic Lawrence Alloway offered a definition that provides a useful criteria for its overall stance:

> Pop art, in its original form, was a polemic against elite views of art in which uniqueness is a metaphor of the aristocratic, and contemplation the only proper response to art. . . . In place of an hierarchical aesthetics keyed to define greatness and universality and to separate High from Low art, a continuum was assumed which could accommodate all forms of art, permanent and expendable, personal and collective, autographic and anonymous. (*Topics* 120)

In spite of the fact that Alloway was referring to late 1950s British pop art, his definition recalls much of the momentum of early New York pop.[1] Take, for example, Jasper Johns's painting of a lightbulb or Rosenquiest's painting of 7-Up bottles. These are works that championed common everyday objects and translated them literally onto canvas with no further comment or allusion. Such paintings, at least initially, suggested an integration of high art with low art in that these "serious" artists had borrowed directly from the anonymous world of advertising—the world of everyday consumption that is so rarely noticed or questioned. What made these paintings even more unusual was that they seemed to deny the application of an authoritative critical discourse. In fact, many New York art critics simply assumed that Johns and Rosenquiest were either engaging in a trivial experiment or that they were intentionally constructing a private joke. Either way, the artists' frivolity could be justified if viewed as a temporary endeavor that would soon be abandoned in favor of the canonical responsibilities of "proper" artists.

By the early 1960s, such assumptions were quickly dismantled as Johns and Rosenquiest were followed by a variety of pop artists, all of whom employed commercial imagery in their art. Indeed, as pop developed into a loosely defined movement, the consistent repetitiveness of commercial images began to raise uncommon questions concerning authorship (Who is the actual author?). In addition, such images fostered a series of debates concerning the objectification and aestheticization of the everyday environment.[2] Initially, such questions may have seemed ironic because most earlier modern art movements from impressionism to abstract expressionism had maintained a relationship to the industrial world, the world of human-produced objects, by portraying aestheticized segments of this world on canvas.[3] Pop art, however, did not put a protective layer over the outside world by attempting to make it aesthetically pure or by emphasizing uniqueness. Instead, pop reproduced the environment "as it is," thereby "tainting" the fine arts with seemingly uninterpreted reproductions of popular iconography: magazine commercials, brand names, images of television and film stars, commercial package designs, billboard logos, and comics. In so doing, pop art, unlike many prior moments in modern art, neither attempted to resolve some impending problem in art, nor did it provide a platform for advocating change.[4] More than any previous artistic mode (outside of, perhaps, Dada or Surrealism), pop simply opened up the passageways of artistic venture by breaking down the boundaries between fine art and graphics, commercial art and the decorative.[5] In this sense, pop art was not a movement, for it only provided open-ended possibilities; its authors appeared to have no clear-cut philosophical agendas or aesthetic aims except to present cultural images as they are: ready-made, fleeting, and autonomous.

As pop art quickly flourished in New York during the early 1960s, the urbane, formalist traditions of art criticism were subsequently forced into a crisis. In fact, both art critics and the general public began asking themselves: How long can one actually stare at a painting of a Coke bottle or a Campbell's soup can? How can the art establishment, rooted in conventional, formal values, analyze such work? Is pop art a serious art? Is the canvas being desecrated by tawdry, commercial forms? If we hate pop's simplicity, why are its images so irresistible? These questions will become critical as we attempt to assess Andy Warhol's pop art and, subsequently, his relation to rock and roll. For Warhol, more than any other pop artist, both undermined and accentuated the boundaries of fine art through his repeatedly contradictory pop art projects. With Warhol, we find that the questions stimulated by pop art are unveiled through an almost indistinguishable series of oppositions.

Andy Warhol: The 1950s

In June 1949, Andy Warhol graduated from the Carnegie Institute of Technology in his hometown of Pittsburgh. By the end of the month, he had relocated to New York and acquired a job illustrating short stories for *Glamour.* These drawings were admired by the art director of I. Miller, one of New York's most fashionable shoe sellers. As a result, Warhol managed to procure a prestigious position in the store's art department, where he established himself as one of the city's finest commercial artists. By the mid-1950s, Warhol found further work as an illustrator for Tiffany's and Bonwit Teller as well as for publications such as *McCall's* and *Vogue.* In addition, he designed record jackets for Columbia Records and even drew the clouds and suns onto weather maps at a local television station. From 1954 through 1959, Warhol maintained his status as a thriving commercial artist. And his graphic illustrations were so ornate and decorative that he had them published in a series of books. But during this time, he had not yet developed a solid and distinctive painting style of his own.[6]

Nonetheless, these job experiences did have an impact on Warhol's later pop aesthetic. First, the energetic and fast-paced world of New York advertising taught Warhol a great deal about the hypocrisies of fame. He was highly influenced by the maxim that people's *ideas* in the world of commercial art were simply items to be bought and sold. In addition, he must have realized that in the advertising business the illustrator's product remains anonymous.[7] In marked contrast to assumptions concerning fine art, the artist is not at the center of commercial art; it is the design instead that receives the most attention.

Second, through understanding these features of commercial art and artists, Warhol developed a monotype style that was used to symbolically "collapse" the distinction typically made between an original drawing and one that was mass produced. In executing this style, Warhol drew an ink illustration onto nonabsorbent paper. While still wet, the ink drawing was pressed onto another sheet of paper—which Warhol labeled "the original"—because it was the first copy to receive treatment. The actual original was then saved so that further copies could be made and so that the drawing could potentially undergo various transformations (Crone 12). Warhol expanded this technique in the late 1950s through the increased use of stencils and rubber or wooden stamps. Such methods were not only innovative in the field of commercial art, but they also laid the foundation for Warhol's future pop projects.

Third, because all of his drawings were easily reproduced, Warhol realized that his assistants could simply paint the suggested colors onto the stamped reproductions. And although this procedure was introduced to maximize time and effort, it was also inspired by an aesthetic decision: the *implication* of authorship—when applied to the drawings—was all that was necessary. In the context of the commercial art world, both Warhol's name and his original ideas were the "items" that sold the product; it mattered not if he had actually drawn the details.

Fourth, another distinguishing feature of Warhol's commercial art is that in it he began to experiment with excessive imagery that often hinted at his fascination with celebrity status. For example, in one series of shoe illustrations, Warhol employed the features of stars such as Zsa Zsa Gabor, James Dean, and Elvis Presley. In another set of illustrations, Warhol lavished the shoes with gold leaf, making them appear laboriously chic. Hence we find that although Warhol's early work was quite different in certain ways from that which he would produce in the 1960s, many of his aesthetic ideas and techniques were already firmly in place. Clearly, even in his initial craftsmanship, Warhol was starting to develop themes of depersonalization and anonymity that would eventually become dominant concepts in his later pop art projects.

Warhol, 1960-63: Pop Art Emerges

By the 1960s, pop art had already emerged in Britain, but its initial impact was just beginning to be felt in New York. The unusual factor in pop art's arrival in Manhattan was that the major artists who were creating images of "the popular" were largely unknown to one another. At the time, Henry Geldzahler, a curator at the Metropolitan Museum of Art, noted with amusement that this odd feature begged a comparison to science fiction (Warhol and

Hackett 3). Yet it is not that uncanny that Warhol, Lichtenstein, Oldenberg, and others arrived at comparable themes. It was a time in which the mass media had reached new heights of social influence. In the process, the aesthetics of everyday life had become increasingly intermeshed with the aesthetics of popular/commercial culture. In noting this merger, a number of New York artists began to scrutinize media-oriented culture as a potential source to inspire their work.

In 1960, Warhol began a series of paintings that commented on the manipulative attitudes of advertisers, using as his subject matter the very icons that dominated commercial culture. In the early stages of his work the paintings varied, however, between a lyrical, abstract style and one that was stark and overtly representational. For example, one of his paintings of a Delmonte peach can appeared to drip and run down the canvas.[8] Another was a faithful hand-painted reproduction of an ad for water heaters. It was simple and straightforward: a painted reprint. Other early works that contain no stylistic embellishments include *Dr. Scholl's Corn,* versions of *Before and After, Coca-Cola, Popeye,* and *Storm Door.*

By 1961, Warhol's most immediate concern was the direction his art should take. One friend, art agent Emile De Antonio, encouraged Warhol to move away from the lyrical, expressionistic mode and to experiment further with the representational style. Another friend, art collector Ted Carey, accompanied Warhol as he visited New York art galleries. One day, while visiting Leo Castelli's gallery, both he and Warhol were led into the back showroom to view a Lichtenstein painting. There, Ivan Karp presented them with one of Lichtenstein's early comic strip reproductions: a man in a rocket ship with a woman painted in the background. Warhol mentioned that he did similar work and invited Karp to stop by his apartment later that afternoon. In *Popism,* Warhol's autobiographical account of his experiences in the 1960s, he explained:

> When Ivan came by, I had all my commercial art drawings stashed away and out of sight. . . . I knew that I definitely wanted to take away the commentary of the gestures. That's why I had this routine of painting with rock and roll blasting the same song. . . . The music blasting cleared my head out and left me working on instinct alone. In fact, it wasn't only rock and roll that I used that way—I'd also have the radio blasting opera, and the TV picture on (but not the sound)—and if all that didn't clear enough out of my mind, I'd open a magazine, put it beside me, and half read an article while I painted. The works I was satisfied with were the cold "no comment" paintings.

> Ivan was surprised that I hadn't heard of Lichtenstein but he wasn't as surprised as I was, finding out that someone else was working with cartoon and commercial subjects, too! (Warhol and Hackett 7)

A few weeks later, Warhol showed his work to Karp's employer, Leo Castelli, a man known for promoting experimental artists. Castelli admired Warhol's work but found it to be too similar in format to the comic strip art (Lichtenstein) that was already hanging in his gallery. Still, Castelli was intrigued by Warhol's use of pop images and decided to provide word-of-mouth promotion with the expectation that a showing would result. Warhol, excited by the prospects ahead, immediately mailed Ivan Karp the original *Nancy* painting. It was a gesture that furthered Warhol's friendship with both of these influential men.

By April 1961, minor progress was achieved in presenting Warhol's work to the public. The window designer at Bonwit Teller agreed to exhibit five Warhol paintings as the backdrop for his mannequins. On the surface this decision wasn't unusual; Warhol was, after all, well regarded among commercial artists and advertisers as a result of his enterprising achievements during the 1950s. But the clientele and employees of Bonwit Teller provided scathing remarks when confronted with Warhol's *Advertisement, Little King, Superman, Before and After,* and *Saturday's Popeye.* The consensus was that the pop representations were distasteful and decidedly inappropriate for the window of such a selective boutique. Paradoxically, within a two-year span, Bonwit Teller would be selling garments that were saturated with the same pop images that echoed throughout Warhol's work. Yet in 1961, pop art was considered too trivial and insulting to be taken seriously, and it certainly did not seem to blend with the refined context of galleries, museums, or even fashion store windows.

Over the next eight months, however, several of Warhol's paintings made their way to the back room of Castelli's gallery, a prominent 1960s "testing ground" for innovative and arresting art. In addition, a few of Warhol's paintings were placed in the back rooms of the Bellamy and the Allan Stone galleries. But the overall response was negative, if not brutal. On the whole, buyers and collectors in New York had no interest in such conspicuous representational paintings. And the lack of traditional aesthetic value made the paintings seem pointless and amateurish. Despite such negative responses, Warhol, Karp, and Castelli continued making proposals to gallery owners and curators. But most of the prospective clients felt such requests were hypocritical. If Castelli and Karp found Warhol so momentous why didn't they hang his paintings in the main display room at their gallery?

Early in 1962, a personal event led Warhol to develop a series of new ideas, ones that proved fruitful in gaining him an opening. One evening, Muriel Latow, the owner of a financially failing museum, paid Warhol a visit. Knowing that he was struggling for new ideas and desperately needing money herself, Latow proposed that Warhol pay her $50 for a suggestion. Amused by the odd nature of her proposition, he immediately wrote out a check. Latow then said that he should paint Campbell's soup cans because these objects were so common that their aesthetic value had never been redeemed. Warhol liked the idea, and the next day began work on the first of the Campbell's soup can paintings (Tomkins 12).

At first he painted only a barren singular image. Soon after, he began to place these paintings alongside one another to achieve a regimental effect: *32 Campbell's Soup Cans.* This was the beginning of an entire series in which Warhol replicated a number of common, commercial images. *18 One Dollar Bills, 210 Coca-Cola Bottles,* and many variations on the soup can theme. After spending time painting row after row of the same image, however, Warhol quickly realized that he could apply the monotype technique that he had developed as an illustrator. He simply designed the selected images, made stencils and rubber stamps, and swiftly created duplicated rows of soup cans, postage stamps, dollar bills, and Coke bottles.[9] After stamping out these rows, Warhol returned to the canvas and provided the appropriate colors, thereby re-creating the very methods he had used in his commercial art.

In July 1962, an ecstatic Irving Blum exhibited some of the hand-painted Campbell's soup cans in the Ferus Gallery in Los Angeles.[10] Although six of the paintings sold at $100 each, most Los Angeles critics and connoisseurs were repelled at the thought of validating Warhol's work. For example, one block away, a gallery owner stacked 32 soup cans in his display window; beside them, a sign read: "Get the real thing for 29 cents a can." Warhol, never fond of West Coast art sensibilities, remained unconcerned with this blatant mockery of his work. He simply turned all of his attention to a new method of visual duplication.

By August 1962, Warhol had begun his system of silk-screening, and with the assistance of a young art student, Gerard Malanga, he turned out multiple portraits of film stars. In explaining the process, Warhol stated:

> The rubber-stamp method I'd been using to repeat images suddenly seemed too homemade; I wanted something stronger that gave more of an assembly-line effect.
>
> With silkscreening, you pick a photograph, blow it up, transfer it in glue onto silk, and then roll ink across it so the ink goes through the glue. That way you get the same image, slightly different each time. It was all so simple—quick and chancy. I was thrilled with it. My first experiments with screens were heads of Troy Donahue and Warren Beatty, and then when Marilyn Monroe happened to die that month, I got the idea to make screens of her beautiful face—the first Marilyns. (Warhol and Hackett 22)

The silk-screening process epitomized the culmination of many of Warhol's ideas concerning authorship, mass production, and the role of consumerism in modern American life. This process and its implications help to illuminate certain central themes that permeated Warhol's career at this time: (a) The aesthetics of silk-screening denied formalistic values about how to produce art. The technology negated the standard relationship one commonly assumes when considering artistic "intentionality" and creativity. (b) The subjects and the flat yet gaudy look of Warhol's silk screens brought to the forefront his obsession with fame as appearance—"surface"—and its fetishization in American culture. (c) The operation of silk-screening raised further questions concerning authenticity because most of the sources were publicity stills or photographs taken from magazines or newspapers.

In giving consideration to the above points, I would suggest that outside of extremist movements such as Dada and Futurism, art had typically been considered a process that required a special relationship between the artist and the desired medium, typically oils or acrylics. In most traditions, the artist drew a series of sketches, engaged in contemplation, and then brought the conceptions into realization through drawing or painting. (For example, among abstract expressionists, the planning stages were tedious and sequenced so as to reveal a proper "painterly" aesthetic). In an opposite manner, Warhol developed a simplistic yet vital method, one that was devoted to consistency in format. By taking images from a preexisting repertoire and transferring them onto silk with only slight alterations, Warhol furthered the notions of mass production and impersonality that had fueled the shoe drawings as well as the first pop paintings. The rows and rows of "Marilyns," "Troy Donahues," "Elizabeth Taylors," and so on resonated with the maxim of "flatness," thus offering an art with reference only to itself. Furthermore, such works called into question the limits of copyright laws, as Warhol chose to exploit "found images," which he then silk-screened in newspaper format—printing them and rolling them out by the hundreds. In ignoring his original sources, Warhol made clear the notion that these faces were "public domain" because they were among the most commodified in our culture. These film stars had been bought and sold for their looks—they were people who had become, in essence, public property.

As Warhol continued to produce the silk-screened photographs, he frequently experimented with singular as well as multiple images. In addition, he often added to the silk screens garish, cartoonlike colors (bright reds, purples, and golds) that commented on the already established public image of the star. The effect was to construct images that appeared both radiant and intentionally crude—Marilyn Monroe as if she had garnished her face with cheap makeup from Woolworth's.

In considering the details of the silk screens, we might also appraise the importance behind the particular gaze present in the photographs. In each case, Warhol chose to reproduce photographs in which the star appears robotic and distant; the smiles seem mechanical and self-conscious. In viewing these gazes, then, we are asked to confirm both the "uselessness" as well as the importance of fame. These mass-consumed, cool, and distant stares remind us of the expendable and varnished nature of the images we choose to embellish with our own private fantasies. Thus, through examining Warhol's "silk screen period," we find a serious departure from the methods associated with traditional art. The images used by Warhol were altered and reproduced in a form that stressed many of the contradictions between popular culture and fine art, artist and medium, fame and its fetishization, subjectivity and objectivity, celebrity and ordinariness, individuality and uniqueness, and anonymity.

By August 1962, Warhol began to employ new ways for investigating the notion that pop art could be used as a way to speak of, and to, our perceptions of everyday life—and thus our contradictory feelings about it. Such an investigation became apparent at Eleanor Ward's Stable Gallery in November 1962. For there, Warhol gained his first official New York public opening, one that spawned controversy yet won him critical acclaim from prestigious factions of the New York art community.

The Stable opening was highly publicized and, as a result, the gallery was filled with New York's most prestigious curators, critics, and buyers. For the first time, many of them viewed the single Marilyns, the duplicated Marilyns, the huge gold Marilyn, the Elvis paintings, the Campbell's soup cans, and the

Do It Yourself paint-by-number series. In the process, Warhol was accepted posthaste within circles where he had once been criticized. In a published conversation with interviewer Patrick Smith, Eleanor Ward provided the following insight:

> Well . . . (sighs), you must remember that in 1962 people weren't lining up on 59th street and spending three days to get into the Metropolitan Museum of Art. The art world was a much more closed world than today so that the people who were interested in art were, primarily, artists, art historians, museum people, and collectors. They were not the mob scenes that you see at the Whitney today. Art hadn't been properly covered, you know as a cultural phenomenon of the world. It was still the closed world of the artists, the museum people. So, my gallery had a prestigious name, and I had shown a great many important people so that almost automatically . . . I would show someone and he would be taken seriously, and so it was with Warhol. (Smith 203)

Rainer Crone has pointed out that Warhol's paintings during this period were particularly enticing, in part, because they were "open to and understandable to everyone," thus no longer requiring "unraveling by the expert" (23). In light of this claim, we might consider the interaction between Bill Seitz and Peter Seltz, otherwise known as the Bobbsey Twins of the Museum of Modern Art. After contemplating Warhol's reportorial matte style, Seltz hurried from Ward's gallery in exasperation. He telephoned Seitz from a public booth and quickly declared that it was one of the most ghastly shows he'd ever endured. Seitz paused and then responded, "Yes, it was horrible. But I bought one." Such was the irresistible attraction to Warhol's hyperreal/commercial/graphic style. Many viewers and critics may have felt the desire to loathe Warhol's seemingly simple proficiency, yet few could resist his startling results.

The Pop Art Explosion: New York in the Early 1960s

By the end of November, Warhol and other pop artists had gained widespread attention following a two-gallery showing at the Sidney Janus Gallery. Besides Warhol, this show included the work of Rauschenberg, Johns, Dine, Lichtenstein, Wesselmann, and Oldenberg. Although these artists' styles varied significantly, each had created art that made explicit reference to American popular/consumer culture. For example, through the use of stencils and overhead projectors, Roy Lichtenstein had continued his line of comic strip art, presenting the viewer with oversized figures and direct quotations from comic texts. Drawing on representations of advertising, Rosenquiest's inspiration often came straight from billboard signs. Wesselmann's paintings featured collages of television sets, telephones, and other everyday objects, as well as hand-painted, glossy, nude figures. Rauschenberg typically used mimeographed and silk-screened images of both common objects and famous paintings while adding his own sweeping brush strokes. In 1962, the work produced by these various artists formally acquired the term *pop art.* It is a term that has been used ever since to describe an art that attempts to represent the modern consumer-oriented/media-saturated environment as it is, and in doing so, no particular emphasis is placed on orthodox painting styles or techniques. During the early 1960s, however, many of the so-called pop artists did not want to be limited by a term that might restrict the expansion of a developing "pop aesthetic." As a result, artists and critics raised questions concerning the implications of the term: perhaps this art is better labeled "neodada." The term *new realism* was also frequently used. In addition, some critics and artists simply referred to the new art as "representational." But when Lawrence Alloway, the originator of the term pop art, made the connection between pop art in Britain and the new trend in art in New York, the term gained a sense of legitimacy. Even though the following passage was written several years after pop art's arrival, it demonstrates a definition that many of the pop artists came to agree on:

> Pop art is neither abstract nor realistic, though it has contacts in both directions. The core of Pop art is at neither frontier; it is, essentially, an art about signs and sign-systems. Realism is, to offer a minimal definition, concerned with the artist's perception of objects in space and their translation into iconic, or faithful, signs. However, Pop art deals with material that already exists as signs: photographs, brand goods, comics—that is to say, with precoded material. The subject matter of Pop art, at one level, is known to the spectator in advance of seeing the use the artist makes of it. Andy Warhol's Campbell's soup cans, Roy Lichtenstein's comic strips are known either by name or by type, and their source remains legible in the work of art. (Alloway, *Topics* 119)

As a result of the Janus showing, the topic of pop art increasingly became a central point of discussion in New York art circles. The once-admired abstract expressionists were being reconsidered; concurrently, pop art emerged as the vanguard trend of the moment. Amid the fanfare, in December 1962, the Museum of Modern Art held a symposium at which factions of the New York art world convened and discussed the validity of this new trend. And although opposing factions engaged in heated debates, pop art's supporters claimed it to be an important new art form that had a legacy in the work of Duchamp, the early German dadaists, and the Bauhaus artists. But the lines that had to be drawn were apparent. Certainly, pop begged a comparison to these artists and movements, for it confronted audiences with obvious and mundane images. But unlike dada and Bauhaus, pop did not maintain a resistant strategy toward established artistic modes, and it certainly had no central radical manifesto or creed. Pop was a novel expression for a modern decade; it represented a collective response to the escalating, industrialized world. Along these lines, art critic Mario Amaya provides an excellent summation of pop art's central features:

> Such art seems to direct attention towards the strange, inhuman, synthetic, elements that man has produced, not for basic existence, but as a by-product of it. The pre-fabricated, plastic reality of a package's existence, as it arrives after endless processing through Madison Avenue, the glossy magazines, and multiple stores, has more meaning than the product it contains. In fact the entire image of the commodity has been commercially transformed before it gets to us: bread becomes Wonderloaf, cereal becomes Snap, Crackle, and Pop. . . . Everything comes in a box: our job, our pleasures, our dreams, our love life. (12)

Increasingly, as the modern environment became the focal point of pop artists in 1962 and 1963, Warhol began a series of reproductions that held up for inspection a number of discomfiting images. Fascinated with America's ironic attitudes toward violence, Warhol began his death series: the severe orange and blue silk screens of a single electric chair and silk screens of car wrecks, race riots, and gangster funerals. Unlike Warhol's earlier choice of subjects, these images tended to chastise the modern world rather than simply expose it on its own terms. By pointing to America's infatuation with horribly violent acts in 1963, Warhol conveyed the often chilling impact of modernization and industrial life. These compositions, moreover, suggested the perverse sense of distance that most viewers are encouraged to maintain when viewing "realistic" representations of violence. Warhol's reproduction of confrontational images thus began to shift the overall tone that had come to be associated with pop's central themes. In turn, the questions raised most frequently by observers were, Is Warhol humanizing objects, while dehumanizing people? Is he criticizing or glorifying a society that has become indifferent to both violence and mass consumption? Is Warhol engaging in both technological and aesthetical nihilism?

Such questions, however, have no easy answers: certainly, none from the artist himself. Warhol, when asked, refused to comment on his work. In adding fuel to the darker suggestions raised by critics, Warhol offered claims that suggested that dehumanization might actually be his intention. In an interview with G. R. Swenson this stance comes through most clearly:

> I think everybody should be a machine. I think everybody should like everybody.
> Is that what Pop Art is all about?
> Yes. It's liking things.
> And liking things is like being a machine?
> Yes, because you do the same thing every time. You do it over and over again.
> And you approve of that?
> Yes. (Russell et al. 116)

Warhol's odd sense of reasoning was not taken lightly by the entire New York art community, however. With all of the attention that he and other pop artists were gaining, traditionalist critics such as Clement Greenberg and Harold Rosenberg were among those who vehemently attacked Warhol and pop art in general for what they perceived to be its lack of individuality and its insensitive approach to the urban landscape. With the hope that abstract expressionism would continue its reign into the 1960s, these critics fiercely resisted an art form that they saw as possessing strong references, both in content and form, to fascism, nihilism, pornography, sexual deviance, and overall despair. In 1965, several years after the attacks became less regular and forceful, Mario Amaya claimed:

> The younger critics and historians, among them Henry Geldzahler, G. R. Swenson, Barbara Rose, Donald Judd and Robert Rosenblum, found themselves in the embarrassing position of defending a movement which was made to appear as if it were the "enemy" of a previous movement. As for the artists themselves, their frank admission of a debt to their forbearers did little to prevent their being assailed as cheap, meretricious, unworthy heirs of the "heroic" years of American painting. (44)

If the aesthetics of pop were the basis for such a strong defense and analysis at the time, it was Warhol's flippant relation with the press that—continuously—exacerbated the already anxious tensions between artistic factions. Warhol repeatedly deferred all analysis, leaving it to his critics and observers, thus confusing some and outraging others. The most blatant example of this anti-authorial technique occurred when he began a live interview with an assertion that became the most infamous one of his career: "You should just tell me the words you want me to say and I'll repeat them. I'm so empty. I can't think of anything to say" *(Warhol: Portrait of an Artist).* He once asked an interviewer at the end of an interview, "Have I lied enough?" (qtd. in Tomkins 14). In line with such public remarks, Warhol's repeated allusions to boredom and mass assimilation often forced critics and followers to question his tactics and even his artistic depth. Many times, he professed that it would be "great if everyone were alike" and that he wanted "to be a machine." He asserted that "in the future, everyone will be world-famous for fifteen minutes." Was he serious? Was he pulling a series of publicity stunts? In one of his most telling quotes, written years after pop art had gained acceptance, Warhol summed up his view:

> I've been quoted a lot as saying, "I like boring things." Well I said it and I meant it. But that doesn't mean I'm not bored by them. Of course, what I think is boring must not be the same as what other people think is, since I could never stand to watch all the most popular action shows on TV, because they're essentially the same plots and the same shots and the same cuts over and over again. Apparently, most people love watching the same basic thing, as long as the details are different. But I'm just the opposite: if I'm going to sit and watch the same thing I saw the night before, I don't want it to be essentially the same—I want it to be exactly the same. Because the more you look at the same exact thing, the more the meaning goes away, and the better and emptier you feel. (Warhol and Hackett 50)

If Warhol appeared to be nonchalant, it was clear that the American public felt otherwise. By the summer of 1963, it seemed as if the pop art aesthetic could be found—intentionally or unintentionally—in reigning fashion trends, popular music styles, and in the broader everyday atmosphere that dominated urban America in the 1960s. For example, the subcultural British mod style not only paralleled pop's infatuation with everything modern, it also defined the major international fashion trends of 1963. Likewise, the Beatles (a pop group) and the Rolling Stones (who had a "pop" manager) were playing the club circuit in London, while Motown, Phil Spector's famous girl groups, and California surf music dominated in the United States. In most urban areas medical doctors were freely prescribing amphetamines for dieting. And the nation was infatuated with the seemingly timeless atmosphere of Camelot as John F. Kennedy and Jackie provided a fashionable youthful exuberance for the White House. In essence, the nation seemed to lean toward beauty, the image of youth, and the fast-paced excitement of city life. Warhol, always the implicit sociologist, took note of the changing environment and became increasingly convinced that the pop attitude was becoming *the* mainstay of American culture in the 1960s. At the same time, as he claimed, pop art also represented a vision that only "insiders" could truly grasp.

He recorded such perceptions during the summer of 1963 when he was invited to provide an exhibition at the Ferus gallery in Los Angeles. Riding in a station wagon with Gerard Malanga and two friends, Taylor Mead and Wyn Chamberlain, with rock and roll blaring from the radio, Warhol noted:

> The further west we drove, the more Pop everything looked on the highways. Suddenly we all felt like insiders because even though Pop was everywhere—that was the thing about it, most people still took it for granted, whereas we were dazzled by it, to us it was the new Art. . . . All you had to do was know you were in the future, and that's what put you there.
>
> The mystery was gone, but the amazement was just starting. (Warhol and Hackett 40)

In New York, during the summer of 1963, to really "get" pop one needed to have an insider's knowledge of the subcultural trends that were permeating Warhol's pop practices. In essence, this meant that all roads led to Andy Warhol's Factory studio, where pop art suddenly took on a new meaning: it became the term that defined not only a series of related aesthetic trends but one that also implied a particular kind of lifestyle.

Notes

1. Lawrence Alloway is often cited as first using the term *pop art* in 1954. He has claimed that such citations are incorrect; he used the term prior to this date as a reference to the actual "products of mass media," not "the works of art that draw upon popular culture" ("Development" 27). For a specific assessment of Alloway's use of the term, see his "The Development of British Pop."

2. For further clarification, see Dick Hebdige's "In Poor Taste: Notes on Pop" in *Hiding in the Light* (1988).

3. The abstract expressionists, by the very nature of their medium, acted as interpreters of the industrial world. Among other things, their art was about the use of paint as a medium to comment on the relation between paint, the canvas, and the perceiver.

4. Most pop artists refused to even consider pop a movement.

5. See Roselee Goldberg's *Performance: Live Art 1909 to the Present.* Goldberg explores the subversive techniques of both dada and surrealism while presenting the reader with modern parallels: "To Be with Art Is All We Ask."

6. Warhol's pencil sketches (e.g., *Self-Portrait,* 1948) and watercolor paintings (e.g., *Living Room,* 1946-47) were a reflection of the training he received at the Carnegie Institute of Technology. They offer, however, definitive proof that Warhol was quite capable of following in the line of traditional modernism. His late 1940s and early 1950s paintings were sometimes viewed with bewilderment by critics who had solidly denounced his pop art of the 1960s.

7. See Rainer Crone's "Commercial Art" in *Andy Warhol* (1970) for a comparable explanation.

8. Warhol often kept the abstract paintings close at hand for observation by friends, whereas he tended to hide the more straightforward pop pieces. Initially, he viewed all of this work as a mere chance experiment—something he wanted to pursue further, but he was unsure about how the paintings would be perceived.

9. Warhol also created monotype images of a number of other commercial objects. These, however, are the most notable.

10. For an extended account, see David Bourdon's *Warhol* 109-11.

The Factory 1964–67

POP ART AS POP LIFE

During November 1963, Warhol's Factory studio at 231 East Forty-Seventh Street became the central focus of his work and his everyday life. There, he and his newly acquired assistant Gerard Malanga created the huge silk screens, the Brillo boxes, and the other paintings that became Warhol's staple output in the mid-1960s. By the onset of January 1964, Malanga's input resulted in two formal changes at the studio: most important, he helped to alter some of Warhol's customary procedures for creating pop art by developing certain practices that became mainstays in the pop medium. In addition, Malanga had social connections with a number of artistic, "underground" New York subcultures, and many of these eventually claimed the Factory studio as their headquarters.

Certainly crucial to all this was the fact that the quick-witted and talkative Malanga had established himself as a regular in many of the most notorious coffeehouses and clubs in the Village. In 1964, when he wasn't helping Warhol, he was attending up to five parties a night, developing a growing interest in the avant-garde Village dance and art scenes, and spending a considerable amount of time at the San Remo coffeehouse. Soon, the somewhat introverted Warhol began taking fascinated interest in Malanga's social activities and, in turn, Warhol began to make the nightly rounds with Malanga.

Warhol was immediately accepted among the flamboyant regulars at the coffee shops and bars, and as a result, he decided that a more conspicuous "visual look" should replace his standard outfits, which consisted of paint-splattered work clothes and worn tennis shoes. Malanga agreed with Warhol's assessment, and as a team they began dressing in the style of many Village gay males:[1] black and white striped T-shirts, tight black jeans, black leather jackets, and high leather boots. In addition, during this time, Warhol began to accent his pasty white complexion by dyeing his hair a shocking shade of silver-white; eventually, he also began wearing his infamous "white, tousled wigs." Thus, with their commanding visual presence, Malanga's sharp tongue, and Warhol's growing reputation as the pop art master, the twosome became a focal point for an already thriving art, dance, and poetry scene.

One of their most frequent hangouts was the San Remo on the corner of MacDougal and Bleecker streets. There, the crowd was composed mainly of hustlers and "A-men," a colloquialism used to suggest both gayness and speed addiction. In addition, many of the cafe's clients were poets, dancers, and underground filmmakers. A subgroup of these regulars was also involved in writing and publishing *The Sinking Bear,* one of the 1960's first mimeographed political/arts newsletters. This lively, energetic crowd therefore represented a unique coalition of subculturally based individuals, with many sharing a common heritage in leftist politics, drug use, and the avant-garde. A core faction of this crowd eventually became instrumental in laying the foundation for the chaotic social-aesthetic atmosphere at the Factory. More specifically, by spring 1964, many patrons of the San Remo became vital participants in a number of art and film projects overseen by Warhol.

One of the first San Remo regulars to help instigate the Factory scene was Billy Linich (aka Billy Name), a 21-year-old A-man who was best known as the lighting coordinator for Village dance shows.[2] Name was intense and attractive, and Warhol was of the belief that he and his friends were the "precursors of a new style" (Bockris 144). When Name was forced to leave his New York apartment, Warhol invited him to live at the Factory studio in an area in the rear ("Billy's room") that was screened off and made private, even to most insiders.

One of the most significant aspects of Name's arrival at the Factory was his ability to encourage a lived merger of pop art with everyday life to create a complete "pop" lifestyle. In fact, both Name's and Malanga's input forcibly signaled the beginning of a distinctly postmodern moment in which the disparate and previously separated worlds of high art, pop art, classical art, and contemporary popular culture became consolidated within the Factory's walls. This phenomenon occurred because, to put it simply, the studio was open to anyone, and so *everyone* came. Abruptly, the Factory became not only the place where one could observe Warhol at work but also the pop site where rock and roll and classical music blared both day and night and amphetamines were so abundant that time often seemed irrelevant; the definitive locale where "posing" became a full-time career; the spacious, decadent mecca where the most pallid, downcast thrill seekers mingled with those who aspired to celebrity status. Within the walls of the Factory studio, Warhol's notions of fame as an immediate yet deceptive quality existed provocatively alongside his own already verified notoriety in both New York art galleries and Village night spots. By the end of 1964, the Factory was represented by a multitude of shared visions that came to epitomize the embodiment of a "living art form."

In many ways, the notion of pop art as living art form was ushered in from January to April 1964, as Name converted the dour Factory studio into a luminous pop arena. During these months, Name spent most of his days covering the walls with tin foil and bits of broken glass, after which he spray painted the entire creation silver. Warhol claimed, "Silver was the future, it was spacey—the astronauts . . . and silver was also the past—the Silver Screen. . . . And maybe more than anything else, silver was narcissism—mirrors were backed with silver" (Bockris 144).

During the time that Name worked on his project, a number of his friends from the San Remo began to meet at the studio so they could spend time with Name, gossip, inject speed, and simply wander around the glittering walls. One by one, the streetwise Narsissy, the flagrant Pope Ondine, and the bitchy Rotten Rita, all made daily visits to the Factory. Soon, it became filled with others: Binghampton Birdie, Silver George, Stanley the Turtle, and The Mayor.

As the weeks passed, Warhol encouraged the A-men to continue their daily procession into his studio. He was especially intrigued by their speed-inspired sensibilities and their personal artistic ventures. Silver George, for example, sat for hours, creating bright drawings with magic markers; others tacked painted decorations to the walls and used feathers and beads as additional props. Warhol was also inspired by the A-mens' taste in music, which was reflected in their valuable collections of largely of out-of-print opera records or private recordings of opera performances. In turn, Warhol decided that his taste in rock and roll could provide for an interesting contrast to singers such as Maria Callas; thus, opera was played on a phonograph while Warhol blasted

"Louie-Louie" and "Sugar Shack" from his always present radio. As the two opposing musical forms roared, Warhol and Malanga produced series after series of silk-screened designs. All the while, curious visitors began to enter through the Factory's elevator doors, all of them lured by the style and attitude that was developing at the studio. Film scholar and Factory regular Stephen Koch describes a typical gathering in those early days:

> The silver room was crowded with a-heads, street geniuses, poor little rich girls, the very chic, the desperately unknown, hustlers and call boys, prostitutes . . . the best artists of the time, and the worst hangers-on. The people "in" thought the place had everything: intensity without demands, class without snobbery, glamour without trying. Not to mention a lot of sex, a lot of art, a lot of amphetamines, a lot of fame. And a door that was always open. (4)

By Summer 1964, the Factory's admits-all policy—as well as its reputation as a living art form—had raised interest in New York's pop art community as well. Artists such as Rauschenberg and Jasper Johns often dropped by to discuss art with Warhol and survey his paintings. Similarly, art dealers and collectors established their presence at the Factory, as did columnists and society reporters. In addition, curators, art critics, and other "established" members of the art community all began to make regular visits to the studio (see Koch 4-7).[3] And as the Factory increasingly became a meeting spot for eclectic individuals and subgroups, word began to spread that Warhol had created an exceptional scene—and it was open to anyone.

By the end of 1964, the Factory studio was undergoing further changes as it became the weekend destination for artistically oriented Harvard students. Concurrently, as the word spread further, the Factory was soon transformed into a regular venue for those who knew of Warhol but did not know him as a friend. Village dancers, poets, artists, and writers began to mingle daily with the A-men, the curators, the transvestites, the call boys, and the collectors.[4] In the process, the Factory came to epitomize a veritable 24-hour open house for all those who cared to enter.

Many who were integrated into this social scene claim that Warhol intentionally attempted to promote the Factory as a place where distinct groups could merge. But others felt that the Factory lifestyle worked in a backward manner. That is, Warhol never attempted to lure people into his studio. He simply watched and worked as the painters, hustlers, A-men, dancers, and others found a way to hold their ground there. Once the activity between and among these various groups was somewhat regimented, Warhol borrowed what he could from those who were around him. He used their ideas, manipulated their skills, and prudently attempted to control them to gain some sense of who he really wanted to be—a powerful and famous socialite.[5] All the while, however, Warhol developed the reputation for being extremely distant and aloof. Repeatedly, those who were regulars at the Factory have pointed out that Warhol had the most illuminating *and* the most vacant presence in the room. Always standing, Warhol could simply march to the center of the studio, stare at those around him, and the mundane soon became "an event." So, with the controlled chaos of the Factory regulars pitted against the enigmatic presence of Warhol, it's no wonder that opinions vary widely as to the reason behind—and the effects of—the unique interactions that occurred at the studio. Warhol himself claimed that

> a lot of people thought that it was me everyone at the Factory was hanging around, that I was some kind of big attraction that everyone else came to see, but that's absolutely backward: it was me who was hanging around everyone else. I just paid the rent, and the crowds came simply because the door was open. People weren't particularly interested in seeing me, they were interested in seeing each other. They came to see who came. (Warhol and Hackett 74)

Stephen Koch, however, offers a more analytical opinion:

> The old Factory was about decadence, about the wasted pallor on Warhol's boyish face, about his silence, his affectless gaze, the chic freakishness of his entourage, about all the things he was able to endow with the magic of his fame and transform into the image, par excellence, of a subterranean world of beautiful people and geniuses and poseurs, the obsessed and the bored, who had come at last into their glamorous own. To the people gathered around him, Warhol was fame; he shed fame's redeeming light on them, and they basked in it, refugees from an invisible secret world that had been growing and steadily defining itself through the late 1950's. One senses that, in those days, a thrilling complicity united the artistic and sexual and drug subcultures, that some kind of shared refusal threw together mute seriosos like the composer LaMonte Young with hardened, quick-witted, druggy street performers with names like Rotten Rita, Narsissy, and Ondine, people living on drugs and their wits, doing numbers in bars and apartments and lofts, of the existence of which the straight world had only the merest dreadful imitations. (5)

As the diverse population at the Factory began to swell in numbers, the social atmosphere increasingly seemed more and more like a self-referential emblem of pop art. At the studio, Warhol was surrounded by the downtrodden and streetwise as well as the rich and glamorous—all of those who appeared to get on by their looks and their illusions. They came to Warhol and the Factory to be noticed and to be on display. Amid all this, Warhol became much like the Coke bottles and soup cans that he had painted. He had little obvious allure, but the associations linked to him made him powerful and attractive. And the more Warhol became sought after, the more he became aloof and mysterious—the living parallel to the distant, yet compelling, gazes of Marilyn and Liz in his "Face Series." Yet, at the same time, Warhol's persona also seemed to recall the "Death Series"—Warhol's annihilation of the celebratory features of pop art. In a comparable manner, Warhol's Factory seemed to promise fame for at least 15 minutes but only if one also happened to be exceedingly lucky.

As it turned out, some were more favored than others, and their position on the social continuum remained steady during the Factory years. Malanga, for example, was always at the forefront during the Factory's heyday, serving not only as Warhol's assistant but also as a major social instigator. Also, Malanga was responsible for actually introducing Warhol to many of the techniques that allowed for the production of the silk screens and sculptures. Warhol needed Malanga in ways that he didn't need the others.

In the early days, Warhol also needed Billy Name, not only for his artistic sensibility but also for his spontaneity in encouraging A-men and other Village artists to frequent the Factory. As Warhol stated, "I picked up a lot from Billy, actually—just studying him" (Bockris 9). For approximately two years, however, Warhol overlooked Name entirely—for no clear reason. This resulted in one of the many Factory "casualties": Name decided to become a recluse in the screened-off area of the Factory where he resided. As Name remained alone in the room, deeply depressed, Warhol never asked questions about his former colleague and refused to check on him even once. Such was the more morbid side that a connection with Warhol could bring.

In the heyday of the Factory, the type of treatment Name received at Warhol's hands manifested itself most clearly among Warhol's female "superstars": the chi-chi and glamorous women who were allowed, for a time, to share some of the benefits that Factory fame provided. The first among these was socialite Baby Jane Holzer, who from 1963 through 1964 was frequently seen accompanying Warhol to parties. As "This Year's Girl"[6] of 1964, Holzer possessed many of the qualities that Warhol so admired in other people: she was wealthy, fashionable, urbane, and she had the kind of charming filmic presence that Warhol found so dazzling. For roughly a year she remained in

Warhol's limelight. Then, after 1964 she was succeeded by a series of new pop princesses, including Edie Sedgwick, Nico, International Velvet, Viva, and Ultra Violet. These women, like Holzer, were able to live out brief moments at the top of the Warhol hierarchy because of their looks, their money, and/or their heritage in high society.

In addition to the preceding individuals and groups, there were others who (for brief periods and under shifting circumstances) were able to bask in the limelight of the Factory and reap some of the rewards of instant fame. Perhaps what distinguished these people was that Warhol not only enjoyed their presence, but he *needed* them to execute his film and art projects during the mid- to late 1960s. Included in this category were the self-invented superstars (such as "Viva" and Baby Jane), as well as underground film actors, would-be models, A-men, and transvestites. Warhol liked to surround himself with notably eccentric groups of people; at the same time, these groups provided the Factory with an overall sense of noisy harmony—they made the Factory famous. Thus the "poor little rich girls," the butch gay icons (Paul America, Joe Dallesandro), and the "wanna-bes" (Rod La Rod), all were able, at one point or another, to enter the Factory's inner circle and emerge as superstars. In the process, such transformations suggested an egalitarian premise: the Factory encouraged the reinvention of self, which subsequently involved the adoption of spectacular, shocking, and transformative styles. In this sense, Warhol enfranchised a number of subalternate individuals by providing them with a social environment whereby they could try on roles and take on the qualities of celebrities with little struggle—except that of maintaining their wits once Warhol's attention was on them.

Finally, established names in the entertainment field and street people passing time between drug deals and tricks defined the extremes of the Factory's continuum. The two groups were very much a staple during the Factory's frantic heyday because both had the same quality: they knew how to strike the perfect, irrepressible pose. They knew the system because they had played it most of their lives. And these people and their trades had a common ground that must have fascinated Warhol, for in his world these two groups could merge and form the perfect bond with edgy Factory regulars, because all groups represented some combination of "real" fame and the glamour learned (literally and/or figuratively) on the streets of cities like New York, where the pose was endemic to the process of everyday life.

The diverse groups and individuals at the Factory collectively gave themselves the label "the Factory subculture" because, although representing divergent backgrounds and interests, they all had a number of things in common: most had come to the Factory, in part, to escape their past and present social conditions. For many, the Factory offered refuge, and it was an unmatchable showcase where they could display their talents. In addition, gay men, the A-men, and transvestites found that the Factory had no protocol when it came to the categorization of sexual identity. Thus one could indeed come to the Factory and escape the confines of the religious and class-based social systems that didn't provide an open-door policy. Similarly, wealthy socialites could find a comparable haven; they could come to the Factory and experiment with bohemian ideas, ones that may not have been acceptable within the strict boundaries of their class system. Finally, the street people and would-be artists found that the Factory offered temporary sanctuary; if one was literally living on one's wits, the Factory's open-door policy allowed a retreat into a world that was accepting. In these ways, then, the Factory offered escape from class, escape from religion, escape from the drudgeries of street life, and escape from the boredom and mundanity of everyday life.

And even though Warhol was a master manipulator, in many ways his manipulative skills worked to the advantage of the Factory regulars. At the studio, and in the public eye, they suddenly became underground superstars, models, avant-garde performance artists. And in many cases, these regulars rose to fame so quickly simply because they used their self-invented Factory personas as credentials. Thus, although Warhol has been criticized for taking advantage of those around him, those around him should also be recognized as people who often indulged in the rewards offered by membership in the Factory subculture. As Koch points out, "Everybody at the Factory knew he was being watched, and a glowing theatrical self-awareness was built into the place's very life. . . . You couldn't make a wrong move; every impulse signified" (6).

Warhol's Art during the Factory Period

From November 1963 throughout the mid-1960s, the Factory's chaotic social environment provided the ideal context for an exploration of pop's ambiguities. During this period, Warhol began to fully examine the tensions already suggested by his previous work. In other words, Warhol was increasingly interested in advancing the contrast he had created between pop as celebratory form (Coke bottles) and pop as a means for producing disturbing and confrontational responses ("Death Series"). In April 1964, these tensions were examined most directly through a number of projects, including the *Thirteen Most Wanted Men* mural, Warhol's "box sculptures," and his minimalist films. Each endeavor revealed that certain subversive textual strategies yielded quite contradictory and controversial opinions. In this sense, Warhol increasingly embraced a conceptual notion of art; the ideas behind the production and layout of the silk screens, sculptures, and films were much more significant to him than the actual works themselves. In addition, in the conceptual tradition, Warhol was consumed with the reactions that were given to his art projects; if they inspired utter confusion, he felt assured that his work was successful.

Perhaps the most explicit example of this approach to art is provided by Warhol's *Thirteen Most Wanted Men.* The piece initially consisted of 48- by 40-inch screens of the FBI's most wanted men of 1957. Warhol then transferred the screens onto 26 canvases that were connected to form one 20- by 20-foot mural. And although the mural may have implied an extension of his ideas on "death and disaster," it, in effect, represented a more confrontational effort. For the mural was funded by a commission from architect Philip Johnson of the New York State Pavilion at the Worlds Fair of 1964 (Crone 30). Johnson had provided Warhol with the funding precisely because the artist's work seemed to already represent a promotional theme of the Fair: "New York is an all-American city that loves and supports the arts!" Johnson's underlying motive was to convince other nations that New York had a "fun-loving" attitude toward art.[7]

The mural was to be hung on the front of the New York Pavilion, a building located near the entrance gates of the fair. Thus it was one the first images noticed by visitors. But when Warhol actually hung the piece, both Johnson and Governor Nelson Rockefeller were appalled by fact that all of the men portrayed on the panel were Italian Mafioso. Also, they recalled that most had been tried for criminal acts and the courts had found them not guilty. And, of course, Johnson and Rockefeller thought that the mural in no way reflected the promotional theme of the fair.

After a series of heated arguments with Johnson, many of which implied legal action, Warhol and Malanga covered the mural with silver spray paint. As a result, by the time the Fair opened, attendees were presented with nothing more than an obtrusive series of glimmering boards. But this was not the end of the *Thirteen Most Wanted Men.* The silk-screening process allowed Warhol and Malanga to reproduce the panels, and eventually the piece was shown in numerous galleries both in the United States and abroad.

In March 1964, during the wake of this controversy, Warhol's *Brillo Box* sculptures made their debut at the Stable Gallery. According to Victor Bockris, "Andy had said he wanted the gallery to look like the interior of a warehouse, and Alan Groh had lined the boxes up in rows and stacked them in corners." (150). On entering the gallery, critics and viewers were immediately bewildered, because they were implicitly forced to contemplate what appeared to be the actual mercantile products themselves.

As a result, the most common question was, "Couldn't we simply walk into a grocery store and view the same thing?" Some critics thought this was precisely the case, and they felt that this time Warhol had extended the limits of a practice (pop) that perhaps already seemed rather limited. In fact, the negative controversy over Warhol's Brillo boxes was so fueled that it continued for 16 years. For example, in late 1980, long after the wooden sculptures had initially appeared, Peter Fuller issued a scathing attack on Warhol in his much acclaimed *Beyond the Crisis in Art.* In an excerpt from the book, he states:

> Warhol was a vandal. The key renunciation he made was that of his expressive relationship to his materials, by which I mean both the paint itself and his representational conventions. . . . His pictures might just as well have been made by anyone else, and indeed they often were. . . . But Warhol's real crime is that he threw away what Marcuse called the power of art to break the monopoly of established reality. In his hands, or rather out of them, painting came close to being a mere reflection of the prevailing ideology and the dominant mode of production. (21)

Although this position has remained customary among some critics since the Brillo box series, Warhol has continued to find supporters, such as the *New York Times* and *Rolling Stone* critic John Rockwell:

> What Warhol and pop artists are trying to tell us and what composer John Cage has been telling us all along is that art isn't necessarily a product crafted painstakingly by some mysterious removed artist-deity, but is whatever you, the perceiver, choose to perceive artistically. A Brillo box isn't suddenly art because Warhol puts a stacked bunch of them in a museum. But by putting them there he encourages you to make your every trip to the supermarket an artistic adventure, and in so doing he has exalted your life. ("Art Rock" 352)

Whether Warhol agreed or disagreed with these assessments is, of course, not known. Again, his refusal to comment on his work thus left it open to multiple interpretations by critics and viewers. At the same time, Warhol's conceptual ideas and his confrontational approach certainly assured him a great amount of media attention. By the middle of the decade, Warhol had become the first American artist to construct himself as media superstar. As Carter Ratcliff points out, "Warhol arrived at a point where judgements of art critics were irrelevant to his reputation" (46). Hence his proclivity for provoking critics and confronting viewers only worked in his favor. The art-viewing public lined up to be a part of *any* Warhol opening, and by the mid-1960s, the self-invented Andy Warhol became "Andy Warhol";[8] he was the living illustration of the myths that he had helped to perpetuate.

The Films of Andy Warhol

Because Warhol's Factory studio was a mecca where members of the Factory subculture were always on stage and because Warhol was often preoccupied with the shock value of conceptual art, it is no surprise that one of Warhol's central filmmaking aesthetics was, "Just turn the camera on and photograph something. . . . [And] leave the camera running until it runs out of film" (from a 1968 Warhol interview; qtd. in Mekas 141). In the early 1960s, this attitude toward "passive" direction was in evidence in a series of films in which Factory superstars devised bizarre characterizations, impromptu dialogues, and frenzied modes of behavior for Warhol's usually static camera.

In gaining an understanding of Warhol's films, however, we cannot simply note what his actors did; we must instead give preference to Warhol's inaction as an auteur to and his action as a conceptual artist. For Warhol's lack of presence as an auteur (i.e., the static camera and his passive directorial style) usually resulted in the creation of hyperreal visuals, similar to those found in the films of Godard or Brakhage, but without the self-conscious stylistic references that often bracket their works. Unlike many of his contemporaries in early 1960s avant-garde cinema, Warhol developed a uniquely simple approach, one that is inimitable for the mere fact that it should not be imitated. As Parker Tyler critically contends,

> There are certain technologists of the avant-garde—VanDerBeek, Landow, Kubelka come to mind—who spend all their time thinking of more or less fruit-

ful ways of modifying the image produced by simply pointing a camera at something and faithfully registering it (Warhol has overparodied that same antediluvian occupation). (206)

All of this points to a central paradox of Warhol's cinema: the hyperreal, outlandish scenes created before the camera make objects and subjects seem to be superstars, to be the center of attention, whether the subject is the Empire State Building or Edie Sedgwick. Actually, it is Warhol's near invisibility as an auteur, his self-effacing, "negative" directorial style that allows these subjects to be showcased in such compelling manner. "For it is Andy Warhol who holds the camera, and it is through his eyes that we see the scene" (Geldzahler 301).

Warhol's first film of major importance was *Sleep,* the six-hour marathon of poet John Giorno doing just that—sleeping. In filming *Sleep* Warhol simply set up his 16 mm Bolex in front of Giorno's bed, and once the subject was in place, Warhol turned on the camera. After several nights of shooting, Warhol simply taped the segments together and the result was the film that gained him initial notoriety among the Jonas Mekas/New York avant-garde contingent. After viewing *Sleep,* Henry Geldzahler predicted, "It is an indication of what Warhol will soon be able to do; make countless movies that are exactly still lifes with the minimum of motion necessary to retain the interested attention of unprejudiced viewers (301).

Geldzahler was indeed accurate in his prediction. Some months later, Warhol filmed *Blowjob,* which focused for 30 minutes on the face of a man who is receiving fellatio. Again, the film is in black and white; it is lengthy; and it contains only one still-framed shot of the man's face. Then there are other films of the period (1963) that could be classified as minimalist pseudodocumentaries: *Kiss* (50 minutes of close-up shots of numerous Factory regulars kissing), *Eat* (Robert Indiana eats a mushroom), *Haircut* (Johnny Dodd, one of Billy Name's friends, gets a haircut), and *Empire* (8 hours of a singular, still-framed shot of the Empire State Building). To add to the spare, minimalist style, these films were often silent, no credits were presented, nor was any effort made to cut off the leaders at the ends of reels. Also, when screened, Warhol slowed the speed from 24 frames per second (standard sound speed) to 16 frames per second (standard silent speed), thus creating a slow-motion effect on an already less than action-packed image.

When these films opened in New York in 1963 at the Film Maker's Cooperative, Jonas Mekas forewarned audiences of the unusual length and "special" techniques of these productions. With this in mind, audience members usually came to the six-hour marathons prepared to do more than sit in front of static footage. Typically, they watched one of these films for twenty to thirty minutes, then exited to the lobby for conversation, food, and drinks. Occasionally, audience members returned to the theater to note a slight camera or subject shift on the screen. For example, John Giorno's stomach might be exposed, as opposed to, say, a close-up of one of his arms. But this doesn't mean that the films went unnoticed as important projects worthy of contemplation. On the whole, these films were discussed for longer periods than they were actually viewed.

So audience members did not actually need to sit through these cinematic endurance tests to grasp their meaning. As Mekas makes clear, "That's the story of Warhol's art: it's always so unbelievably a simple thing that makes it work" (139). From Warhol's minimalist stance, the banality of everyday life, the boredom of eating, sleeping, and simply staring at objects are topics that seem to be worthy of an audience's uninterrupted contemplation. At the same time, it was the *idea* behind such films that made them keystones of avant-garde cinema in the 1960s. As film critic Peter Gidal states, "What is defined here as 'boring' is the substance of a large segment of life" (50). Thus, if this is the case, Warhol's passive directorial techniques allowed audiences to become the "artists of perception." When audiences did watch the films, they had no alternative but to stare, and the banal, nonnarrative subject material made viewers realize that their observations were the major event of the film(s). In this sense, Warhol turned cinema going into an art form—the audience became the center of attention; its reactions were the art piece.

In 1964, when Warhol began experimenting with sound in his films, his passive directorial approach continued. Warhol simply filmed the Factory regulars as they created a number of impersonations, often following loosely defined "plots." By 1965, however, Warhol turned much of his authorial control over to writer Ronald Tavel and to camera operator Buddy Wirschafter. In addition, Chuck Wien directed some of the Warhol projects, followed by Paul Morrissey, who directed many of the most notorious projects associated with Warhol's name. Numerous critics have already spoken in excess of the anti-authorial techniques that Warhol employed during this period, and my intention here is not to repeat the most cited arguments.[9] Instead, I want to consider the main premises that I dwelled on earlier, focusing on the *context* in which many of the silent films were used. This brings us to a description of the "Exploding Plastic Inevitable"—Warhol's multimedia production that employed the films, the Factory subculture (as performers), and the rock and roll band, the Velvet Underground. As we will discover, the films produced at the Factory became the perfect accompaniment to a rock and roll event that, like Warhol's Factory subculture itself, embodied the maxim that pop art could be translated into pop life.

Notes

1. Of course, most of Warhol's friends knew that he *was* gay but that he always remained at a far remove from politicized gay culture. Also, it has been noted that he rarely acknowledged—in an open manner—his gay orientation (except among very close friends). In addition, very few sources discuss Warhol's sexuality, except to mention in passing that he was gay or to deal with his "voyeuristic obsessions." Some exceptions include Stephen Koch's *Stargazer,* a book that forthrightly analyzes the gay themes in Warhol's films and assumes (somewhat modestly) that these were related to the artist's sexual orientation. For a more frank discussion, see Victor Bockris's *The Life and Death of Andy Warhol,* a biography that discusses the artist's gay affairs in some detail and provides an honest and nonsensational account of Warhol's sexuality. For a direct reference to one of Warhol's early 1960s relationships, see the first volume of Winston Leyland's *Gay Sunshine Interviews.* In an interview with John Giorno (129-62), the poet reflects briefly on his gay love affair with Andy Warhol. For a somewhat diverse assessment of the more general topic of sexuality see John Wilcox's *The Autobiography and Sex Life of Andy Warhol,* especially the interview with Charles Henri Ford.

2. Specifically, those that occurred at the Judson Church.

3. In the complete version of the preceding quotation from Koch, such people and groups were mentioned. I purposely left them out of the quote to show the "flow" within and between distinctive categories and subcultural groups. See pages 1-4 in *Stargazer* for more details.

4. Also see Koch for a longer and more detailed explanation of the "concentric social circles" that filtered through the Factory.

5. At times, Warhol even had Factory regulars churning out the silk screens and signing his name to them. In an even more absurdist move toward anti-authorship, Warhol made a rubber stamp with his signature and had Factory members simply stamp his name onto the bottoms of silk screens.

6. A moniker given to her by Tom Wolfe.

7. For a particularly insightful examination of the *Thirteen Most Wanted Men* and the fun-loving attitude, see Crone 30.

8. See Duncan, *The Noise.*

9. See Koch; Boultenhouse; Crone; Coplans; Mekas.

The Velvet Underground

POP ART MERGES WITH ROCK AND ROLL

The Velvet Underground Begins

In the early 1960s, Lou Reed was attending Syracuse University, where he was determined to have a career in writing and music.[1] In addition to his literary pursuits, Reed was committed to creating an outlandish public persona while at Syracuse. For example, he was dismissed from the ROTC program after holding a pistol to the head of his commanding officer. During the weeks following the incident, Reed consistently disrupted ROTC practices by blasting his electric guitar from the window of his dorm room. With these "credentials" in hand, he went on to become a disc jockey at the campus radio station, where he played black rhythm and blues as well as 1950s rock and roll. But his stint at the station was cut short after he dared to poke fun at a muscular dystrophy commercial. Thus, by the time Reed had completed his college career, he had begun to experiment with notions of everyday disruption and confusion. He later found that college life had actually prepared him for his role as "rock and roll's leading punk aesthete."

Several months after graduation, Reed moved to New York, where he became a staff writer/studio musician at Pickwick Records. The Pickwick strategy was to produce songs that cashed in on current Top 40 trends, such as surf music. Therefore, Reed was allowed little creative input; the job required that he simply imitate the kind of music that was riding high on the nation's charts. At the same time, however, his work at Pickwick did have advantages in that Reed learned studio procedures and techniques. In addition, he began to privately compose his own rock and roll music and lyrics.

During the fall of 1965, Reed submitted some of his compositions to John Cale, who was best known as an avant-garde violinist. Cale had studied musicology at London University Goldsmiths' College, but his ideas were far from traditional. He was highly influenced by the random electronic music of artists such as John Cage and LaMonte Young. As a result, Cale was searching for a project that would allow him to develop his talents as an experimental violinist. Hence Reed's guitar work seemed as if it might provide an interesting accompaniment to the kind of atonal music that Cale was attempting to produce. In relating the details of his first meeting with Reed, Cale has explained, " 'He played "Heroin" . . . and it totally knocked me out. The words and music were so raunchy and devastating. What's more, his songs fit perfectly with my music concept' " (Bockris and Malanga 18).

As Cale and Reed began some collaborative efforts, both realized that they were in the process of creating an atypical form of rock and roll. Reed's dark and venomous tales of drug addiction and street life and his heavy-handed guitar rhythms supplied the perfect contrast to Cale's droning viola. In other words, the combination of discordant musical forms proved to be satisfying; in fact Cale and Reed believed they were developing a form of rock and roll that would destroy many of the precepts that had dominated rock of the 1950s and early 1960s. In writing songs, then, they forthrightly rejected any notion of developing a formulaic style; their compositions were intentionally designed so that Reed's dark, poetic lyrics meshed with the assaultive intonations of their music. In the process, Cale and Reed self-consciously sought to fracture two popular conventions: the traditional, romantic rock and roll "poem" and folk songs that were designed to raise the social consciousness of their listeners.

As the ideas flowed and the rehearsals continued, a core band was formed during the summer of 1965. Initially called the Warlocks, the band included one of Reed's Syracuse friends, Sterling Morrison, who was "entranced by the possibilities of creating music that reduced the simple structures of rock and roll to a one-note tone" (Doggett 33). For a few months, Angus MacLise also joined the unit, although he was later replaced by Maureen Tucker, another one of Reed's Syracuse friends.[2] Once the rehearsals had became regimented, the four band members began to deliberately confront the boundaries of contemporaneous rock by focusing on themes that dealt with urban despair and alienation. In addition, the band developed a consistent visual style that was intended to provide a parallel to the kinds of topics that were being explored in their music. Therefore, typical attire consisted of black jeans and shirts, black leather jackets, and wraparound shades. In line with this image, the band adopted the name the "Velvet Underground," a title that was actually lifted from the front jacket of Michael Leigh's exposé on "America's sado-masochistic subculture." But as Sterling Morrison has explained, the band wanted a name that immediately suggested their "involvement with the underground film and art scenes" (Bockris and Malanga 21).[3]

By December 1965, this eclectic group had actually achieved some notoriety among Greenwich Village music and art aficionados. The Velvets had gained steady employment at the Cafe Bizarre, where they stunned audiences with harsh vocals and droning electronic music. During this time, the band also performed on stage at the Cinematheque Theater, where artists such as LaMonte Young, Jack Smith, and Robert Whitman were experimenting with theatrical methods for combining film with live music. In addition, the Velvets released their first demo tape, which received positive responses from European music industry executives who were attuned to the avant-garde.

In the meantime, Andy Warhol had decided to indulge in his lifelong passion for rock and roll. He had formed a band with Jasper Johns, Claes Oldenburg, Lucas Samaras, LaMonte Young, and Walter De Maria. However, mutual collaborations were difficult among such an eclectic group of individuals, and Warhol had trouble producing the style of singing that was requested by the musicians and artists. Consequently, after 10 trying rehearsals the group disbanded.

Despite the failure of the group, Warhol continued to develop a growing interest in live rock and roll. As a result, he determined that his talents were best suited to management, and through a stroke of luck, he was soon put into such a position. Michael Myerberg, a prominent Broadway producer, contacted Warhol and offered to pay him a salary if he, Paul Morrissey, and the Factory entourage agreed to socialize at what was to become New York's first disco. Although the idea seemed intriguing, Warhol and his crew quickly sought more direct input into the actual ambience of the disco.

Morrissey proposed that Warhol manage a band that would provide the nightly music at the club. In addition, he suggested that Warhol project films directly above the band as it performed. After all, multimedia events were very much in vogue at the artistically oriented Cinematheque. Why not combine rock and roll with film at the discotheque? Warhol liked the idea and decided that Myerberg's club should be named "Andy Warhol's UP." Myerberg wholeheartedly supported all of these suggestions and sent Morrissey on a search to find the perfect "Warhol band." Victor Bockris and Gerard Malanga explain:

> As Morrissey began his search, Barbara Rubin, a boyishly attractive, precocious 21-year old art groupie came to the Factory and invited Gerard Malanga, who was Andy's Prime Minister without portfolio, to go with her to see a group called The Velvet Underground. Malanga had been a dancer on Alan Freed's "Big Beat" TV show when Freed got busted in a payola scandal (that also affected, among others, Dick Clark) and the show got closed down. Rubin was an intimate of, among others, Allen Ginsberg, William Burroughs, Bob Dylan, Jonas Mekas and Andre Voznesensky, who had, according to Ginsberg, "Dedicated her life to introducing geniuses to each other in the hope that they would collaborate to make great art that would change the world." It was the middle of December 1965. (8)

At Cafe Bizarre, Malanga was immediately impressed by the Velvets' provocative music style. In Malanga's opinion, the screeching guitars, the feedback, and the abrasive rhythms worked in harmony to create a number of haunting and seductive melodies. In fact, the music so inspired Malanga that he began to engage in free-form dancing. The audience at the cafe was then stunned when Malanga pulled a whip out of his back pocket and began cracking it against the dance floor. The impromptu performance was so hypnotic that Lou Reed felt he should compliment Malanga after the set. In turn, the cordial interaction between Malanga and Reed helped to lay the foundation for further collaborations.

The following day, Malanga suggested that Morrissey should investigate the possibility of hiring the Velvets. Coincidentally, that very evening, Malanga's friend, Barbara Rubin, was supposed to film the band at the Cafe Bizarre. So, Malanga invited Morrissey to come along and help with the production. By the end of the evening, Morrissey had decided that the Velvets' belligerent musical style would indeed be appropriate at Andy Warhol's UP. Also, he found it unique that a rock and roll band dared to sing of heroin and sadomasochism. At the same time, he saw an irony in the Velvet's approach; they had included a few songs that spoke of innocence, songs that seemed almost childlike when compared to the more sophisticated appraisals of urban paranoia. Finally, the use of the term *underground* also impressed Morrissey. Certainly, it was a term that had been associated quite frequently with Warhol's art and films, and it had wider currency in the New York avant-garde community of the mid-1960s.

The next day, Morrissey described the Velvet Underground to Andy Warhol, who immediately envisioned them as the house band at Myerberg's disco. As Warhol considered the possibilities that the Velvets might pose in terms of his own career, he also considered that the band's overall musical approach might be too agitational; perhaps the Velvets were *too* dark and decadent. With this thought in mind, Warhol decided that Nico (a German singer and a recent Factory arrival) might provide the Velvets with the essential ambiguity that he always sought in any artistic endeavor:

> Another idea we had in mind when we went to check out the Velvets was that they might be a good band to play behind Nico, the incredible German beauty who'd just arrived in New York from London. She looked like she could have made the trip over right at the front of a Viking ship, she had that kind of face and body. (Warhol and Hackett 145)

On the evening that Warhol watched the Velvet Underground, he was immediately impressed by their unsettling approach to rock and roll. The guitars were so deafening and the amplifier volumes were turned so high, that Warhol felt as if he'd been engulfed by the Velvets' piercing rhythms. When Malanga again took to the dance floor and pounded his whip, Warhol became even more enthused. He saw a definite connection between the band, pop art, and the Factory lifestyle. After the performance had ended, Warhol exclaimed: " 'We have to think of something to do with the Velvets. What can we do? What could it be? WE HAVE TO THINK OF SOMETHING!' " (Bockris and Malanga 10).

The Velvets Enter the Factory

By January 1966, the Velvet Underground had found a new home at Warhol's Factory, where the group set up a rehearsal space at one end of the room. Warhol, however, had plans that went beyond the mere acquisition of new regulars. He had commercial designs on the band, but to achieve these, he decided that he would have to infuse the members with his own pop sensibilities. He began his mission by attempting to convince Reed and Cale of Nico's potential as a band member. Warhol argued that her delicate physical features created a paradox when she spoke or sang—her voice had a peculiar monotone quality; it seemed devoid of all emotion. In Warhol's view, Nico would provide the group with yet another striking contradiction; their menacing sound would be complemented by Nico's voice, while their image as protagonists would be offset by her exceptional beauty. Although Reed and Cale were initially reluctant to accept Warhol's premise, they eventually allowed Nico to join the group, and after a few sessions with Nico, Cale and Reed agreed that her hollow voice and her captivating visual beauty would help to advance the band's cacophonous musical style. In turn, Reed and Cale began to implement other suggestions made by Warhol.

By February 1966, Warhol's influence on the Velvet Underground was even more apparent. He had convinced the members to change their name to the "Velvet Underground and Nico." Concurrently, he had proposed that Reed write songs specifically for Nico. This suggestion resulted in compositions that forthrightly demonstrated the group's collective musical outlook ("All Tomorrow Parties," "Femme Fatale," and "I'll Be Your Mirror"). As Frith and Horne point out,

> Lou Reed's songs, particularly as sung by Nico, were flat accounts of pain and fear and lust with apparently no personal involvement (or moral response) at all—the group's aim was to "express uptightness and make the audience uptight." (112)

As the band rehearsed at the Factory, the studio increasingly became a showcase for both rock and roll and films. In the process, the Factory subculture, more than ever, seemed to be preoccupied with the ambiguities of pop art.

For example, Edie Sedgwick, the reigning queen of pop, was frequently upstaged by Lou Reed and Nico, because both personified many of the aesthetic principles that had dominated Warhol's art of the early 1960s. Whereas Nico was beautiful, aloof, and moody, Reed was tough yet sensitive, boyish yet manly, streetwise yet astute. In Warhol's terms, Reed and Nico represented the living parallel to his pop canvases: they were enigmatically sexual and glamorous, yet simultaneously, they were distant and aloof. By February 1966, under Warhol's careful eye, Nico and Reed had transformed themselves into local pop icons. In the case of Nico, the transformation was less extravagant; however, she suddenly found herself at the top of the Factory's social hierarchy. In Reed's case, the Warholian impact was more direct. To Reed, the Factory was a haven where he could remake himself in Warhol's image.[4] Indeed, as Peter Doggett claims,

> Before the Factory, Reed had the scenarios for his songs; Warhol provided the cast and the telling details. Reed soon abandoned the sweaters and casual jackets he'd affected since leaving Syracuse, and took on the Factory image—Warhol's leather and shades. It became the Lou Reed look, and in its turn, the look of the rock New Wave. (42)

Here, we can also consider additional ways in which Lou Reed was drawn to the subcultural milieu at the Factory. For one, Reed was enthralled by the Factory's open acceptance of gay sexuality. His enthusiasm was prompted in part by a horrifying boyhood experience; his parents had forced him to take electroshock treatments to "cure" his sexual urges. Therefore, for Reed, the Factory seemed like an escape into a world that he'd always imagined: a world in which gay men were held in high esteem, a world that was dominated by gay aestheticism. Second, Reed was inspired by Warhol's premise that "there's nothing beneath the surface" of pop art. In pondering the implications of this idea, Reed developed a method for writing lyrics that also spoke of "surfaces": he created images and semifictional characters that were to be taken at face value. As Doggett points out, "It's purely coincidental, he seemed to say, that my creations toy with death and sexual perversion; that's what they are, and it has nothing to do with me" (43). Thus, in using the Factory as a refuge, Reed found that he could openly experiment with the sexual feelings that had long been repressed. The Factory also provided him with the idea that his art could be used as a "disguise." As Reed has stated,

> "I have songs about killing people . . . but Dostoevsky killed people too. In reality I might not do what a character in my songs would do, if only because I'd be jailed. I've always thought it would be kinda fun to introduce people to characters that maybe they hadn't met before, or hadn't wanted to meet." (Doggett 12)

When Reed's Factory-inspired lyrics were then combined with the caustic music already being produced by his band, the result was a pop art group that was decidedly anticommercial. For this reason, the Velvets maintained the status of a "cult band" in New York; they found a following among those who were already predisposed to the Factory's subcultural endeavors. By February 1966, the Velvets were best known as another product of the Factory, one that perfectly embodied the turbulence that was associated with Factory life.

Multimedia Experimentation

The first public enactment of Warhol/Factory/Velvets' collaboration occurred at the Cinematheque Theater, which already had an established reputation as a premier experimental art movie house. There, the Velvet Underground performed with films such as *Vinyl, Lupe, Eat,* and *Empire* projected onto the stage backdrop. In addition, Malanga continued to perform his whip dance, and other Factory members often joined him onstage. Also, Barbara Rubin frequently accompanied the Warhol troupe to film audience reactions. The performances were titled "Andy Warhol's Uptight," and they were met with both curiosity and respect by quite a diverse crowd. Not only had Warhol and his cohorts managed to combine a number of artistic forms (e.g., films, rock and roll, dance, and filmmaking itself), but they had also engineered a performance art production that attracted rock and roll fans, avant-garde film fans, pop artists, filmmakers, and curiosity seekers. Thus the collaborative multimedia presentations represented a unique development in that they opened new territory for experimentation within the visual and musical arts. As Gerard Malanga suggests,

> Everybody involved with the week at the Cinematheque was very excited about what we were doing together, although it was still more of an art than a rock event and there were a number of kinks to be ironed out before "Andy Warhol, Up-Tight" would bloom into the "Exploding Plastic Inevitable." We all went out to dinner after each show. Andy's question to everybody was always the same, "How can we make it more interesting?" (Bockris and Malanga 25)

Within weeks after the shows at the Cinematheque, several East Coast and midwestern college film departments contacted Warhol with inquiries concerning the multimedia production. One inquiry came from Joseph and Anne Wehrer, who invited the "Uptight" cast to perform at the University of Michigan Film Festival. It was a trip that proved worthwhile, not only because of the passionate reception of the audience there but also due to the interpersonal connections that were made with members of this particular rock/art "scene."

On the evening of the performance, the Velvet Underground and Nico offered their standard brand of frenzied rock and roll. Simultaneously, the dancers moved about the stage and Warhol's films served as a backdrop. But what added a new visual dimension to the performance was the use of strobe lights, a quite uncommon concert device at the time. In addition, the Velvets engaged in an activity that was not only unusual, but it was almost unthinkable at the time. During several of the songs, the band members turned their backs to the audience. This resulted in cries of outrage from a few hecklers, but Warhol found the overall response to be positive:

> Ann Arbor went crazy. At last the Velvets were a smash. I'd sit on the steps in the lobby during intermissions and people from the local papers and school papers would interview me, ask about my movies, and what we were trying to do. "If they can take it for ten minutes, then we play for fifteen," I'd explain. "That's our policy. Always leave them wanting less." (Warhol and Hackett 154)

That evening at a party at Anne Wehrer's home, the Warhol cast mingled with university film students, professors, and local musicians. Much of the discussion centered on the implications of combining rock and roll with other aesthetic forms, such as film. Entering into the discussion was Jim Osterberg, a high school student, who was also the drummer for a local garage band. Warhol thought Osterberg to be an attractive person but somewhat young and naive in comparison to the rest of the people at the party. Others, such as Nico, John Cale, and Factory regular Danny Fields, concurred. But none of them could then realize the strong impact they had on Osterberg's life. For within a few years, Osterberg and Warhol became close friends; Nico became Osterberg's lover; Cale, his record producer; and Fields, his manager. And through following the custom that was endemic to the Factory, Osterberg created a persona by transforming himself into the white-haired protopunk, Iggy Pop. Simultaneously, Osterberg found himself infatuated with the subcultural activities at the Factory. Consequently, the chance meeting between Osterberg and the Warhol troupe actually helped to lay the partial foundation for many of the ideas that emerged through glitter rock.

In the meantime, the Uptight entourage returned to New York with the hope of conducting frequent performances at Andy Warhol's UP. But after unsuccessful attempts to persuade Myerberg to sign a contract with Warhol and the band, it seemed as if the original plans for UP were doomed. Unexpectedly, Myerberg hedged on all deals, and concurrently, a strong gangster presence at the club tended to discourage Morrissey. Finally, UP did open with the Young Rascals as the house band, but it was closed on opening night due to liquor law violations. Several weeks later, the club was destroyed by a fire. In turn, Warhol and Morrissey were forced to completely abandon the Myerberg deal.

With UP a thing of the past, Morrissey and Warhol were indecisive about what to do with the Velvet Underground and Nico. Warhol had purchased the band's equipment, and a management contract had already been signed. At the same time, the group's theatrical style had been self-consciously geared toward nightclub performances. Facing such predicaments head on, Morrissey and Warhol quickly negotiated a deal with the owners of a large hall called the Dom. Hence, during the last week of March 1966, Factory denizens were busy loading projectors and films into the building. And as the work transpired, Morrissey decided to christen the Warhol troupe with a new, more emphatic name: the Exploding Plastic Inevitable. Just meeting the *Village Voice*'s March 31, 1966, weekly deadline, Morrissey placed an ad that announced the rather rushed event. It was an invitation to come and "blow your mind" on Friday, April 1, from 9 p.m. to 2 a.m., when the Silver Dream Factory would present the First Exploding Plastic Inevitable along with music and food, light works and ultra sounds, dancing and movies such as *Suicide, Kiss, Sleep, Vinyl,* and *Haircut.*

Staring at this page in the *Voice,* one immediately notices the range of work that Warhol was producing during this time. Just above the notice is an advertisement for *My Hustler,* which was opening that week at the Cinematheque. In addition to the film and the Exploding Plastic Inevitable events, Warhol was receiving further visibility at the Castelli Gallery, where his silver, helium-filled balloons were hanging amid his "cow wallpaper." As Warhol elaborated,

> So now, with one thing and another, we were reaching people in all parts of town, all different types of people: the ones who saw the movies would get curious about the gallery show, and the kids dancing at the Dom would want to see the movies; the groups were getting all mixed up with each other—dance, music, art, fashion, movies. It was fun to see the Museum of Modern Art people next to the teenyboppers next to the amphetamine queens next to the fashion editors.
>
> We all knew something revolutionary was happening, we just felt it. Things couldn't look this strange and new without some barrier being broken. (Warhol and Hackett 162)

Other Warhol cohorts have provided similar descriptions regarding this phenomenal moment in New York art and music. In the most impassioned accounts,[5] the details focus specifically on the Dom, which became the premier showcase for the Velvet Underground during the month of April 1966. The band's performances—combined with the atmospheric qualities of this

Warholian club—helped to establish a central meeting ground for rock and roll fans, pop music stars, film stars, artists, speed addicts, and numerous other individuals and subcultures. In *Popism: The Warhol '60s*, Warhol provided an illuminating account of the spectacle:

> All that month the limousines pulled up outside the Dom. Inside, the Velvets played so loud and crazy I couldn't even begin to guess the decibels, and there were images projected everywhere, one on top of the other. I'd usually watch from the balcony or take my turn at the projectors, slipping different-colored gelatin slides over the lenses and turning movies like "Harlot," "The Shoplifter," "Couch," "Banana," "Blow Job," "Sleep," "Empire," "Kiss," "Whips," "Face," "Camp," "Eat," into all different colors. Stephen Shore and Little Joey and a Harvard kid named Danny Williams would take turns operating the spotlights while Gerard and Ronnie and Ingrid and Mary Might (Woronov) danced sadomasochistic style with the whips and flashlights and the Velvets played and the different colored hypnotic dot patterns swirled and bounced off the walls and the strobes flashed and you could close your eyes and hear cymbals and boots stomping and whips cracking and tambourines sounding like chains rattling. (Warhol and Hackett 162 63)

Throughout the month of April, the Exploding Plastic Inevitable events continued to draw capacity crowds at the Dom. As a result, Morrissey felt that if the band could produce such an enthusiastic live following, then perhaps its sound would also be adaptable to recorded music. Thus Morrissey and Warhol pooled several thousand dollars and rented time in a small studio on Broadway. But although this decision resulted in the Velvets' first album, it ultimately caused the Exploding Plastic Inevitable to splinter. By the end of April, the Exploding Plastic Inevitable would never operate in quite the same manner as it had before.

Although Warhol was an excellent coordinator of live performances, when he signed on as the band's studio producer his limitations became apparent. He knew very little about musical techniques, and he had even less knowledge when it came to the engineering aspects that would record a band's music properly.[6] Nonetheless, his input continued as he proposed specific visual effects and provided ideas for songs ("Sunday Morning," "All Tomorrow's Parties"). He also suggested which tracks came closest to the true Velvet Underground sound.[7] In addition, he encouraged the band to continue to break with traditional forms of rock and roll. Thus, as the band set out to perform in California during the spring of 1966, it seemed as if Warhol would remain integral to the Exploding Plastic Inevitable events.

From May 3-29 (1966), the Exploding Plastic Inevitable was booked to play the Trip in Los Angeles, where the Mothers of Invention were scheduled as the opening act. Unaccustomed to West Coast conventions,[8] the Velvets produced their typical multimedia floor show. It is no surprise, then, that many of those in attendance cheered the Mothers of Invention and heckled the Velvets. In fact, Frank Zappa, lead singer of the Mothers, prompted the negative responses, making derogatory remarks about the Velvets during the opening set. As a result, on the second evening of their performance, the Velvets ended the last set by laying their instruments on the stage and turning their amplifiers to the highest possible decibel levels. "It will replace nothing, except suicide," stated Cher Bono to the local press (Warhol and Hackett 167). Barry McGuire also expressed the sentiments of many audience members when he claimed, "The Velvet Underground should go back underground and practice" (Bockris and Malanga 42).

On the evening of the third performance the Trip was closed by the local Sheriff's department,[9] thus leaving the Velvets in a disheartening position. Because of union restrictions, the group was required to stay in California at least until the 29th, but it seemed unlikely that they would find further bookings. In addition, the Velvets so despised the "hippie music scene" that members eagerly awaited their return to New York. At the same time, however, the Musician's Union demanded that Trip pay the group, even if the club had been temporarily closed. In turn, the band rented studio time and was able to complete some of the master tracks for its first album.

Around the time of the recording session, the band decided to end some of Warhol's managerial duties. Steve Sesnick was hired as their booking manager, even though Warhol and Morrissey were still under contract.[10] But neither objected to the decision because it seemed as if Sesnick would actually be helpful in gaining additional club dates. This assumption proved correct in that Sesnick was able to arrange a few dates in San Francisco at Bill Graham's Fillmore Auditorium.[11] As a result, when the recording sessions were finished, the band headed toward San Francisco with the hope that the city's diverse population would yield an appreciative audience. But this was not the case. Graham despised the Velvets' music, and the San Francisco audience reacted negatively to the Exploding Plastic Inevitable events.

During the summer and fall months that followed, several personnel changes occurred within the Exploding Plastic Inevitable. For one, Nico was dropped from the group, and she began to work on a solo album and career. Second, Warhol's direct input also subsided, because he was convinced that his role with the band was indeed limited by his own lack of experience. Thus, with Steve Sesnick taking complete managerial control over the group, it seemed as if the Velvets were becoming more committed to developing as a rock and roll band, and less committed to the notion of rock as spectacle. Hence, from October through December 1966, the Exploding Plastic Inevitable gradually began to present themselves as the Velvet Underground. Still, for the sake of recognition, their posters included in small print, "Andy Warhol's Exploding Plastic Inevitable." But this reference only reflected a reoccurring problem: What was the precise direction that the band would take, now that Warhol's input had waned? The question resulted in numerous arguments among band members; in fact, as the Velvets attempted to decide on an autonomous image, the social situation among group members had become extremely "uptight" (Bockris and Malanga 65).

During this time of transition for the band, Warhol began to frequent Max's Kansas City on Park Avenue South. There, he once again became the master of a social scene that was attracting Village dancers, artists, writers, and musicians. In fact, Warhol described Max's as the "ultimate hangout," attesting to the fact that "everybody went to Max's and everything got homogenized there" (Warhol and Hackett 185-86).

While establishing himself at Max's during the winter of 1966-67, Warhol also preserved some ties to the Velvet Underground, because he had previously been commissioned to design the cover for their first album. The result was a bright yellow paper banana that could be peeled away to reveal a purple-toned "pop banana." Although the cover was simple in concept, Warhol was one of the first to experiment with the notion of album cover as art piece. That same year, the Rolling Stones and the Beatles also presented album covers that violated the traditional standards of record jacket design.

In March 1967, *The Velvet Underground and Nico Produced by Andy Warhol* was released. The album was dominated by Lou Reed's observations concerning the Factory and New York urban street life. These observations were complemented by Cale's droning viola, Reed and Morrison's pounding guitar rhythms, and the occasional use of Nico's eerie voice. Most indicative of the Velvets' sound and image was "I'm Waiting for the Man" in which Reed extolled the paranoia and humor involved in attempting to score drugs in Harlem. In addition, cuts such as "Venus in Furs" emphasized the psychosexual ambiguity that the band had attempted to create in its visual presentations. The song also contained melodic chords that were superseded by aggressive guitar work. "Heroin" operated in a similar manner in that Lou Reed's voice is somewhat tranquil during the opening segments. But as the song builds to a noisy crescendo, Reed churns out words of desperation. Other cuts include "Run, Run, Run" (a tribute to Union Square), "Femme Fatale" (the story of a woman doomed to failed romance), and "All Tomorrow's Parties" (Warhol's favorite cut due to its celebration of the virtues of endless party going).

Although the album brilliantly described urban street life at the time, it was not well received, even in New York City—where its messages might have seemed particularly appropriate. In retrospect, it seems quite likely that the first album was victimized, not only by radio censorship and poor management but also by the era in which it was released. After all, this was the spring before the "Summer of Love," and youth culture trends were rapidly moving toward nonviolence, the peace movement, long hair, "do your own thing," and an infatuation with the San Francisco/Haight-Asbury scene. These trends probably fostered sentiments against the alienated, nihilistic visions of the Velvet Underground. Perhaps their songs seemed too jaded and barbaric for a generation that was rallying against nihilism and despair.

During the months following the album's release, the members of the Velvet Underground became increasingly distraught over the fact that the album did not become popular among New York cohorts. Certainly, they realized that the response outside of the city would be marginal. But they never expected local radio stations, critics, and audience members to react negatively to their first effort. Given their labor and frustration, however, it is likely that the band ignored one important reason for the album's poor reception in their home city: on vinyl there was no way to re-create the agitated atmosphere that had dominated the Dom. Still, the Velvets found no way to justify the negative reactions, and, in turn, they flatly refused to play New York clubs and dance halls until 1970.

In the late spring of 1967, the Velvets decided to move to Boston. This was a wise career move in that Boston critics and fans nurtured an appreciation of the band. But just as the band began to reach another pinnacle of success, self-image problems among the group's members seemed to escalate. As rock historian Diana Clapton points out,

> With the approach of genuine publicity, egos began colliding. Lou began to grow into the part of the junkie desperado that a large part of his audience saw as the real person behind "Heroin." "People assume," he mused in *Rolling Stone* eleven years later, "that what's on a record applies to the person singing it, and they find that shocking." The Warhol divine-decadence blessing gave them much of their

> clout. Too much, felt Cale. "That made us nervous—we really wanted to make it as a band." (27)

So as the direct connection to Warhol was more clearly severed than ever before, in the summer of 1967 the band began to lay down the tracks for a second album (*White Light/White Heat*). This album was released in December 1967, just as the music of San Francisco was beginning to dominate the U.S. charts. But although most popular acid rock was harsh and laden with jams, the music on the Velvets' *White Light/White Heat* had a much different grain. Overall, the music was abrasive, dominated by speed-inspired guitar rhythms. And once again the lyrics were uncompromising in their appraisal of urban angst. The subjects addressed on the album included amphetamine addiction (the title cut), transvestite parties ("Sister Ray"), and unrequited love that results in unintentional murder ("The Gift"). These topics provided further proof that the Velvets were attempting to self-consciously denounce the limits of contemporary rock and roll. As Ronnie Cutrone explains, " 'The Rolling Stones were making 3-D album covers, The Beatles had beautiful little pictures of them looking cute, and then this dark album comes out with a very subdued picture of a tattoo [on the cover]. It didn't fit in anywhere, so that was strange' " (Bockris and Malanga 91). But as Rock critic Lester Bangs claims,

> White Light/White Heat was the album, though, that firmly proved the Velvets to be much more than a Warhol phase, and established them for any one with ears to listen as one of the most dynamically experimental groups in or out of rock. This great album, which was all but ignored when it appeared, will probably stand to future listeners looking back as one of the milestones on the road to tonal and rhythmic liberation that is giving rock all the range and freedom of the new jazz. ("Dead Lie" 46)

Although the Velvet Underground continued to play in the Boston area, the release of the second album did little to create success outside of their already established musical networks. Still, the continuing social interactions between band members, Warhol (as friend), ex-Velvets associates, and other rock and roll musicians were instrumental in developing European contacts. In fact, by the late 1960s, the Velvets were generating some interest among record executives in Britain. For example, by late October 1967, Beatles' manager Brian Epstein had approached the band with the hope of arranging a European tour.

Just prior to finalizing the deal, however, Epstein died and the plans were never realized.

Although the Velvets never had the chance to carry out a European tour as planned, their growing impact overseas was becoming increasingly apparent. For example, Lou Reed received numerous letters from bands in Italy, France, and Britain, all requesting permission to record his songs. In addition, Kenneth Pitt—David Bowie's manager—saw a connection between Bowie's work and that which had been produced by Warhol and the Velvets. As a result, Pitt flew to New York during late 1967 with the hope of representing and managing Warhol in Britain. The deal was never realized, but the two did strike up a friendship. As a result, Pitt returned to London with quite a bit of information concerning the artistic and musical techniques of Warhol and the Velvet Underground. He also brought Bowie some acetates of the band, and Bowie listened to them with intense interest, deciding that he could also create a mesmerizing musical/theatrical production. Thus, as the Velvet Underground continued to perform from 1967 to 1970, their influence was building in various interconnected areas of art and music. This influence, however, would not become wholly apparent until the advent of glitter rock.

Notes

1. Reed studied under poet Delmore Schwartz. His studies also took him to the works of Sartre, Hegel, and Kierkegaard (see Doggett 19-23).
2. The formation of the Velvet Underground has been documented in a number of sources. See *What Goes On*, No. 3 (published by the Velvet Underground Appreciation Society, 5721 E. Laguna Avenue, Stuart, FL 34997-7828). For additional information also see the Spanish fanzine, *Feedback*, which is produced by Ignacio Julia and is translated and published by the Velvet Underground Appreciation Society (no further information available). The most comprehensive book on the Velvet Underground is Victor Bockris and Gerard Malanga's *Up-Tight: The Velvet Underground Story.*
3. During this time, members of the Velvet Underground were directly involved with multimedia happenings at Jonas Mekas' Cinematheque on Layfette Street. Mostly, they were helping to stage productions that were billed as "environmental assaults."
4. See Doggett 42.
5. See Bockris and Malanga 30-37 for the assessments of Paul Morrissey, Ronnie Cutrone, Walter De Maria, Richard Goldstein, Ed Sanders, Sterling Morrison, Danny Fields, Maureen Tucker, John Cale, and Phil Milstein.
6. Ultimately, then, Warhol did very little in terms of the actual studio engineering. Instead, Lou Reed relied on the knowledge he'd gained at Pickwick, and he served as the unofficial producer of the first record.
7. See Bockris and Malanga 33-34.
8. See Warhol and Hackett 168-69.

9. The raid had nothing to do with the Velvets but, instead, was due to liquor violations and other legal infractions.

10. At first, Sesnick worked with the band purely on a freelance basis. The reason for asking him to take on managerial duties had much to do with Sesnick's music industry connections. Warhol was an excellent coordinator of projects, but he had little clout in the competitive world of rock and roll, and he knew virtually nothing about managing a band on the road.

11. Although some of the tracks had been laid down in New York, there was further work to do in an L.A. studio; thus the Fillmore date provided a way to bide time as a result of the aforementioned requirements of the Musicians' Union.

The Foundations of Glitter Rock

Glitter Rock: The Guiding Principles

Warhol, the Factory, and the Velvet Underground all had a phenomenal impact on the musicians who came to be associated with glitter rock, and subsequently, on the style that came to be defined as "glitter." In this chapter, I will consider the ways in which this impact began to surface among a particular group of musicians and performers who were living in Detroit and London during the late 1960s. First, I will provide a broad overview that will define the main "principles" apparent in the glitter genre. An analysis of these principles will provide an understanding of the way in which Detroit and London musicians drew on a broad range of interrelated aesthetic ideas, ones that can be directly or indirectly traced to the Warholian ethos.

We can begin by considering that the New York/Warholian tradition (1965-69) provided glitter performers with the primary themes of flamboyance, style and image construction, polymorphous sexuality, and multimedia montage as performance art. The Detroit scene (1967-70), also loosely inspired by the New York underground and best represented by Iggy Pop and Alice Cooper, had as its basis a dramaturgical focus not unlike the one posed by the Factory and the Velvet Underground. In Detroit, the performance schemata was analogous in principle to Artaud's "theater of cruelty" (74) in that the technique was to "incite a kind of virtual revolt" by absolving the boundaries between audiences and performers through impulsive physical confrontations within the concert arena. Such "disturbing of the senses' repose" (Artaud 74) occurred quite literally as Iggy Pop often bounded from the stage directly *onto* audiences, a tactic that always induced concerted mayhem among his fans. Similarly, the androgynous Alice Cooper frequently prowled the corners of stages, while spitting newspaper and propelling objects (feathers, mannequin parts, dollar bills) out toward the crowd, thus forcing an immediate clash/reaction. In these instances, performer/audience "unification" was effectively achieved through an anticommunal affront to the senses. Audiences often became a part of the "living theater" regardless of their own decision in the matter.

In London (1968-71), David Bowie (the eventual king of glitter) was experimenting with rock and roll that was at times derivative of that being produced by the Velvets and Iggy Pop. In addition, he incorporated into his own work notions of media manipulation (Warhol) as well as exaggerated theatrics (the Velvet Underground and Iggy Pop). Concurrently, by openly announcing his bisexuality and by presenting androgynous images both on and off the stage, Bowie helped to advance subversive propositions that eventually worked toward "sexualizing" glitter in a manner that was uncommon to rock and roll.

By 1972-73, these musicians (Lou Reed of the Velvet Underground, Iggy Pop, Alice Cooper, and David Bowie), emerged with a collective agenda that many rock critics labeled "glitter" or "glam" (Shaw 141). Through the medium of glitter, Bowie, Lou Reed, and others translated their somewhat insular, context-specific ideas for a broader audience, thereby recasting situational notions of sexual/performance subversion through commercial means. Within the framework of glitter, commercialization thus served to "recontextualize"[1] fanatical (stylistic) ensembles and perspectives that were previously used by those who were either directly immersed in Warhol's Factory/Velvets milieu or in the London/Detroit scenes and their offshoots.[2] Most significant, through this process of recontextualization, glitter rock provided 1970s adolescents with ways to experiment with what were once quite unobstructed (and perhaps unattainable) bohemian conventions.

In giving consideration to the principal glitter artists (Bowie, Lou Reed, Iggy Pop, Alice Cooper, and Brian Ferry, among others), I propose that the marketing of the New York/London/Detroit factions via this mass-produced rock and roll genre was not a simple case of ideological or commodity incorporation. For even though glitter rock performers lifted elements from the Warholian underground, they also precisely rearticulated the essence of these elements. As a result, a wide range of possibilities opened for fans, many of whom were limited by backgrounds or geographical locations. Thus their predominant subcultural experience in the early 1970s occurred through the application of subcultural precepts that were transmitted by way of a mass-mediated and highly commercial format.

In light of these claims, we can consider a broad question: Were fans who were unaccustomed to the egalitarian structure of subterranean subcultural groups (e.g., Warhol's Factory) able to see beyond the sometimes obvious seductive titillation imposed on them by Bowie and his cohorts? I believe the answer to this question is both yes *and* no. Some avid glitter fans recognized the direct textual relation between the glitter anthems, performance techniques, and the bohemian traditions that had laid the foundation for the genre's emergence. Others didn't necessarily *need* to grasp such connections: glitter's style produced a discourse that was metaphorically translatable without referents. In other words, no matter the background or location of fans, glitter's most pertinent motifs made possible a collective liberatory reprisal that reversed dominant conceptions of sexuality, mainstream style, and commercially informed fandom.

Given the context of the early 1970s, however, the detractor's question, of course, becomes, If one is given a number of (popular) references from which to choose, *why choose this one*? The answer, again, lies in the identification one may have had (consciously or unconsciously) with the subtextual, subcultural bohemian foundation from which glitter arose. As I will ascertain, glitter rock's "propositions" were in fact largely derivative of the Factory ethos, in that homosexuality and bisexuality were givens: sexual orientation was not an issue that necessarily had to be overtly politicized or defended. Like pop art—as both aesthetic form and as lifestyle—glitter rock was nonapologetic about embracing an open-ended approach to sexual themes.

In one sense, then, glitter had its own ironic subtext: one could pose as gay or bisexual or pose as an androgynous Bowie fan, and these acts *in themselves* were considered to be central and acceptable features of glitter style. In other words, many of the "Bowie boys and girls" who identified with glitter and adapted its styles were reveling in the process of identifying with the sexual other, whether this other was or was not intrinsic to their own sexual orientation(s). And in other cases, glitter rock provided gay and bisexual fans with a method for expressing themselves, a way of being that allowed for a distinct pronouncement of their sexual orientation. In both cases, this celebration of sexual difference provided a key into another world, a world that was not often made available to those who were living within the confines of particular localized cultures (for example, small towns). As such, then, glitter cross-pollinated the values of a flagrant underground with the commercial sensibilities that had always in one manner or another been a part of rock and roll style. But in this case such sensibilities reflected the values of subcultural practitioners whose ideas had been exhumed in a highly dramatic and forceful manner.

In giving consideration to these claims, I also propose that glitter rock maintained a strong alliance with many equally invigorating themes that were vividly apparent in pop art (both as aesthetic and as lifestyle). Through incorporating Warhol's notion that fame could result from the self-creation of a particular style and persona (posing), and through implementing the Velvets' proposition that musical performances need not have a straightforward narrative, glitter rock "cut up" performance styles both on and off the stage. Alice Cooper, for example, dramatized his role (as Alice) with a live boa constrictor wrapped around his body, and he often chose to haphazardly dance with a broom. Likewise, David Bowie often sang "Rebel-Rebel" while punching the air with red glitter boxing gloves, or he included a hand-held skull as part of his stage repertoire, acts that had little literal reference to the content of the songs being performed. Similarly, Iggy Pop often donned makeup and bikini underwear only to offset the erotic image by engaging in various forms of self-mutilation.

Such theatrical forms of bricolage found their parallel among glitter rock fans whose mismatched apparel consisted of platform shoes, second-hand mink coats, ripped fishnet hose, "obscene" cutoffs, satin scarves, costume jewelry, feather boas, sequined jackets and pants, "retro" tuxedos, satin lounging pajamas, slips, and space makeup. Here, stylistic bricolage was linked in part to the posturing of difference so apparent within the Factory, where the notion of instant transformation had become the mainstay. In a manner analogous to that which was common to the Factory, glitter rock provided fans with the premise that they could become superstars. In fact, posing became a regimented form of behavior, with fans providing offstage performances during concerts. In this manner, glitter rock was homological in form—it connected notions of sexual difference with ways to cut up fashion, and in so doing, it provided confirmation that fans could be famous for 15 minutes. In this sense, I believe that the glitter genre can be analyzed as a particular type of subcultural style (and lifestyle) that both extended and revealed the excesses already established through Warhol's art and his Factory studio. In assessing all of the preceding points, I will continue to provide a historical, contextual analysis of the major proponents of glitter rock—those musicians who directly or indirectly entered into the Warhol/Velvets milieu and helped to establish glitter as the rock and roll equivalent to pop art.

Detroit-Ann Arbor (1967-70): The Midwestern Foundations of Glitter Rock

In April 1967, the Detroit-Ann Arbor rock and roll scene could be loosely divided into two subcultural camps: (a) Those who were committed to leftist politics and (b) Those who were involved in the artistic avant-garde. By no means were these camps mutually exclusive; at the same time, their obvious differences becomes apparent when one gives consideration to the self-appointed leaders of each group. On the one hand, there was John Sinclair, an avowed Marxist revolutionary whose Trans-Love Commune provided both a meeting place for the Rainbow People's Party and a practice site for select rock musicians.[3] On the other hand, there was Anne Wehrer, whose home served as "the 'George Washington Slept Here' house of contemporary culture in the Midwest during the sixties and seventies" (Pop and Wehrer 119). Whereas Sinclair purported to create outright revolutionary action through his political manifestos and through the rock bands he promoted, Wehrer took a no less forceful but more indirect political stand. She organized and promoted numerous avant-garde theater, art, film, and music events that provided area artists with some of their only outlets for conducting experimental work. Within and between these two environments, several local rock and roll acts—The MC5, Iggy Pop and the Stooges, the Alice Cooper Band—found refuge.

Although the Detroit-Ann Arbor bands did not adhere to any one musical style, two interlocking threads linked them together: each band maintained a protopunk visual image complemented by the maxim that one need not be a professional musician to play an instrument. Thus Detroit-Ann Arbor musicians were known for their ripped jeans and leather apparel, and their music was noted for its rambunctious aural textures. Although inhibitions were dismantled on all fronts, the most direct result was that songs often contained no more than three or four chord progressions. In a corresponding manner, lyrical messages were straightforward, as short, choppy phrases reflected an incessant and uncontrollable anger. In addition, the majority of bands in the area presented a street-smart attitude that announced a contention with prevailing middle-class ideologies. At the same time, Detroit-Ann Arbor rock toed no explicitly identifiable party line, even though many adherents were strictly to the left of center. As rock historians David Dalton and Lenny Kaye explain:

> There was, however, little choice. Given the factory climate of Detroit and much of the Midwest, rock won its battles by default, politicized as a natural response to repression. The outlaw stance was in itself attractive and set in the context of an ongoing revolution, it both reacted against and partook of the city's assembly-line air. Where Detroit tried to smooth over interior violence, its rock was consciously and defiantly brutal; where Detroit emphasized middle class virtues and restraint, its rock promoted running wild in the streets, drugs, and any former taboo. What could not be turned about was simply subverted. Shying away from musical excellence, the music was raw, performed with intensity and total belief. (202-03)

One of the most unrefined bands in the area was the MC5, a group of local performers whose minimal equipment was used to produce a riveting and unsettling form of rock and roll. Initially attracted by the band's brutal sound, John Sinclair convinced the MC5 that their music might actually provide the blueprint for a number of revolutionary political ideas. In Sinclair's view, the MC5 had the ability to literally transmit his Marxist agenda through the medium of rock and roll, "a more powerful means of mass communication than any type of traditional propaganda, be it pamphlets or speeches" (Nilsen and Sherman 12). Taking the band into his fold during the summer of 1967, Sinclair served as its manager, and he attempted to infuse the members with his ideas concerning a Marxist revolution.

But even though the band members were committed to Sinclair's political ideology, they thought it naive to suggest that a cultural revolution might occur through the medium of rock and roll. Following Sinclair's lead, however, band members wrote lyrics that focused on "guns and ammunition" and "the killer forces of capitalism." At the same time, the lyrical messages could not offset the fact that in the concert arena the MC5 had only one main goal: they wanted to become the "most avant-garde band the world has ever known" (Marsh, "MC5"). As a result, the MC5 produced a primal form of rock that was reinforced by Who-inspired stage antics. While performing, band members would leap into the air, push one another, and kick their instruments. And at every show they turned the volume on their amplifiers to maximum level, insuring a manic fusion of screeching vocals and thick metallic noise.

As the MC5 gained a cohort of fans and as the raw Detroit-Ann Arbor sound was filtering into the musical styles of other local bands, *Creem* magazine served the area with articles and reviews that supported the local scene. Initially, *Creem* was as a regional fanzine, a newspaper that focused almost solely on midwestern rock and roll. Consequently, during the early months of publication, *Creem* strictly adhered to the wants and needs of area bands and their fans. In part, this meant that *Creem* writers were determined to re-create on paper the kind of frenetic energy that dominated Detroit rock. In this sense, the writers followed few traditional journalistic rules. Reviews and essays were written to produce a "rock and roll tone," not necessarily to provide "accurate information." By the late 1960s, this approach to rock journalism led *Creem* to proclaim that it was "America's *only* rock and roll magazine." Most important, this phrase was also intended to suggest a distinction between *Creem* and "hippie publications" such as *Rolling Stone*:

> This [*Creem*] school saw rock music as a revolutionary force: rock generated "energy" which was then transformed into socio-political action. Groups such as the MC5 were presented as "killer bands" that produced loud music with exaggerated performances: Subtle, long lauded "in" folk rock and Beatles material was considered too "intellectual" and bourgeois. (Denisoff 297)

Whereas *Creem* writers were using rhetoric as a method for reconstructing the assaultive approach of Detroit-Ann Arbor rock and the MC5 were attempting to transcend comfortable sound barriers, Iggy Pop and the Stooges emerged as a band that was bent on dramatizing the anger and frustration that was already endemic to the Detroit-Ann Arbor scene. In the process, the Stooges produced a stage act that deliberately mocked Sinclair's proposal that "we need the music to hold us together. Separation is doom" ("MC5" 48-49). As if to exaggerate this proposal in a quite literal manner, lead singer Iggy Pop would often swan dive directly onto the outstretched arms and bodies of audience members. During his performances he sometimes stabbed himself; he frequently beat his head with a microphone; and on many occasions he stripped off his clothes. In some instances, he baffled audiences as he poured hot candle wax on his bare chest. And he often caused outrage when he attempted to engage in various sexual antics with his fans.[4] As far as Pop was concerned, separation was doom and audiences were forced to participate whether they cared to or not.

Much of Pop's stage behavior was derived from an attempt to exceed the performance antics of the MC5, but band rivalry was not the sole source of his inspiration. For one, Pop took some of his cues from Jim Morrison, who was known for his sexually charged, improvisational stage behaviors. Second, Pop was attentive to the Velvet Underground and was greatly inspired by their corrosive style of instrumentation. Third, the Stooges created an even more primitive version of midwestern garage music than their contemporaries in that they often produced songs that were dominated by the essentials of loudness as well as speed. Fourth, the name "Stooges" reflected a self-conscious attempt to announce the band as a group of violent misfits. As Pop has explained, "We loved the one-for-all/all-for-one of the Three Stooges, and the violence in their image. We loved violence as comedy" (Nilsen and Sherman 11). Hence, on the night of his first performance as "Iggy" (October 31, 1967), Pop had already developed a strong association with protopunk imagery, and his aim was to demonstrate that in the Detroit-Ann Arbor area he had no contenders. In other words, Pop and his band members were not content with merely reproducing yet another version of midwestern garage band rock. For here we must note that in the context of October 1967, Pop was surrounded by fans and musicians who considered the MC5 to be *the* most radical rock and roll band in the area. Pop was thus determined to open a gap in Detroit rock. He wanted to perform with retaliation, showing the Detroit-Ann Arbor crowds that his form of punk dementia had no limits.

With a lipstick covered smirk, bleached hair, ripped clothing, and a backup band producing rock and roll at decibel levels higher than those of the MC5, Iggy Pop gained his credentials as "the madman of rock and roll." This title produced a significant amount of recognition in the area, and subsequently, his performances ensured capacity crowds. In turn, *Creem* launched a journalistic campaign to champion Iggy and the Stooges as new local heroes. As one *Creem* critic claimed of the Stooges, "They are reminiscent of the early Velvet Underground music, carrying it to even more bizarre levels. This is probably the guitar style of the future" ("1969" 9).

In a broad respect, this critic was on the mark in that the Stooges, like the Velvets, were not sympathetic to the current mood of West Coast youth, nor did they abide by the notion that peace and love would lead to social change. Likewise, Pop and the Stooges were unimpressed by the revolutionary proposals of John Sinclair. Pop's idea was that rock and roll had become too closely associated with a number of serious political agendas; it had lost its edge, its spontaneity. In part, then, Pop wanted to "reclaim" the feisty spirit of teenage rock, and in the process, he hoped that his lyrics would allow audiences to come to terms with their own everyday frustrations, their own sense of boredom. Pop's songs therefore addressed the concerns of Detroit's "underdogs," the kids—who like himself—had grown up in trailer parks with only the assembly line to look forward to. As Nilsen and Sherman point out,

> The Stooges music tapped into the true pulse of America's youth, not the glamorous hippies converging on Capitol Hill, but the kid down the street with nothing to do; the kid so bored and angry that he throws a brick through his neighbor's window. (122)

Even though the Stooges' approach to rock and roll had little to do with Sinclair's political leanings, the band's relentless "anti-anthems" and its riotous stage performances made obvious the fact that the members were attempting to rival the efforts of the MC5. As a result, Sinclair tried to draw Pop into his Trans-Love fold. But as might have been expected, Sinclair's efforts remained unsuccessful. Instead, Iggy Pop found refuge at Ann Wehrer's house, where avant-garde ideas were discussed and encouraged.

Through interacting with Wehrer's friends and cohorts, Iggy Pop became convinced that his act was a form of performance art. This qualification makes sense, given that many of those involved in Wehrer's scene also had direct ties to the Warholian underground. When compared to Warhol's protéges, the Velvets, Iggy and the Stooges seemed to be producing a musical/visual form that provided the midwestern parallel to New York primitivism. Yet, even though Pop realized that his performance style was distinctive, the comparison to the Velvets would only serve to further establish his reputation as an artist who demanded the attention of those who were attuned to innovative trends in the New York/Detroit rock and roll.

During the month of September 1968, Pop's most immediate connection to the Warhol contingent was Warner Brothers' talent scout, Danny Fields. Fields was an ex-Harvard student who was a central player in Warhol's Factory subculture. Among his closest friends were Lou Reed, Nico, and the other members of the Velvet Underground. As a result of these friendships, Fields had a good working knowledge of the rock and roll business.

By the fall of 1968, Fields had acted as an editor at *Datebook* and *16* and he had acquired a job as a talent scout for Elektra/Warner records. When he heard the MC5 and the Stooges on September 22, 1968, at the University of Michigan, however, he was faced with a contradiction. Here were two bands whose music was so anarchistic that each seemed unlikely candidates for a commercial record label. At the same time, Fields was impressed by the noise-as-music approach of these bands. Also, it struck Fields that the Velvets' live performances had been enthusiastically received at the University of Michigan. In considering this idea, Fields decided that perhaps New York/Detroit underground rock and roll would become the wave of the future. This premise in mind, Fields met with his employer Jac Holzman, the president of Elektra Records. Already riding on a lucky streak after signing the Doors and Love, Holzman agreed to sign contracts with both the Stooges and the MC5. In turn, both bands began work on their first albums during the spring of 1969.

Whereas the MC5 opted for a live recording, the Stooges decided to take the studio approach. They recorded their album in Elektra's New-York based studio, and as a result Iggy Pop developed even closer ties to the Warhol regime. For one, John Cale was hired as the record's producer. Cale's involvement with the band served to encourage audiences that were already predisposed to the Velvet's musical style. In addition, Danny Fields believed that Iggy Pop would be inspired by the chaotic lifestyle that had been established at the Factory. Therefore, Pop decided to stop by Warhol's notorious studio.

On the day of Pop's visit, Warhol was not present. Nonetheless, Pop interacted with a number of Factory regulars, including Nico. She and Iggy became enamored with one another and eventually became lovers. Most important, at the time of their first meeting, she encouraged Pop to intensify his erratic and sometimes dangerous theatrical techniques. But in Nico's terms *danger* translated as *heroin,* which she regarded as a necessary form of "poison":[5] " 'We do not want to see a person on stage, no, no, no, we want to see a performance, and the poison is the essence of the performer' " (Nilsen and Sherman 21).

Some weeks later, back on his home turf of Detroit, Pop began to explore Nico's propositions. At Detroit's Grande Ballroom, he dove from the stage, often intimating that his microphone was to be used as a weapon for attacking fans. As audience members carried him with their hands and shoulders, he often made explicit sexual gestures, sometimes going so far as to expose his genitals. All the while, it appeared as if Pop was in a daze; heroin allowed him the uncanny ability to have his way with the crowd, and this often resulted in physically dangerous behavior. In fact, not only did Pop "attack" his fans, he also engaged in various forms of self-abuse. At this point even the open-minded John Sinclair claimed that Pop was "too weird," adding that the Stooges had gone beyond "psychodrama" (Nilsen and Sherman 23).

In studying the dynamics of Pop's stage performances, we can also consider the way in which his music translated onto vinyl. Here, I would point out that when *The Stooges* was released in August 1969, the rough mix and the tormented vocals seemed to suggest that on record Pop could be just as abrasive as he had been in concert. In a manner similar to that of the Velvets, Pop had incorporated a dark, streetwise urban attitude into his lyrics. Likewise, he was unconcerned with the utopian views that dominated many hippie bands of the period. In fact, the week that the album was released coincided with the Woodstock festival. Accordingly, as the "Woodstock Nation" was proclaiming communal harmony, Pop was announcing 1969 to be just one more boring year in the lives of American youth. In "I Wanna Be Your Dog" Pop's nihilism was also apparent as he glorified sex for the sake of sex. "No Fun" and "Real Cool Time" solidified the Stooges' image: everyday life was boring and oppressive and their mission was to bring a critical edge to this view. And on all of the cuts, the music added magnitude to the verbal messages. The sound was brash and firmly based in a rough, clanging, Velvets-like beat of guitars and drums.

Yet, although the two groups were similar in these regards, it should also be noted that Pop took aggravative rock one step further than the Velvets. He did not aspire to generate a noise-as-music-as-art sound; instead, he created what eventually became known as "shock rock" (and later as the "metal" quotient of glitter). This meant that the chords were stripped down to four or five and there was a strong reliance on pace—the rhythms were fast and jerky without much adherence to texture or form. Combine, then, the exhibitionistic stage performances of Iggy Pop with his antistructure-as-structure approach to rock and roll and one can see how the Stooges produced a musical form that defied easy classification in 1969. For all of the these reasons, rock critics who associated themselves with the counterculture found that they had little tolerance for Pop's form of musical insurrection. *Rolling Stone* critic Chris Holdenfield, in fact, proclaimed, "The Stooges appeal to base broken tastes. . . . Iggy is boredom and repression and he appeals to boring, repressed people. No cool times. . . . The Stooges are really dungeon material (134-35).[6]

With a boisterous approach to both music and performance, the Stooges managed to acquire pockets of fans throughout the Midwest-East Coast area. Still, like the Velvet Underground, the band was largely ignored or misunderstood on the West Coast, where rock and roll fans maintained a strong alliance with the precedents being forwarded in acid rock. West Coast dates, however, were not completely unproductive for Iggy and the Stooges, especially during the band's stay in Los Angeles. At the Tropicana hotel, Pop managed to make connections with Andy Warhol, and they spoke face-to-face for the first time since Iggy was known as Jim Osterberg in 1966. Pop explained:

> Andy Warhol, Paul Morrissey and the whole cast of *Heat* or *Light* were also staying there. And so I met Andy Warhol. I was swimming at the pool at the Tropicana. . . . He said, "My you swim well." The exact words—"My you swim well." So we had a little chat, you know. He was very nice and said, "Come to see me sometime." I was very nervous. . . . So anyway, he'd always leave his door ajar, just to see if I'd come in. I was very shy. I finally did come over one time, and we managed to talk a lot. (Pop and Wehrer 89-90)

The first "official" meeting between Warhol and Pop served to foster the ties that developed between the Detroit and New York camps during the end of the 1960s and the dawn of the 1970s.[7] In the meantime, the Detroit rock scene continued to emerge as America's midwestern parallel to the arty and aggrandized musical scene that had been established by the Velvets.

During the stay in Los Angeles, Iggy Pop and the Stooges also established common ground with another artistically oriented rock band that eventually chose Detroit as a temporary home base. On several occasions, the Alice Cooper Band had opened for Iggy and the Stooges. Later that year, the Alice Cooper Band became renowned among midwestern and eastern audiences. For, like Iggy and the Stooges, Alice Cooper took an assaultive approach to rock and roll. In fact, Alice Cooper provided the impression that his band was forthrightly attempting to challenge the clamorous musical styles that had come to dominate Detroit/New York rock and roll of the late 1960s.[8]

The Alice Cooper Band: The Style of Glitter Rock Begins to Gel

In the summer of 1969, the Alice Cooper Band arrived in Detroit direct from a mediocre American tour. During the year prior to its arrival, the band had managed to offend and ostracize audiences, especially in Los Angeles, where it became known as "the band you love to hate." As Cooper has stated, the popular thing to do was to pay admission to see them only to walk out on them *(Alice Cooper Prime Cuts)*. One reason for this response was that the Alice Cooper Band's guttural sound did not coincide with the music being produced by West Coast groups. Needless to say, within the contexts established by Beat-inspired "happenings" and "freak outs," the band's abrasive, heavy-handed riffs only served to annoy those who were attuned to the psychedelic scene. And as a way of adding fuel to the already hostile reactions, the band deliberately mocked the standard rhythms that were customary among orthodox acid rock groups. Accordingly, the band members lashed at their guitar strings with agonizing fury, often prompting audiences to flee nightclubs in disbelief.

In addition to the band's music, Cooper's stage image provided yet another reason for the negative responses on the West Coast. As the band performed, Cooper pranced about the stage, sporting greasy shoulder-length hair, his face accented by macabre black makeup that darted from his eyes and mouth. At times Cooper donned a pink ballerina dress, topped off with a black leather jacket. And in a manner similar to that of Iggy Pop, Cooper would prowl the stage, contort his body, and spit newspaper directly onto incensed hippie onlookers. In reference to this period, Cooper has stated that they plunged a stake into the love generation's heart *(Alice Cooper Prime Cuts)*.

After two albums and a tour fraught with financial problems, the band arrived in Detroit. Despite dire circumstances, Cooper had decided that his band should make one final attempt at finding an appreciative audience. After performing at a large outdoor pop festival, Cooper was immediately accepted among local musicians and fans. In a context that had been established in Detroit, the Alice Cooper Band did not seem foreign. Instead, the group represented another extension of the primitive performance aesthetic that had come to dominate the area. David Marsh observes:

> It was the heyday, Detroit's angry revolution/street-fighting rock bands, the Stooges and the MC5. Here at last Alice found an audience which understood what his band was trying to say. The Detroit fans encouraged them and began treating them like stars. By the fall [of 1969] the group was living in a downtown seedy motel [by choice], playing midwestern gigs almost nightly and becoming an integral part of the then burgeoning Detroit scene. ("Introduction" 5)

Following in the tradition of local rock bands, Cooper was soon grappling with ideas that would accentuate his already absurdist performance schemata. He attempted to combine fast-paced harmonies with lyrics that reveled in a comic book approach to lurid subjects, such as murder and insanity. The overall idea, according to Cooper, was to incorporate into rock and roll many of the surreal tenets that had surfaced in the work of artists such as Salvador Dali. Thus his stage sets contained props, such as mops, brooms, and articles of clothing, and Cooper often used these in a haphazard manner. The only form of visual coherence was found in Cooper's clothing, which usually consisted of tight mesh jumpsuits, silk pants and scarves, rhinestone jewelry, and feather boas. And, of course, there was the ever present makeup, the dark lines that "dripped" from his eyes and mouth. Other band members also dressed similarly (silk pants, scarves, lamé, bracelets), although they tempered the accessories so that Cooper remained the focus of attention. In considering all of the preceding, it can be claimed that a more precise prescription of surrealism had not been designed by any contemporaneous rock and roll group. If the idea was to confuse audiences, it was an idea that worked toward establishing the band as one of the most popular acts in the Detroit area.

By 1969, Cooper began to increase his efforts to shock and confuse audiences. But he found that in some cases, audiences provided *him* with the props that were necessary if he was to gain widespread notoriety. For example, an incident occurred at the Toronto Rock and Roll Revival that led to his band's distinction as a shock rock group. There, during a long set of primal music, Cooper's fans threw several live chickens onto the stage. The birds, which were not adept at flying, were retrieved by Cooper who tossed them back into the crowd. Immediately, the birds were ripped apart *by* crowd members, who attempted to catch the chickens in flight. However, the word that spread throughout Detroit rock circles was that Alice Cooper had sadistically maimed the live chickens during his performance—and that he had drunk the blood. This story also spread among the nation's rock promoters who were already suspicious of Alice Cooper and his act. As a result, Cooper acquired the label "chicken killer," and many music industry employees vowed that they would refuse to book such a revolting act. Little did they know that what was termed *repulsive* in 1969 would be termed *commercially successful* two years later. In developing his shock rock tactics, Alice Cooper (like Lou Reed and Iggy Pop) soon found himself at the forefront of a then-unclassified trend in American/British rock and roll: glitter rock.

New York/Detroit/London
Rock and Roll at the End of the 1960s

As the 1960s ended, the musical careers of the bands treated here were at a turning point. Both the MC5 and the Velvet Underground were on the verge of breaking up. On the other hand, Iggy Pop was gaining widespread "cult" popularity, and the Alice Cooper Band was on the brink of national success. Recovering from an assassination attempt, Warhol was busy working on films, art projects, and *Interview* magazine in his Factory studio. In addition, he was presiding over social gatherings at Max's Kansas City's notorious back room. In a description of his newfound followers at Max's, Warhol provided an indication of the sensibility that fueled underground rock's up-and-coming "second arrival" (as glitter) both here and abroad:

> The cast was a new, younger, post-Pop group of kids (like Jane Forth, a sixteen-year-old beauty with great shaved eyebrows and Wesson-oiled hair). All the morality and restrictions that the early superstars had rebelled against seemed so far away—as unreal as the Victorian era seems to everybody today. Pop wasn't an issue or an option for this new wave: it was all they'd ever known. (Warhol and Hackett 298)

As Warhol was busy holding court at Max's, another artist and performer, David Bowie, was in London constructing plans to upstage the American underground. Driven by artistic creativity and a desire to become famous through theatrical rock and roll, Bowie was consciously harboring ideas that would merge the somewhat loosely defined concepts that had been established by Warhol, the Factory subculture, Lou Reed and the Velvets, and Iggy Pop. Bowie's strong background in art and music and his yearning to become a worldwide superstar gave him inducement to create a rock spectacle that would eventually mesh many of the concepts that had been used by *all* of these individuals and groups. In the process, Bowie emerged as the ultimate self-created star, the supreme king of glitter rock. Before examining his transformation in detail, I will briefly consider some of the background conditions that led to Bowie's infatuation with the American underground.

In the early 1960s, David Bowie was employed as a session musician. But unlike Lou Reed, Bowie was not involved in mimicking current rock trends, nor was he immersed in writing novelty songs. Instead, Bowie provided backup guitar and occasional vocals for musicians such as the Kinks, Gene Pitney, and Gerry and the Pacemakers. By the mid-1960s he had played on 15 British singles and he had served brief stints in several bands. He had also decided to pursue a solo career.

Highly influenced by the literature of Kerovac and Burroughs and the music of King Curtis, Cliff Richard, and Bob Dylan, Bowie aspired to become a coffeehouse singer. Thus he presented himself in the traditional "freak" mode of the day (long hair, torn denims, lyrical music). In addition, Bowie recorded five singles in 1965, and each presented listeners with a folk-inspired version of rock and roll.

Early in 1966, Bowie signed with manager Kenneth Pitt, a man who viewed Bowie as a multitalented artist who was in need of guidance. Following Pitt's advice, Bowie did some commercial modeling and he acted in a short avant-garde film. By 1967, after releasing a few more folk-oriented singles, Bowie decided to develop additional artistic skills. At this point he entered Lindsay Kemp's London mime school. Also, by late 1967, he became involved in London's growing "arts lab" movement.

These labs were usually small coffee shops that were used as work spaces by experimental artists. The labs were, quite simply, accessible to those who were involved in the production of avant-garde paintings, films, poetry, plays, music, and sculpture.[9] More precisely, the labs appealed to London aesthetes who were endorsing vanguard artistic movements: pop art, experimental rock and roll, cut-up poetry, and so on. Bowie was particularly impressed by these labs, and with his limited financial resources, he opened his own at Bromley. As a result, Bowie became a somewhat small-scale Warholian figure. And although his main interest centered on his own music and mime performances, he suddenly found himself surrounded by a number of diverse artists and musicians.

June 1968 to January 1969: Bowie Experiments with Rock Theatricality

In June 1968, Bowie's artistic career took another direction. He befriended Marc Bolan, who was the lead singer for Tyrannosaurus Rex, an acoustic band that based its imagery on Tolkien's *Lord of the Rings* trilogy. Bolan's mellow, elfin-styled image was, at the time, quite attractive to the arts lab following that had developed at Bowie's Bromley studio. In turn, Bolan found Bowie's arts lab fascinating, and he asked Bowie to create a mime piece to serve as the opening act for an upcoming Tyrannosaurus Rex performance.

By the end of June, Bowie had formed his own mime troupe, Feathers, which began performing regularly in London concert halls. Later that year, Pitt arranged for a commission to film Feathers in an avant-garde video with Bowie's "Love You Till Tuesday" single as the soundtrack. Once the video was completed, Pitt anticipated its premiere on national British television. But his intentions were stalemated because station directors believed that "Love You Till Tuesday" was not appropriate for commercially oriented audiences. Even though the project was shelved, Pitt believed that he had created a unique kind of visual "art document" that would flourish with Bowie's development as an artist.

Convinced that Bowie should write more video-oriented material, Pitt encouraged him to develop a conceptual piece that resulted in a commercially viable product. The result was "Space Oddity," a composition that was inspired in part by the film *2001: A Space Odyssey.* Most important, the theme of "Space Oddity" was among the first to suggest Bowie's philosophical alignment with many of the conceptual ideas that had been explored by Andy Warhol, the Velvet Underground, and other like-minded American artists and musicians. The overriding message of the song proclaimed the dangers of technological nihilism and alienation in a society that had increasingly become dehumanized. This was also Bowie's first attempt to create a theatrical character in his compositions; Major Tom actually became a "mask" through which Bowie could enact a persona.

In the narrative of the song, Major Tom is adrift in space, alone and cut off from all of humankind. In an act of technological treason, the major disconnects the transmitters in the spacecraft, purposely barring his communication with Earth. While the rocket spins uncontrollably, he proclaims that his situation is hopeless. Alone and absorbed in his suicidal destiny he mockingly screams the viewpoint of his commanders in charge, as if he is boasting about, yet damning, his act of anarchy. Such a message suggests an odd sense of irony in Major Tom's decision; he is to spend his last days of human existence differently from all those who have died before him, as he will terminate his life in space—by his own hand.[10]

The video production of "Space Oddity" accentuated the lyrical narrative: Bowie wore a sliver lamé space suit and boots, and his face was covered with vague traces of makeup. While crawling through a mock space capsule, Bowie enacted the thoughts and feelings of "Major Tom," whom he viewed as an extension of his own alter ego. Although the video was not seen by the general public until years later, it was a landmark composition that had strong bearings on much of Bowie's later work.

If this conceptual piece of rock filmmaking and recording seems to connote more than a passing parallel to the work of Bowie's American counterparts, the connection has some basis in fact. Several months before the production of the video, Ken Pitt had flown to New York with the hope of managing Warhol in London. Although the proposed deal fell through, the trip did prove to be fruitful on other fronts. In an interview with George Tremlett, Pitt claimed that he met Warhol in New York and found him to be an articulate, although not extroverted, man. There was a spare seat on the plane that the Warhol troupe had chartered for their concert in Toronto, and Pitt was invited to come along and see the show. Pitt later brought the acetates of the first Velvet Underground album back to London, and he gave these to Bowie, who sat next to the "loudspeaker, listening to that album and another one by the Fugs . . . playing them again and again, late into the night" (Tremlett 96).

What Pitt had brought Bowie was much more than a few tapes. He had also provided him with a new sense of image making, a new sense of style. As a result, Bowie developed an increasing fascination with Warholian iconography. Not only did he study the Velvets' musical form, but he became a distant student of Warhol's, absorbing as much as he could about the artist's work and his life at the Factory studio.

The Year of Transitions: 1969

Nineteen sixty-nine was full of directional changes for David Bowie. He met his future wife, Mary Angela-Barrett, at a party given for King Crimson. During this time, Bowie also continued to experiment with music at his arts lab. Then on June 20th, Bowie's musical career took an upswing as he signed with Mercury Records. On this day, he also rerecorded "Space Oddity," which was released in time to coincide with Neil Armstrong's July 20th moon landing. The single was on the British charts for 13 weeks and rose to number eight by September. It was withdrawn and rereleased a few weeks later, this time reaching number five on the charts. This success gained Bowie some immediate media coverage, most of which focused on the "message" of the song. In turn, Bowie's responses to questions of meaning quite likely appealed to those who found "Space Oddity" intriguing:

> The International Times interview asked David if he saw Major Tom as an alter-ego figure: "Well we drew this parallel that the publicity image of a spaceman at work is an automaton rather than a human being and my Major Tom is nothing if not a human being. It comes from a feeling of sadness about this aspect of the space thing. It has been dehumanized so I wrote a song farce about it to try and relate science fiction and human emotion. I suppose it's an antidote to space fever really."
>
> He explained it as an attempt to express the totality of all things, a common sixties underground preoccupation, "At the end of the song, Major Tom is completely emotionless and expresses no view at all about where he's at. He gives up thinking completely. . . . He's fragmenting. At the end of the song his mind is completely blown. He's everything then." (Miles 26)

Although this single gained Bowie the recognition he had desired for so long, it also proved beneficial in other ways. Ken Pitt encouraged Bowie to write more songs in the same musical vein. The result was *David Bowie,* an album of diverse rock and folk ballads. Like many critically acclaimed artistic ventures, however, *David Bowie* was not a commercial success. During the fall of 1969, it maintained a low position on the U.K. charts, which caused Mercury records to halt further distribution and production of what it had considered to be *the* album that would launch Bowie's career.

Oddly enough, although Bowie did not reap financial success in the recording marketplace, he was successful as a performing musician. He received positive responses from audiences who saw his opening act for the blues-based Humble Pie. In turn, his public image took a dramatic shift as he was suddenly faced with mobs of teenagers who pushed and shoved to be near their new idol.[11] On the basis of such attention, he began to perform solo acts—a propitious move: concert halls in London were sold out as soon as a Bowie performance was announced. Because Bowie was used to playing before hundreds of fans, not thousands, this quick shift in his popularity provided a strong reason to further his musical experimentation. It seemed as if rock and roll was to be his launching pad after all.

During November and December 1969, Bowie and Barrett moved into a large Victorian home, where they set up a small recording studio. This setup provided a space where Bowie could carefully study the American artists he hoped to borrow from and then transcend. In the studio, he spent much time listening to the music of Iggy Pop and the Velvet Underground, and he took to heart the Warholian notion of creating a persona. Amid a barrage of potential ideas about future performance styles, one particular inclination was becoming clear: Pitt (Bowie's manager) believed that the origin of the later gimmicks, including the ingenious image-making Bowie used to convince *Melody Maker* that he was bisexual, came from Warhol, and much of Bowie's musical inspiration came from the Velvet Underground, too.

As these influences became stronger, Bowie decided to form a rock and roll band that would take less of a folk approach to popular music. By the onset of 1970, he was experimenting with the idea of using flamboyant costumes on stage and he was loudly proclaiming he wanted to be "more outrageous than Iggy Pop." He also wanted to develop an enticing musical approach strongly linked to visuals, as in the Warhol/Velvet Underground productions. Within the span of roughly one year, these Warholian pop influences and ideas culminated in one of the most elaborate rock and roll productions of all time: *The Rise and Fall of Ziggy Stardust and the Spiders from Mars.* With this album and stage production, Bowie found himself the avatar of a new rock and roll movement, as the rock press labeled him "the king of glitter rock."

Notes

1. The notion of recontextualization here should not be confused with Hebdige's explanation of bricolage. The dominant glitter musicians who emerged from these subcultural locales simply translated predominant notions about style and sexuality for a wider population, one that lived outside the parameters of New York/Detroit/London.

2. I am not suggesting that without glitter rock, such fans would have had no knowledge of these subversive styles and attitudes. Yet glitter did provide immediate access to stylistic territory that was previously *not* directly available to many rock-and-roll-oriented youth. In the process, glitter promoted progressive notions concerning sexuality. During a time (1972-73) in which bisexuality and homosexuality were not openly treated in pop music, glitter made acceptable that which was previously considered forbidden.

3. Sinclair referred to his political beliefs as Marxist to disassociate himself from "intellectual Marxism."

4. During Pop's early performances, fans were often quite terrified of him. Many accounts present images of fans scuffling to retreat as Pop snarled closer.

5. Nico certainly can't be held responsible for Pop's embracement of the "heroin philosophy," as he was already well into the experimental stages of drug abuse. Nonetheless, she did encourage him to use heroin to lose "the ego" while performing.

6. Some years later, Holdenfield regretted this assessment. Nonetheless, at the time of these remarks he was quite serious in his attempt to denounce the Stooges.

7. The quotation from Pop suggests that this was the first "official" meeting. In other words, at the time of the first Velvets' Ann Arbor date, Pop was known as Osterberg and he was virtually an unknown in the music business.

8. Iggy Pop later claimed that he provided Alice Cooper with many of his ideas concerning performance and music.

9. The London art labs functioned mostly as makeshift nightclubs, providing entertainment space and coffee. Some labs also functioned as work spaces by day, and they catered to artists and musicians at night. However, the labs did not contain the kind of subcultural factions that could be found at the Factory. Nonetheless, the labs did attempt to democratize music and art with an "anyone-can-do-it" philosophy.

10. Interpretations vary as to whether Major Tom actually commits suicide at his own hand. Still, the song provides suicidal metaphors, while drawing on Bowie's self-acknowledged fear of space-age technology.

11. At this stage, Bowie's career seemed analogous to that of Iggy Pop's. Although most of Pop's albums sold poorly by record company standards, he could be assured capacity crowds in concert halls. In essence, during this brief phase in Bowie's career, he faced a similar situation. It was also during this period that he decided to change his last name from Jones to Bowie, so as to not be confused with the teen idol Davey Jones (of the Monkees).

Alice Cooper

THE THEATRICAL GROUNDWORK OF GLITTER ROCK

Although the rock press used the term *glitter rock* in reference to Bowie's early 1970s music, Alice Cooper is often considered to be the forerunner of this musical genre. Early in 1970, the term *glitter* was not yet used, but in 1972-73 when it became a common classification, Cooper was often referred to as the original "glitter rocker." As we will see, the term did not necessarily apply to Cooper, but in retrospect it is understandable why he was associated with glitter. His costuming and makeup were designed to have an androgynous flair, and like many other future glitter rock performers, his act included numerous theatrical devices, such as mechanical props and sophisticated lighting devices. Because Cooper was partially responsible for generating the kind of image affiliated with glitter, I will give brief consideration to his performance techniques and to the ways in which they were manifested during the developmental stages of the glitter genre.

Early in the winter of 1970, as David Bowie was on the verge of customizing a unique theatrical style, the Alice Cooper Band was attempting to gain additional recognition in the Detroit/Ann Arbor area. Although the band had no difficulty acquiring midwestern concert dates, it continued to pose a risk to national booking agents, many of whom were still frightened by Cooper's reputation as a "chicken killer." However, in the winter of 1970 a hit record changed the relationship between music business executives and the "demented" Cooper. His first single, "I'm Eighteen," established his act as one that was capable of drawing capacity crowds.

Even though the song was self-consciously constructed as a commercial product geared to reach an adolescent audience, its popularity was also due to a series of ironic events that took place within the music industry. Consider the following account provided by Dave Marsh:

> Early in 1970 Shep Gordon [Cooper's manager] made a deal with Nimbus 9 productions of Toronto to produce Alice. Nimbus 9 was Jack Richardson and his assistant Bob Ezrin. Richardson was known for his records with the Guess Who and a bunch of Canadian Coke commercials and Ezrin was a nonentity in the biz. The record they produced for Alice, *Love It To Death* [which contained the single "I'm Eighteen"], was made in Chicago. But Richardson and Ezrin were both Canadian citizens, so it was presumed that the record qualified as Canadian product and was subject to that government's new ruling that a certain percentage of all records programmed on Canadian radio stations had to be made by Canadians.
>
> This was a lucky stroke, and particularly significant in Detroit and the Great Lakes region where the dominant A.M. station was the 50,000 watt CKLW in Windsor Ontario. CKLW blankets the north central area from Pittsburgh to Toronto and west as far as Chicago. It is the number one station in Detroit and also has a large audience in Cleveland. Because it was presumed that the first single from *Love It To Death* ("I'm Eighteen") was Canadian product, the CKLW programmers began to give it heavy airplay.
>
> As it turned out, the station was informed that two Canadian producers did not make a record Canadian—the artists had to be Canadian, or the writer, or it had to have been cut in the Dominion. But it was too late: "I'm Eighteen" was a hit and it was on its way to the top of the charts. It was a fluke of the strangest kind, admittedly; but the record was a good one—some might even say a great one. ("Introduction" 5)

The steady airplay on CKLW resulted in a barrage of requests at local radio stations across the northern half of the United States. This strong response was effected by the immediacy of the song's message. The lyrics spoke directly to an emerging post-1960s generation, one that seemed to feel dislocated because it had *grown up old*. What made the song cathartic was the way in which Cooper celebrated this generational dilemma. On the one hand, his age connoted a reason for exhilaration; but on the other hand, he felt trapped by the societal constraints imposed on 18-year-olds. In these two connected ways, then, Cooper proclaimed to possess all the idealism of a young boy, and all the cynicism of an old man. In the process, he professed that listeners should sneer at the dilemmas posed by adolescence because there was no other option. Hence Cooper did not provide a platform for survival, but instead, he offered the simple suggestion that one should present the "face" of a contented old man who can't hide the fact that inwardly he is seething. The song consequently managed to focus on an emotional spectrum that was strongly felt by the myriad adolescent listeners who were in the process of forming a unique generational identity during the early 1970s. As Robert Christgau has stated, "This song changed Cooper from the 'group that destroyed chickens' to the group that destroyed stadiums" ("Alice Cooper" 7).

The Surreal and Warhol at Max's Kansas City

As "I'm Eighteen" rose on the nation's charts during the summer and fall of 1970, Alice Cooper and his band played a total of 12 midwestern dates. The group then toured the East Coast with the hope of establishing legions of fans. Subsequently, the band's biggest concern was the response it would receive from the audience at Max's Kansas City. For it was there that Warhol was holding court in the infamous "back room." Also, the club had the reputation for giving credence to idiosyncratic rock acts that might have been shunned at most commercial venues. With its well-established status as an eccentric midwestern group, the Alice Cooper Band was ready to demonstrate its commitment to onstage provocation. The time was October 1970, and the Cooper Band desired the kind of credibility that could be granted only by those who dominated the underground scene at Max's:

> Years ago in the late 1960s and early 1970s, it was a haven of decadence, of the unreal, theater of the absurd becoming life of the absurd. At the time the infamous back room at Max's was restricted: freaks only. Mickey Ruskin, who owned Max's didn't care if the place was empty. If you weren't hip enough to belong there, you had to sit up front with the tourists. It was the Algonquin of its day. (Cooper and Gaines 198)

Cooper and Gaines show an upside down world where "drag queens" and "leather boys" were accepted and even highly regarded for being different. And for the people at Max's, the creativity involved in being different made all the difference. On the night of the band's performance, his unwashed and stringy hair complementing chunky high heels and eyelashes caked with mascara, Cooper shredded newspaper and spit at the audience and smelled his hands after rubbing his crotch. And then something unheard of happened at Max's: A police officer came into the club after receiving a complaint about the noise and at first only wanted the volume turned down. But when he saw Cooper sashaying and spitting and scratching himself, the officer pushed his way toward the middle of the room, and the show did not go on. But Cooper couldn't have been more pleased: "Nothing more perfect could have happened. Not even if the cop had been hired. Maybe he was" (Cooper and Gaines 198).

The regulars at Max's provided the band with a spirited response. For Cooper, the emphatic reactions thus validated his own sense of artistic authenticity: there was the Warholian entourage—the subterranean network of artists, musicians, and "superstars"—giving its endorsement to the group. In Cooper's terms, this approval signified that he had not only presented an arresting performance but that he had also created an "artistic event" in the tradition of Warhol's Factory subculture. This critical notice provided Cooper with the encouragement to experiment with theatricality in a more lavish manner. He would attempt to create a highly commercial production that would still find its appeal among a subcultural audience.

After returning to Detroit, Cooper decided to advance the surreal aspects of his act. Specifically, Cooper began to investigate methods that would allow him to replicate the "disorderly structure" of dreams. Drawing once again on the ideas of Salvador Dali, Cooper decided to incorporate a number of odd items into his stage show: dolls, sheets, pillows, a live boa constrictor, mannequins, and an electric chair. The intention was to juxtapose these objects so as to construct a "dream-like montage," thereby providing the audience with a bombarding series of images void of continuity and logical meaning. In Cooper's view, this approach was intriguing because it would force audiences to make their own decisions regarding the "theme" of his performance. Cooper explains his goal at the time:

> I love the idea of confusion. I think a valid point of art is chaos. I love the idea of not really knowing what the audience is thinking, and not really caring what they're thinking.
>
> For instance, if you pull a snake out, it's going to mean 15 things to 15 different people. If I pulled a snake out right now, this person would be scared, this person would think it was funny, and this person might be sexually aroused. A snake is that kind of thing.

> That's how Salvador Dali works, he pulls out a brain—that's dripping. When people see it they're all going to get different ideas about it, but all it is is an image. My whole idea is not to preach anything. Just to give them images to fantasize with. (Swift 62)

From 1970 throughout 1971, Cooper's *Love It to Death* production came to reflect both his artistic visions and his commercial intentions. For one, Cooper developed a hypnotic rock and roll stage play that was filled with phantasmagoric imagery. Second, he and manager Shep Gordon were hypersensitive to the commercial potential of this spectacle. It would not only attract the audiences who had identified with "I'm Eighteen," but it would ensure new fans who would, they hoped, be lured by the dazzling potpourri of incongruous images. In the process, Gordon and Cooper were quite cognizant of the manner in which the performance might generate the condemnation of the nation's reporters. Such attacks, however, worked only in their favor: Cooper's reputation as a madman reached new commercial heights as a result of the negative publicity. In turn, all of their calculations proved correct. The *Love It to Death* tour established Cooper as a financial asset to Warner Records. In addition, Cooper gained an enormous amount of media coverage that focused on the "decadence" of the stage act and on the "abhorrent" state of those American youth who were so willing to accept Cooper as a hero.

In particular, rock commentators who were still embedded in 1960s counterculture themes and philosophies found that they couldn't bear the idea that this "comic book madman" with "no values" was emerging as an idol to 15- and 16-year-olds. Consequently, they often approached interviews with the hope of exposing Cooper as a fraud. In their terms, he seemed to represent an adversary; after all, hadn't counterculture musicians been striving to *raise* the audience's collective consciousness? Couldn't audiences see that Cooper was the master of manipulation? After interviewing Cooper, however, critics usually came away with a simple, yet seemingly logical, point of view. For instance, in questioning Cooper's sexuality—time and time again—reporters were often told this:

> People are really surprised when they meet us and find out that we're all straight. It's really very simple. Everyone is part man and part woman, and you've got to accept all parts if your head is together. It's natural law. The people who are threatened by us haven't really dealt with their own sexuality, so after they've

> seen us we've given them something to think about. One of the things I'd like to do would be to play for Women's Liberation and Gay Liberation since so many people are trying to liberate themselves from the roles our society has imposed on them. (Gross 13)

Even though rock commentators may have found Cooper's explanations reasonable, his performances provided them with an opportunity for negative evaluation, especially when considering that in months past they had been asked to cover the Grateful Dead, the Jefferson Airplane, John Lennon, and Jimi Hendrix. By 1971, Cooper was viewed as a menace to the counterculture, and likewise, *Rolling Stone* frequently portrayed him as a insult to the intelligence of his audience. The main reason for such opinions was that reporters had a difficult time distinguishing between "Alice Cooper" as a persona and the "actual Alice" who was otherwise known as Vincent Furnier. At the same time, Cooper always made it clear that there was a distinct difference between his characterization of Alice and the role he played in everyday life. But most reporters had never witnessed this kind of rock and roll duality: a performer who both did and did not take responsibility for his actions on stage. Of this period, Cooper claims that every day he faced dozens of "cocky and hostile" reporters who called him a money-hungry degenerate, a shrewd operator, a "frightening embarrassment." But Cooper says he thrived on these attacks, and during the interview would try to convince them he wasn't that bad in real life; yes, he was money-hungry because he had once starved, and yes, he probably was a degenerate because he reflected a degenerate society. By the end of the interview, the reporters were really confused—most liked Vincent Furnier but hated the Cooper character. It was much easier for the few who didn't like either one.

Coming from an opposite point of view were the Detroit rock critics at *Creem*. In particular, Lester Bangs found Cooper's performances to be intriguing:

> People who call all this darkness and negativism are merely shortsighted, if not certified candidates for white and red canes. The Stooges were the ultimate Nova blowtorch of savage nihilism, but Alice Cooper has recognized it as his function to take some of the irritation, hostility, and paranoia around us and demonstrate that it can be capitalized on and transcended with glee if we're just dementedly lucid enough. ("Alice Cooper: All American" 22)

Bangs was certainly on the mark in his assessment of Cooper. By 1971, Cooper's shows routinely included several focal points designed to capture as much attention as possible. For example, during the heavy-handed "Ballad of Dwight Fry," Cooper described the frustrations of a man who had been locked away in a mental institution. As the song's tempo increased, Cooper revealed "his" condition as an insane "victim" who had lapsed into a paranoiac mental state. Toward the end of the number, a "nurse" walked onto the stage and led a confused Cooper to the sidelines. Minutes later he returned, this time wearing a straitjacket. As he darted from one side of the stage to another, he begged for the audience's mercy.

After a number of songs that included a range of special effects, the show culminated with Cooper's "death act." During this scene he was strapped into an "electric chair" and he simulated an electrocution. As the stage darkened, Cooper then reappeared, demonstrating to his audience that the performance was just that: an act. The show came to a fitting conclusion when guitarist Mike Bruce pointed a compressed air tank at Cooper who held ripped pillows in the direction of the machine, thus causing hundreds of feathers to cascade out over audience members. As a way of constructing an encore, Cooper tossed posters and dollar bills toward the audience and he watched triumphantly as they fought to grab these objects. This manifestation of "crowd psychosis" resulted in Cooper's resounding question: "Who is crazy? Them or me?"

The Concept of *Killer*

By August 1971, Alice Cooper and his band had become one of the most financially successful acts in the history of Warner Brothers records. But as the first nationwide tour came to a close, the band needed a new concept for a forthcoming album and subsequent tour. Looking for inspiration, Cooper noted the assessments of critics such as Lester Bangs and Elaine Gross, who had suggested that he should be compared to Dali and to playwrights such as Antonin Artaud. Bangs even offered the opinion that Cooper had "surpassed" Artaud's work, and he claimed that if the playwright had grown up with the bombarding images of a media culture, then perhaps the two artists would have been collaborators ("Alice Cooper: All American" 79).

Focusing on this positive input from critics, Cooper began work on what he later called "the perfect American morality story." During a three-hour layover in Chicago's O'Hare Airport, he constructed the theme for *Killer,* a stage production that "totally captured the imagination of the public and embodied everything we [the band] had been working on up until then. It was a moralistic, dramatic statement, a masterpiece of shock and revenge, the first dramatized rock and roll show with a story concept" (Cooper and Gaines 215).

Cooper decided that the main character of *Killer* would be an axe murderer who would die at the end of a hangman's noose. In Cooper's view, this basic narrative simply elaborated on traditional Americana; the theme was a common one in horror movies, westerns, and television suspense dramas. This notion in mind, Cooper worked on developing a visual image to complement the theme of *Killer.* His eyes were completely blackened with long trails of dark mascara descending down from his eyes and mouth. His apparel consisted of ripped tights, leather accessories, chains, and oversized platform boots, and his hair was purposely greasy and matted.

In creating the *Killer* concept, Cooper believed that he had devised both the "perfect" villain and the perfect straw man for those who claimed to be the "upholders" of the nation's morality. Across the country, PTAs, Parent Leagues, city councils, and various religious groups were certain to find Cooper a public threat—an indecent hero for their children to worship, the cause for much alarm and concern. Just as he had predicted, bans were proposed around the nation, and as a result Cooper became a controversial public figure. Nonetheless, his *Killer* concept resulted in international sell-out performances and an album that sold over a million copies. In turn, the commercial success led to three cover stories in *Rolling Stone* and to articles and exposés in such publications as *Time, Newsweek, Life, Playboy,* and *Forbes.* Most important, Cooper became a dependable source of revenue for Warners; the "depraved" Alice represented hot new record label property.

Killer, Theatricality, and the Foundation of Glitter

In *Killer,* Cooper relied on surreal and violent stage antics that he often contradicted with song lyrics that demonstrated an adherence to mainstream American values. For example, "Dead Babies" presented a story about children who die as a result of swallowing pills that are left unguarded in parents' medicine shelves. But as Cooper sang the song on stages around the world, he hacked away at baby dolls, and laughed as he tossed their arms and legs into the audience. Other songs in the *Killer* repertoire focused on an even more dramatic approach to violence as an alternative to traditional methods of coping with problems. For example, in "You Drive Me Nervous," a teenage boy fantasizes about running over his girlfriend with an automobile. In "Halo of Flies," Cooper turns the buzzing creatures into objects of glory. And in "Desperado," a macho western character describes his fetish for black lace and leather.

Onstage, such songs were accompanied by intensified theatrics and extreme special effects. For example, after singing "Dead Babies," Cooper showed no remorse for the acts committed on stage; thus the band "beat" him with canes. During another portion of the performance Cooper retrieved Kachina, an eight-foot boa constrictor, which wound about his body as he muttered the lyrics to "Killer." Following this segment, he was led to a gallows, and through techniques learned from a magician, Cooper twirled at the end of a noose as blood spewed from his mouth. Minutes later, he reappeared in a white tuxedo, and he and the band danced underneath sheets. At the end of the performance, Kate Smith's "God Bless America" blasted through the speakers only to find Cooper under a spotlight, saluting the American flag. After viewing this production, British critic Chris Welch claimed:

> Alice Cooper gave a most moving performance at London's Rainbow Theatre on Sunday night. She [sic] made me want to move right out of the theatre; out of the rock business; out of the country. . . . America's greatest industry is packaging and its finest culture is advertising. Alice Cooper is the crescendo and finale in gift wrapped emptiness. Buy now. But your values cannot be refunded. ("Alice's Moving Performance" 16)

Regardless of one's opinion of Alice Cooper, several conclusions can be formulated as to the way in which he provided a foundation for the trends that were leading toward glitter rock. For one, Cooper was the first rock performer to incorporate grandiose theatrical sets (props, lighting, "devices"—such as the noose) into his stage act. Second, he was the first rock and roll musician/singer to create a conceptual approach to *all* areas of the music, including lyrics, story lines, and stage design. Certainly, those who disagree might point to the Who, the Kinks, or the Beatles, groups known for creating concept albums during the 1960s and early 1970s. And, of course, the Who and the Kinks performed the music from their albums in a live concert setting. But these bands did not take on theatrical roles as actors; group members did not "become" the characters that they had created in their narratives. In an opposite manner, Cooper attempted to enact the roles of the characters that he sang about; he became the demented psychopath on stage. Thus Cooper's main distinction was that he created the rock and roll "play." As a result, during the 1970s rock and roll saw an increase in many like-minded innovations. More and more, throughout the 1970s, rock performers were expected not only to *perform* their music, but fans increasingly required a theatrical show, an "experience" that would overwhelm the senses. In turn, many critics denounced this approach due to its emphasis on conspicuous consumption and individual glorification. In addition, many parental groups found this new theatricality appalling, and they often cited Cooper as the one most responsible for the moral decline among youth in the early 1970s. But how could these groups acknowledge and understand the connections between art and music that Cooper was attempting to make? Cooper, quite aware of the controversy, thought that critics should have been more astute. Cooper was not on the Top 10 list with mothers and fathers and adults in general. When the group toured the country and their albums rose in the charts and were worshipped by children nationwide, teachers and psychologists protested that no one could imagine a more disgusting display of entertainment. And yet, Cooper says, these same teachers and psychologists require students to read *King Lear* and *Macbeth.* But Shakespeare, Cooper adds, "would have been my biggest fan" (Cooper and Gaines 219).

Ironically enough, like most rock and roll musicians who pose threats to mainstream values, both the rock press (*Rolling Stone*) and the mainstream press began to present a slightly more positive side of Alice Cooper just months after the *Killer* tour. Increasingly, in 1972-73, Cooper was dismissed as a cartoon character who did not warrant attacks by the media. By 1972, fans were also quite well aware of the fact that Cooper was, after all, *an actor.* When combined, all of the above factors worked in favor of legitimating Cooper and thus, by the time that glitter rock emerged, the questions concerning his detrimental effects had been swept neatly away. By the end of 1972, the impulse to label him an "outrage" had lost its validity, because, after all, Cooper had done an excellent job of reinforcing the notion that he was a reflection of culture, not a threat to it. In considering his presentations and the subsequent evaluations given to them during the early 1970s, however, we must remain keenly aware of the foundation that Cooper had managed to build. For Cooper was clearly the first of many who entered the arena of commercial rock in the 1970s while still toying with the subversive elements of his original (surreal) style. In this case, he thus represents a central tension that would not be resolved fully until the arrival of David Bowie's "Ziggy Stardust." As the first to explore this tension in the early 1970s, Cooper successfully crossed the line between the avant-garde popular and the popular avant-garde.

The Early 1970s

THE FOREBEARERS OF UNDERGROUND ROCK FACE THE 1970s AS DAVID BOWIE CHARTS HIS COURSE

Iggy Pop: The Chaos Continues

For Iggy Pop, the early 1970s were years of struggle and (to an extent) demise. In the summer of 1970, the Stooges released *Funhouse,* and the band established faithful followings in cities such as New York, Chicago, and Detroit. But as the Stooges began to gain pockets of fans, Pop found himself on the road to heroin addiction. This addiction increasingly affected his stage performances; he was often incoherent and not "in synch" with the band or with his surroundings. At the same time, heroin acted as a catalyst, one that Pop felt he needed if he was to cultivate the violent stage antics that he had experimented with in the 1960s. From 1970 up through the summer of 1971, Pop frequently extended this assumption by bashing his head so hard with his microphone that he bled profusely. And during one of his last performances in this particular vein, Pop broke a bottle on stage and stabbed himself in the chest. By midsummer 1971, Pop was no longer able to sustain a performance; the Stooges had broken up; and Pop had committed himself to a methadone clinic in Ann Arbor. But his retreat from the rock circuit was brief. By the fall of 1971, he was back in demand, this time due to the associated efforts of David Bowie and his new manager, Tony DeFries—both of whom were plotting a course for Pop within the terrain of glitter rock.

Lou Reed: The Shift

Lou Reed retired from the Velvet Underground on August 23, 1970; subsequently, he went into seclusion at his parent's Long Island home. By the summer of 1971, he had returned to New York but seemed unsure of his artistic direction. On several occasions, he gave readings of Velvet Underground lyrics and gay poems at St. Marks Church, but his friends Lisa and Richard Robinson felt he needed a musical outlet (Clapton 43). As a result, they arranged for a few social gatherings where Reed could mingle with music industry employees and, they hoped, stir some interest. On several occasions, he arrived with a blond woman named Betty, whom he categorically referred to as a "normal girl." In some ways, then, it seemed to those who were close to Reed that he was making a strong attempt to move away from his bisexual/gay "Warholian past" with the Velvet Underground and the Factory. On one occasion, he even confided to rock journalist Lisa Robinson, "I am cultivating heterosexual experiences because one cannot be bisexual—one is either straight or gay" (Clapton 43). As Reed contemplated his sexual orientation, he also seemed to be on a more generalized search for an artistic and personal life that was simply distanced from many of the features that had come to define his involvement with the Velvets. This attitude was emphasized during interviews with the rock press in which he repeatedly indicated that Betty was a woman who was "not very hip," as if this was the highest compliment that could be bestowed on another individual. However, Reed's alignment with such unhip companions was short-lived, and by August of 1971, he was once again frequenting the all-too-familiar Max's Kansas City.

In the meantime, the vice president of RCA's A&R (artists and repertory) department, Dennis Katz, had arranged for Reed to sign a contract with the label. As a result, Reed's producer and manager, Richard Robinson, planned a recording session at Morgan studios in London, seeking out musicians to back Reed's first solo effort. By January 1972, the work was completed for *Lou Reed,* which gained some critical acclaim among rock journalists in New York and Detroit, but outside of Reed's allegiant inner circle, the album was criticized as a mistake in approach. The session musicians seemed to stifle Reed's disharmonious vision of rock and roll, and the production was considered flawless but vapid. Of course many critics were hoping to hear yet another version of the Velvets' clamorous sound; thus, to them, the music on *Lou Reed* seemed too polished, and the vocals seemed awkward when combined with the glossy instrumentation.

During the spring of 1972, Reed self-consciously attempted to refute the opinions of those critics who had suggested that the album was too "stylized" and/or "refined" (Clapton 48). In an effort to reconstruct a rougher edge to his sound, he employed the Tots as his touring backup group. This band, virtually unheard of outside of their hometown of Yonkers, only created an additional burden. The Tots' careless renditions of Reed's songs caused him to dismiss them—due to his increasing fear that audiences might invoke bodily harm on the group (Clapton 48).

By June 1972, it seemed as if Lou Reed was a performer who possessed exceptional musical and lyrical talents, but according to some critics, he needed the proper cohorts to achieve his full potential as an artist. The album's commercial failure also caused a general feeling of uneasiness among the major executives at RCA. Indeed, there was even further remorse over the fact that Reed was under contract to produce another record with the label. But all of this changed during the month of August 1972 because Reed, the master of the New York underground, became aligned with David Bowie. In fact, Bowie aided in the production of an album that resulted in critical acclaim and commercial success. In addition, the album provided fans with a dominant glitter anthem: "Walk on the Wild Side."

David Bowie: The Success

By the spring of 1970, David Bowie had replaced Kenneth Pitt with manager Tony DeFries, the eventual founder of the Mainman Management/Production Company. According to biographer Barry Miles, DeFries was a calculating businessman who "had enormous ambition. He saw David as the most famous rock singer in the world and set about manufacturing an image and a programme of world domination" (38). In part, this plan was initiated when Bowie formed Hype, a band that included producer Tony Visconti on bass, John Cambridge on drums, and Mick Ronson on guitar. Collectively, the band members were intent on creating a stage image that would gain the public's attention in as rapid and as forceful a manner as possible. As Bowie stated at the time, "I'm going to become much more theatrical . . . more outrageous—much more outrageous than Iggy Pop and the Stooges have ever been . . . and I also want to produce much more, working with new artists" (Tremlett 96-97).

During this time, Bowie was concentrating on methods for incorporating many of the themes that he saw as central to the Detroit/New York underground. At his Beckenham home, he continued to investigate press releases on Warhol, and he studied any information that related to the Factory, pop art, and multimedia experimentation. He also took particular interest in the commercial success of Alice Cooper, even though Cooper's conceptual methods seemed slightly unsophisticated compared to the stage techniques that Bowie had learned through studying with Lindsay Kemp. Nonetheless, all of these Detroit/New York sources had a direct impact on Bowie. And even though Hype had not yet cultivated the type of cosmopolitan performance style that Bowie was beginning to envision, he realized that his band's visual image would be a significant factor in attempting to gain widespread attention among audiences and journalists alike. Tony Visconti describes the band's first performance on March 28, 1970:

> I went as Hype Man, wearing a long cape like Superman, David was Rainbow Man with all these scarves, and Mick was Gangster Man, wearing a 30's gray pin stripe suit. We went on stage and half the place roared and the other half booed. (Fletcher 15)

The contradictory responses did not discourage Bowie; instead, he was prompted to think more seriously about the techniques employed by those who had provided him with inspiration. Accordingly, he began to nurture the hypothesis that in the future his music and his stage image would not be limited to any one set of stylistic devices or to any one audience.[1] By 1971, this notion began to surface with the April release of *The Man Who Sold the World,* the brooding predecessor to *Ziggy Stardust.*[2] On the cover of the British release, a photograph showed Bowie reclining on a sofa, holding a queen of hearts card in the direction of the viewer. Coinciding with this pose was Bowie's outfit, which he had often described as a "man's dress"—a long floral velvet gown that was tapered and simplified so as to show off his "manliness."

The U.S. cover of the same record displayed cartoon cowboy characters instead. Such discrepancy between visual presentations is apparently attributable to the fact that Mercury executives believed that the "man dress" cover would greatly offend American buyers. Nevertheless, the album sold roughly 100,000 copies in the United States but failed to make the charts in Britain. The reason for the album's midrange popularity in the States is not completely clear; at the same time, the album did provide listeners with a complex version of hard rock. In addition, the thematic tone of the songs may have been appealing to those who were attuned to abstract ideas concerning theology, the occult, and the role of computers in modern society.

With the hope of gaining further attention among audiences in the United States, DeFries arranged a promotional tour in February 1971. Due to legal complications, Bowie's visa was restricted, which meant that he was not allowed to perform in public venues. Consequently, most of his time was spent traveling to urban radio stations in an attempt to establish contact with music business personnel and disc jockeys. The overall goal was to initiate friendly relations with his American admirers.

In addition to these activities, Bowie did manage to secure a few performance dates; for even though legal restrictions were binding, several clubs in New York, Chicago, Philadelphia, and Los Angeles took risks and booked Bowie. But his performances were not announced because any publicity would have indicated open violation of the law. Because patrons had no knowledge of who was to be performing, they were many times shocked to see a man dressed in floral gowns. Bowie's delicate visual image and his cryptic rock ballads did not allow for easy categorization among club patrons.[3] Each performance therefore resulted in appreciative yet tranquil responses.

Such ambivalent reactions, however, did not have an effect on several important personal connections that were made during this "tour." While attending a Mercury promotion party in Los Angeles, Bowie was introduced by Rodney Bingenheimer, who had helped sponsor the event. Bingenheimer eventually opened Rodneys, an exclusive glitter rock nightclub that catered to fans and performers in the Los Angeles area. At the party, Bowie also gained a great deal of media attention as a result of wearing his floral gown. In fact, the design of this costume caused *Rolling Stone* reporter John Mendelsohn to raise a series of questions regarding Bowie's "intentions." Bowie responded that Mendelsohn and his readers could come to their own conclusions when contemplating the meaning behind his man dress; he even claimed that negative publicity would probably be forthcoming. He went on to nonchalantly suggest that such publicity would eventually escalate to even greater heights "when I'm found in bed with Raquel Welch's husband" (Miles 41). Thus the overall result of the so-called secret tour was that quite a bit of attention was raised; Bowie had succeeded in gaining a great deal of public notice. At the same time, without his rock band, Hype, the musical performances did not produce the kind of ebullient responses that Bowie had hoped to attain.

The Summer of 1971: The Trends toward Glitter Rock Grow Stronger

By 1971, rock critics at *Creem* and a new wave of British critics at rock journals such as *New Musical Express* and *Melody Maker* began to argue that many rock performers of the late 1960s had "sold out" in favor of an establishment image. For example, Roy Hollingsworth ("Pop Establishment" 25) claimed that by the summer of 1971 rock had finally lost its once revolutionary force. He cited the materialism of Mick Jagger and Eric Clapton, two performers who were obsessed with "large houses, large cars, estates, and cocktail parties" (25). This being a prevalent attitude, many critics began to evaluate a new group of rock performers who were relying heavily on flamboyant images. Because Alice Cooper seemed to headline this group, critics began to arrive at labels for defining his performance style. The term "shock rock" (Shaw 348-49) seemed appropriate, yet the classifications "transvestite rock" and "psychiatry rock" also arose (Rudis 29). In response, Cooper claimed that he failed to see how anyone could consider his band to be feminine, given that its on-stage performances were "very masculine" (Rudis 29). Statements such as these became prevalent over the next few months, causing some critics to ask the question, Is the trend toward theatricality becoming "thoroughly predictable?" ("Purging" 22).

During this time, other rock artists were raising further questions concerning predictability. Marc Bolan had changed his band's name to T. Rex and his hobbit imagery had dissolved.[4] In adopting a more pop-oriented sound, Bolan also decided to develop a stage production that contained the kind of flash and frenzy that was lacking in the performances of groups such as Ten Years After, Savoy Brown, and Led Zeppelin. Bolan therefore reversed his elfinlike, hippie image by clothing himself in silver jackets and lamé pants and by covering his face with glitter dust makeup. In addition, he released eight singles during the early 1970s, all of which rose to the number-one position on the British charts. As George Tremlett has pointed out, "Marc Bolan dominated pop music [in the U.K. throughout 1971] in a way no other individual act had done since the Beatles" (115).

During the summer of 1971 and throughout the following year, Bolan's impact became apparent as a number of U.K. bands aspired to create similar approaches to "glam style." Groups such as the Sweet played comparable pop music, and their visual repertoire consisted of bold-colored taffeta, satin, and glitter eye shadow. In a parallel manner, Slade released a number of commercially prosperous singles and albums, and by December of 1971, this band had also begun to usher in further tendencies toward a glam rock style: members wore silver leather, glitter makeup, and high-fashion platform boots. Along the same lines, yet more innocuous, was Gary Glitter, a teenybop idol who produced a string of AM hits and who was best known for his sequined jackets and pants.

In other musical quarters, the pop images of all these groups were skillfully observed, but the music was viewed as lacking in sophistication. In line with this opinion was Roxy Music, a band that derived its theories about musical and visual style from sources such as Richard Hamilton, Andy Warhol, the Velvets, and avant-garde musicians such as John Cage. The first public indication of Roxy Music's abstruse approach to glam/pop style occurred during August 1971 when critic Richard Williams at *Melody Maker* received a demo tape from the group. He reported that Roxy Music had

> produced one of the most exciting demo tapes to come my way. Although it was recorded on a small home tape machine in what sounds like a Dutch barn, it carries enough innovating excitement to suggest that Roxy may well be near the head of the field in the avant-rock states. . . . The band's influences stretch from Ethel Merman to the Velvet Underground to jazz and they want to bring all these elements into the music, creating a very diverse approach. The electronic thing is important to them, but they are also interested in the flash and style of rock—like wearing outrageous clothes, and using some kind of act. (10)

At this point, Roxy Music had not yet been able to acquire gigs in London, but by 1972 the band found a devoted following among an avant-garde fringe of glitter rock fans.

As Roxy Music prepared a stage production, T. Rex was at the height of popularity in Britain, and Alice Cooper was achieving celebrity status in the States. David Bowie, like Roxy Music, was still outside of the spectrum, and like Roxy Music, he was attempting to define the trends toward theatricality from a more labyrinthian point of view. But in April 1971, after recording *Hunky Dory,* the members of Hype decided to leave the group so that they might engage in personal projects. By early June of 1971, however, Mick

Ronson and Woody Woodmansey were back with Bowie, and Trevor Bolder had replaced Tony Visconti on bass. The new group had no name, per se, but during June 1971, studio work began on a concept album that soon described the musicians as theatrical characters—the Spiders from Mars. During that month, a number of tracks were laid down on tape, resulting in the LP *The Rise and Fall of Ziggy Stardust and the Spiders from Mars.* But even though the musical concepts of the group had been well established, the visual motifs were still under development because Bowie was sketching a number of production ideas.

While Bowie and the band were hard at work, DeFries spent much of the late spring and early summer ironing out contractual negotiations with record labels. He wanted to move Bowie from Mercury to RCA, a label that, he hoped, would provide more investment in the artist. In the process of conducting a bargain, DeFries sought out a suitable cohort, A & R Vice President Dennis Katz. At this point Katz, was overly enthusiastic after having recently signed Lou Reed to the label. In sensing that Bowie and Reed were comparable, Katz and DeFries arrived at a contractual agreement that was viewed by RCA executives as beneficial to the label. After all, DeFries had proposed a number of viable promotional schemes, all of which centered on his plan for "world domination."

As Bowie was on the verge of staking his claim as the king of glitter rock, the British press gave only minimal attention to his efforts that summer. But indeed there was not much to focus on. Bowie's public performances were irregular, and a theatrical stage production had not yet fully developed. In addition, coverage during the summer of 1971 was virtually nonexistent in the United States. Still, there was one influential American who believed that Bowie would be an important force in what seemed to be an up-and-coming trend in rock and roll. Rodney Bingenheimer—the man who had held a party/reception for Bowie when he toured the States—had since gained further clout within the music business. By August 1971, he was writing music gossip columns for 60 magazines; he was a talent scout for United Artists; and he had been dubbed "the mayor of Sunset Strip." While conducting business in London, Bingenheimer spoke with rock critic Michael Watts. In referencing Bowie's visual style, Bingenheimer also proposed a label for the kind of rock and roll that Bowie was producing. He began the conversation with an explanation of the reactions given to Bowie at the Mercury-sponsored party in Los Angeles:

> My they were all surprised when he walked in with those clothes on. They just couldn't believe it! Nobody spoke for several seconds. But that's really him. I don't think it's a gimmick. You know, he really digs Andy Warhol and the Velvet Underground, Iggy and the Stooges and Kim Fowley. It's really strange here, they hardly look when he walks down the street.
>
> David Bowie and Christopher Milk[5] are very close, of course you should understand, they are up there with Alice Cooper and Iggy purveying *Outre Rock* (emphasis added). . . . (Watts, "Meet Rodney" 22)

Bowie and the Warhol Regime

During August 1971, Bowie's conceptual ideas concerning outré rock underwent further development. Instrumental to this development was the underground play *Pork,* which premiered in London on August 2, 1971. The critically acclaimed off-Broadway production was composed of members of Warhol's entourage, who re-created on stage the numerous telephone conversations that the artist had tape-recorded during the 1960s. Bowie and his wife Angela were captivated by *Pork. Creem* rock journalist Lisa Robinson describes the essence of the play:

> Warhol assistant Patty Hackett labored for years transcribing the tapes, and Tony Ingrassia edited the transcript together into what became one of the funniest and best of the underground theater productions. Wayne County as "Vulva" was magnificent in the first of his many multicolored afro wigs. Tony Zanetta was unforgettable as Andy Warhol, seated in a wheelchair, drooling and dozing, his hair dyed a frosty platinum. Cyndria Foxe was so tough in her skin-tight lame sheaths and Mamie Van Doren blonde hair. ("Alice Cooper Did Not Invent" 77)

Because the actors in the play were all directly involved in many of Warhol's film and art projects, Bowie was naturally fascinated. He attended as many performances as possible and was completely engrossed with the dialogue that took place between the Warhol character and the others on stage. In addition, he also took note of the gender-blurred costumes of the actors. In fact, Bowie was already in the process of developing a fashion style that he likened to that worn by many of the performers in *Pork.* Increasingly, Bowie was in the habit of wearing tight pantsuits, yellow patent leather shoes, and Garbo-styled floppy hats.

Bowie's atypical clothing style could hardly go unnoticed by the cast of *Pork.* Indeed, several actors were quick to observe Bowie's outfits, and they pointed him out to stage manager Leee Black Childers. Childers approached Bowie and the two struck up an immediate friendship. Concurrently, Childers also took a strong interest in Bowie's ideas concerning musical presentation. As their friendship bond grew, Bowie found himself in the company of the New York *Pork* entourage, as they frequented London's trendiest nightclubs. Bowie was in awe of the cast; he was impressed by their anecdotes concerning Max's and the Factory. He was infatuated by the important fact that they were integral members of Warhol's New York social scene.

Within a period of two weeks, Bowie's fascination turned fanatical. When Childers suddenly styled *his* hair into a 1950s ducktail pompadour, Bowie decided to go one step further. He created the haircut that inspired millions of rock and roll fans and musicians during the 1970s and 1980s. Bowie chopped off his hippie-styled locks and dyed his hair orange, thereby designing the first version of the "spiky" cut that was eventually refined by hair stylist Suzy Fussey (in creating Ziggy).[6] Bowie found that his new haircut—when combined with his androgynous clothing style—gained him immediate notice on the streets of London.

Overall, then, the cast of *Pork* had a profound impact on Bowie. To Bowie, they represented the living embodiment of Warhol's ideas; they symbolized the very facets of pop art and pop life that Bowie found so fascinating. In turn, Bowie began to think more seriously about a number of Warhol-inspired suppositions concerning theatricality and public presentation. He began to consider a method for developing an alter ego stage persona that would fit with the conceptual format of the *Ziggy Stardust* album.

In September 1971, a trip to New York resulted in the solidification of a number of personal connections that had an enormous effect on Bowie and glitter rock. First, Bowie was in the city to finalize a deal with RCA. Second, he once again had the chance to mingle with the members of the *Pork* cast, who were invited to attend Bowie's RCA-sponsored dinner at Max's on September 7, 1971. Third, during the course of the dinner, Bowie also managed to meet Lou Reed. And during the dinner, Danny Fields phoned Iggy Pop, who also arrived at Max's in time to converse with Bowie. The RCA event thus helped to foster the bonds between Bowie and the Warholian actors, and it gave Bowie the chance to meet two of his strongest musical influences.

Finally, by the end of the evening Bowie had suggested to the *Pork* entourage that he'd like to meet Andy Warhol. As a result, before leaving New York, Bowie finally met the artist whom he had idolized for the past five years. And even though Warhol presented his typical self-effacing persona, he and Bowie did manage to converse and exchange ideas. Warhol was most impressed with Bowie's arresting visual presence. Also, Warhol demonstrated appreciation when Bowie sang "Andy Warhol," a personal tribute to the pop master. By the time that Bowie had left Warhol's studio, the artist had snapped dozens of Polaroids, thus suggesting to Bowie that he had the kind of filmic presence that was tantamount to "superstardom."

The New York trip also proved to be significant in a number of additional ways. As a result of the connections made in New York, Bowie had the chance to work directly with the very people who had provided the motivation for many of his aesthetic ideas. For example, after meeting Iggy Pop, Bowie encouraged DeFries to conduct a management deal. In no uncertain terms, Bowie and DeFries saw Pop as belonging within their fold. As Nilsen and Sherman make clear,

> The plans for Iggy evolved over the next few days: as soon as Iggy was through with his methadone program, DeFries would get him a record contract, after which Iggy would go to England to record an album. DeFries wanted the record to be recorded in England for several reasons. Iggy's reputation in the States couldn't have been worse. Everyone in the music business knew of his drug abuse and he was branded an eternal loser. (48)

In addition to acquiring a management contract with Pop, DeFries and Bowie also set their sights on Lou Reed. Without question, he was one of Bowie's strongest influences, but at this point Richard Robinson was in control of Reed's career. Thus a DeFries/Bowie/Reed collaboration seemed unlikely in the near future. Nonetheless, Bowie and DeFries hoped that over the next year a working relationship would develop. By 1972, this was the case as Reed found himself aligned with DeFries' Mainman organization. In the process, Bowie acted as the producer of his glitter-oriented album, *Transformer*. As Lillian Roxon states,

> Richard [Robinson] was ditched after producing Reed's premier LP, *Lou Reed*, and replaced by the very au-courrant antics of David Bowie. With *Transformer*, Reed's career as a slick decadent, a product of the glitter times, was launched. It was Brecht with a backbeat and a hit single, "Walk on the Wild Side," rocketed monotoned Reed to the top ten. (417)

During this time, DeFries and Bowie also made proposals to several *Pork* cast members. As a result, by the time of Ziggy Stardust's arrival, Lee Black

Childers served as the official tour photographer, Tony Zanetta became Bowie's personal assistant, Cherry Vanilla his press agent, and Jamie Andrews an administrative consultant. Thereafter, DeFries' Mainman company operated as the corporate masthead for glitter's major instigators: Bowie, Pop, Reed, and the cast of *Pork*.

In the meantime, on December 17, 1971, *Hunky Dory* was released. In an interview with Steve Peacock of *Sounds*, Bowie was asked to offer an explanation regarding the lyrics on the album. In answering Peacock's questions, Bowie playfully attempted to demonstrate his knowledge of Warhol's pop practices, and he also provided a strong indication that he was attempting to imitate the artist's approach to media interviews by saying that he just made songs out of what other people were saying and didn't think deeply or for himself anymore. But he said he preferred it this way:

> I'd rather retain the position of being a photostat machine with an image, because I think most songwriters are anyway. I don't think there are many independent-thinking songwriters. They're all heavily influenced, far more than any other form of writing . . . because it's such a disposable medium, that's why. (qtd. in Tremlett 110-11)

And songs that aren't studied or analyzed will survive for a few weeks and seem prophetic and deep, Bowie added, which is what makes pop-biz so much fun: "It's so unserious and untogether—an art form of indifference with no permanent philosophy behind it whatsoever" (Tremlett 110-11).

This kind of response came to represent the first among many ploys in which Bowie would be more interested in attracting media attention than he was in providing journalists with insights into his work. In fact, as the ultimate media manipulator, he eventually claimed that his persona was answering all questions, and therefore he couldn't be held responsible for any interpretations given to him by reporters or readers. In such cases, Bowie took Warhol's maxim of "just tell me what you want me to say" one step further. He *knew* what media critics yearned to hear, and in the process he often attended to their fantasies while exploring his own.

Ziggy Stardust Arrives

By January 1972, Bowie was attempting to acknowledge all those who had influenced his work over the past few years. This acknowledgment came in the form of a grandiose rock and roll project unlike any produced by his contemporaries. On January 19th, Bowie spoke with writer and critic George Tremlett, who asked the young star to comment on the kind of performances that could be expected in the near future. Bowie said to expect outrageously theatrical, costumed, and choreographed shows that would be different from anything that had been done before. Entertainment and outrageousness in pop music had now fizzled, he added, and even though the Beatles and Mick Jagger were once outrageous, Bowie said that it is impossible to "remain at the top for five years and still be outrageous . . . you become accepted and the impact is gone. . . . Me, I'm fantastically outrageous. I believe people want to see you if you're being outrageous—and I'm old enough to remember Mick Jagger!" (98).

Another admission was made several days later, only this time Bowie was much more blunt in his approach. In an interview with *Melody Maker*'s Michael Watts ("Oh You Pretty Thing" 19), he drew on all that he had learned regarding pop art, media manipulation, and instant transformation. Bowie decided to arrive at the interview in as flamboyant a manner as possible. He wanted to make sure that Watts was dazzled by his "superstar" presence.

Once the interview was in progress, Bowie announced his sexual orientation.[7] This announcement was so shocking to the interviewer that he ended up asking a barrage of questions and what started out as a small story on Bowie turned into a two-page spread. In fact, the word *bisexual* held such titillating power that *Melody Maker* placed a 13-inch picture of Bowie on its January 22, 1972 cover. The caption underneath stated:

> David Bowie, rock's swishiest outrage: a self-confessed lover of effeminate clothes. Bowie, who has hardly performed in public since his "Space Oddity" hit of three years ago is coming back in super style. (*Melody Maker* Jan. 22, 1972 1)

On page 19 of this issue, Watts reported:

> David uses words like "verda" and "super" quite a lot. He's 25, gay, he says. Mmmmmm. A few months back, when he played Hamstead's Country Club, a small greasy club in north London which has seen all sorts of exciting occasions, about half the gay population of the city turned up to see him and his massive floppy velvet hat, which he twirled around at the end of each number.
>
> As it happens, David doesn't have much time for Gay Liberation, however. That's a particular movement he doesn't want to lead. He despises all of these tribal qualifications. Flower power he enjoyed, but it's individuality that he's re-

> ally trying to preserve. The paradox is that he still has what he describes as a "good relationship" with his wife. And his baby son Zowie. He supposes he's what people call bisexual. ("Pretty Thing" 19)

Later in the piece, Watts predicted:

> Before the year is out all those of you who picked up on Alice are going to be focusing your passions on Mr. Bowie, and those who know where it's at will be thrilling to a voice that seemingly undergoes brilliant metamorphosis from song to song, a songwriting ability that will enslave the heart, and a sense of theatrics that will make the ablest thespians gnaw on their sticks of eyeliner in envy. ("Pretty Thing" 19)

And in his most vibrant prose, Watts came to terms with his perception of Bowie's sexual orientation:

> David's present image is to come on like a swishy queen, a gorgeously effeminate boy. He's as camp as a row of tents . . . and if he's not an outrage, he's at least an amusement. The expression of his sexual ambivalence establishes a fascinating game: Is he or isn't he? In a period of conflicting sexual identity he shrewdly exploits the confusion surrounding the male and female roles. ("Pretty Thing" 19)

This piece, referenced so repeatedly due to its phenomenal claims and subsequent effects, concluded with the following statement, "He and Lou and Iggy, he says are going to take over the whole world. They're the songwriters he admires" ("Pretty Thing" 42).

As a result of this one interview, Bowie's career suddenly took a number of turns. "Within the music business the impact was immediate," stated Tremlett (101), one journalist who was closest to Bowie at this time. Indeed, this assessment was correct; in 1972, rock critics descended on Bowie because many assumed that his admission of bisexuality warranted a great deal of public notice. With RCA's Mainman subsidiary handling the promotion, Bowie's album sales increased, and concurrently, there was a strong demand for more interviews, this time from journals as diverse in nature as *Rolling Stone* and *Club International* (a soft-core men's magazine). But what was most significant about the media coverage was the fact that it had broader consequences. For Bowie had chosen to speak out on a subject that most in the entertainment business had decided to avoid. He chose to speak in a way, moreover, that allowed for many of his followers to suddenly feel more open in terms of expressing their own autonomy from heterosexual culture. In reference to this period in his career, Angela Bowie reports:

> My husband could not have possibly envisaged the impact his simple statement was to have on public opinion. Social ethics and structures started to change. Gay people breathed more easily, without fear of recrimination. Newspapers and magazines took up the theme. People were actually speaking about a subject that in the past had remained strictly taboo. Naturally, I was asked to express my opinion. Was I shocked by David's admission? I wasn't going to back pedal. Not now. "We are both free spirits," I said. We decided to make a stand on the subject as a matter of policy. . . . In terms of David's career, all this interest and controversy had no ill effects. (74-76)

Following the interview, Bowie decided that all of his public appearances should qualify as media events. Thus he always appeared in glitter-spangled clothes complemented by large platform shoes. DeFries took advantage of the situation as well. With an album on the verge of being released and a tour already planned, DeFries hired a limousine to transport Bowie to interviews and to other public appearances. Keeping in mind that Bowie had previously had only a mild impact on the rock press, DeFries felt it was high time that Bowie be presented as a superstar.

As the media attention continued, rock journalists grappled for terms that might be appropriate to Bowie's music/image. Certainly the interview came at the onset of what was being referred to as glam rock in Britain. At the same time, Bowie's image seemed more refined than that of performers such as Gary Glitter and the Sweet. Other comparisons were made between Bowie and Alice Cooper (shock rock), Bowie and Iggy Pop (shock rock/avant-rock), and Bowie and the Velvet Underground (art as pop performance/shock rock). As a result, a number of new terms were bandied about by the rock press: "gay rock," "bi-rock," "glam," "glitter rock," "camp rock," "pantomime rock," "theatrical rock," "flash rock," and "trash rock." By the end of 1972, the most common term used in reference to Bowie, Lou Reed, and Iggy Pop was "glitter rock," but umbrella terms such as glam and theatrical rock were at times applied to any or all of these musicians.

Another point of interest in relation to this time period is that once Bowie began to gain attention as a bisexual rock star, many mainstream sources took note of his lyrical and musical attributes. For example, *Billboard,* the most widely read U.S. music trade publication, proclaimed that Bowie was an avant-garde superstar (Tremlett 111). Similarly, another important trade journal, *Cashbox*, referred to him as a "shining genius" (Tremlett 111). Later that year, even the conservatively oriented *Time* magazine listed Bowie's most current album at the top of its "Ten Greatest Releases of the Year." These cases are interesting in light of the *Melody Maker* interview, and they tend to raise questions concerning the incorporation of Bowie. On the one hand, mid-cult publications had no problems dealing with Bowie's sexual pronouncement, because he was concurrently defined within a framework that suggested he had a unique talent. On the other hand, and in an opposite manner, the coverage by the rock press provided fans with information concerning Bowie's sexual orientation. In this way, Bowie's admission—when placed within the context of his visual style—served as a source for the development of a subversive subcultural style among glitter fans. As Polhemus and Procter point out,

> Groups such as Kiss don't really shake up the status quo because it's all clearly just for the stage. This sort of tongue-in-cheek makeup is safe because it's just theatre, but David Bowie in the early seventies was something else. The man was serious. Parents who hadn't raised their sons to wear lipstick, pan-cake and eye shadow, or their daughters to fancy such abominations were scared. (75)

In a more general manner, *Rolling Stone* critic Tom Carson sums up Bowie's early 1970s approach to rock and roll, media, and subversion:

> He also, almost single handedly, moved rock and roll into a new era—redefining rebellion as entertainment, and entertainment as subversion, changing forever his audience's perception of the form, and opening it up to possibilities heretofore unimaginable. (389)

In discussing these same issues in a more uncomplicated manner, fanzine writer David Currie claims of Bowie, "Parents were shocked, kids were delighted. Here was someone who nurtured every kid's secret desire to be a rebel-rebel. Here was Ziggy Stardust—the decadent Rock God" (*Starzone* 8).

Notes

1. See Carr and Murray 10.

2. *Hunky Dory* followed *The Man Who Sold the World.* Here, I am suggesting that the latter preceded *Ziggy Stardust* in terms of visual (album cover) presentation and thematic tone. Certainly, on *The Man Who Sold the World,* the themes that dominated *Ziggy* were beginning to gel.

3. His band, Hype, was forced to remain behind in Britain. Therefore, Bowie had little choice but to perform acoustically.

4. In so doing, he lost much of his hippie audience, which was disgruntled over Bolan's acceptance of a crassly commercial image.

5. An obscure theatrical rock band that had an eclectic following in the United States in 1971.

6. My intention here is not to imply that Childers was the major inspiration for the infamous spiky orange hairstyle. At the same time, Bowie felt a sense of encouragement from Childers and others with the *Pork* entourage. Thus he created an early version of the Ziggy style, one that would be further modified within the following year.

7. It is important to consider the context in which Bowie explained his sexuality. The Stonewall riots had occurred only two and a half years prior to his claim. The gay liberation movement was still in its early stages. Given the rather oppressive attitudes toward gay and bisexual people in Britain and in the United States, Bowie was taking an enormous risk in making such a public announcement. And during this time there was no reason to doubt his claims.

Spring 1971

GLITTER ROCK BECOMES AN OVERT STYLE

From January 1972 throughout the following summer, David Bowie and his band, the Spiders from Mars, performed the stage version of *The Rise and Fall of Ziggy Stardust and the Spiders from Mars.* Critics have often singled out the July 8, 1972 performance at London's Royal Festival Hall as the beginning of Bowie's "superstar period" (Miles 47). Although Bowie had not fully developed his stadium-oriented theatrical concepts, he was still intent on presenting a spectacular act that would be complemented by the Spiders' music. Thus Bowie could be seen leaping about multileveled stages, his orange hair and luminous outfits providing focal points amid the flashing lights and smoke.

During the performance, Bowie included all of the material from the *Ziggy* album as well as several cover versions of songs by the Velvet Underground. After finishing this tribute to the Velvets, Bowie provided the audience with an even stronger indication of his musical roots. To the astonishment of the crowd, he introduced Lou Reed, whose black, sequined outfit and dark mascara presented a bold indication that he'd given up his straight image. As the performance concluded with several numbers by Reed, it became clear that he and Bowie were cohorts. The following week *Melody Maker* proclaimed "A Star Is Born," adding that "the magic was boosted by an unadvertised appearance of Lou Reed." The brief but laudatory review went on to state "David Bowie is the undisputed King of Camp Rock" (43)

During the rest of the summer, one of DeFries's main goals was to arouse further interest among rock critics. As a result, RCA arranged for select American rock journalists to fly to the United Kingdom to attend the Ziggy performances. In a strategic manner, DeFries and RCA organized trips that coincided with Bowie's performances during the second week of July 1972, just one month after the *Ziggy Stardust* album had been released. Therefore, on the evening of July 15, American rock journalists viewed Bowie's highly acclaimed show at Frairs, Aylesbury, and afterward they were transported back to London, where they attended Iggy and the Stooges' "comeback concert" at King Sound. In turn, their reports focused on Bowie, Lou Reed, and Iggy Pop, and in many cases the three were categorized as the purveyors of glitter rock. Specific attention, however, was paid to Bowie, who was described as a strange and prolific rock performer, one who was portraying a bisexual alien character.[1] Critics also noted that Bowie was gaining momentum as one of Britain's all-time heroes of rock and roll. And of course, Bowie's repeated claims concerning his sexuality also received extensive attention by journalists who were fascinated with someone so "liberal" and "open."

As "Starman" rose on the single's chart that July, further strength was added to the media's reports. Chronologist Kevin Cann stated, "After the huge success of the tour and many further bookings, David Bowie had really arrived in the eyes of the media and the public. *Ziggy Stardust* was to be the real breakthrough record for David" (90). Likewise, rock critic Tom Carson has pointed out, "David Bowie's timeliness and rock and roll wham-bam-thank you ma'am not only made Bowie a superstar, as it was brazenly calculated to do; it also anointed him as the avatar of the new age" (387). Such opinions were common among rock critics in the early 1970s: virtually all of them[2] praised *Ziggy*, and many argued that the album was one of the great rock and roll testaments of all time.

On the whole, *Ziggy Stardust* (as both album and as stage production) brought together many of the conceptual ideas that Bowie had been working on during the late 1960s and early 1970s. On the one hand, it was the story of a bisexual rock star's rise to international fame. Thus, in an uncanny manner, the story actually paralleled Bowie's own career. On the other hand, the Ziggy tale was one of alienation; the extraterrestrial character arrives on planet Earth, finds that Earth will be destroyed in five years, and attempts to "save" youth through rock and roll. However, as Ziggy's plan unfolds he becomes the ultimate "plastic" rock and roll star. His narcissism takes control and he momentarily abandons his mission to make love to his own ego. After returning from this fantasy, he discovers that his mission has failed, and he comes to realize that he has inadvertently created a fascist state. As a result, the character murders his ego and leaves planet Earth in ruins.

Throughout the summer of 1972, Bowie and his band presented performances that meticulously re-created on stage the story of Ziggy. Typically, a recorded version of "The Alla Marcia" of Beethoven's Ninth Symphony prefaced Bowie's arrival. As it concluded, Bowie danced onto the stage and the Ziggy repertoire began. While bounding about the stage's rostrum, Bowie demonstrated exceptional abilities in both mime and dance. The performance also incorporated numerous costumes—glitter tights, satin pants, floral shirts, and multicolored jumpsuits. In addition, Bowie wore theatrical makeup that gave him the appearance of an androgynous alien.

As performances continued that summer, many fans began to develop their own versions of "Ziggy's style." They wore sequined pants, shirts made of silk and taffeta, glitter-dust makeup, and patent leather platform shoes. Rock journalists took note of these trends and released numerous "hot" stories that focused on the "glitter phenomenon that was occurring in Britain."[3] But even though most British rock journalists were infatuated with Bowie, a number of mainstream writers often demonstrated an opposite point of view. In the same manner that critics had attacked Elvis Presley, Alice Cooper, and other "intolerable" rock performers, they also launched an attack on Bowie. On the fashion pages of the *Daily Express,* Jean Rock described him as "the pop star with the poison green eyelids and the hair like an orange lavatory brush."

And then he had the ultimate pop star's accolade, the publicity stroke of fortune that was bound to make Fleet Street take even more notice—condemnation from one national newspaper, the *Daily Express,* which described him as the star who had gone too far, a 26-year-old who behaved more like a "Soho stripper than a pop star," with all that bumping, gyrating, and hip-wiggling, and flirted with a new audience of boys and girls who would see Bowie rolling on the stage and smirking at his back-up group, the Spiders From Mars. And when one member of the group straddled Bowie, Bowie then feigned to make love to his strident guitar. But where this unwholesome fun starts is also where the controversy begins, the newspaper claims, because Bowie "is a self-confessed bisexual. 'I'm not embarrassed about it. Are you?' he [Bowie] asks. The answer, inevitably, is yes" (Tremlett 119-20).

The Impact Continues

During the summer of 1972, as Bowie was gaining an inordinate amount of media attention, he was also focusing on the music of other individuals and bands. Consequently, a number of performers were virtually (re)molded by Bowie, and in the process, they became identified with the glitter-oriented context that he was responsible for developing. For example, Bowie had long been impressed by the eclectic music of Mott the Hoople, and just as the band was on the verge of breaking up, he proposed that it align itself with glitter rock. Bowie presented lead singer Ian Hunter with "All the Young Dudes," his "anthem to glitter rock." After giving consideration to the composition and to Bowie's proposal, Hunter decided that a glitter image might indeed provide the creative jolt that the band needed. Within weeks, DeFries became Mott the Hoople's new manager and Bowie its producer. The band recorded "All the Young Dudes," and subsequently, it was transformed into a group that—at least for a brief period—seemed to add definition to much of what glitter had begun to champion.

Indeed, "All the Young Dudes" was a glorious affirmation of glitter rock's power as a potent subcultural style, and it certainly possessed all the "hooks" of a bona fide anthem. The song provides listeners with the tale of Billy, an aspiring glitter rock fan who finds that he is incompatible with his older, hippie brother. During the course of the song, we learn of the reason for this incompatibility: Billy has little connection to or sympathy toward his brother's outdated tastes in 1960s music. In addition, Billy is contemplating his own future, and in so doing, he feels inclined toward self-destruction:

Well Billy rapped all night
About suicide
How he'd kick it in the head
When he was twenty-five
Speed Jive
Don't want to stay alive . . .
When you're twenty five . . .
And his brother's back at home
With his Beatles and his Stones
Never got it off on that

Revolution stuff
What a drag!
Too many snags . . .

Billy, however despondent, doesn't resort to suicide. Instead, he finds solace in glitter rock style. As he becomes a glitter rocker, he also notes that the media have constructed a negative portrayal of his subcultural group:

The television man is crazy
Thinks we're juvenile delinquent wrecks
Oh man, I need t.v.?
I got T-Rex
All the young dudes
Carry the news.

But what exactly *was* the news? What was Billy proclaiming? The answer is not as clear-cut as one might assume, given Mott the Hoople's attempt to weave a gay sexual theme with its otherwise heterosexual image.

In effect, "All the Young Dudes" implies a number of double entendres. Hunter's vocals echo these as he shifts from a third-person narrative to one that positions him as a dude who is "gonna raise some cat to bed." This decision to engage in male-to-male sexual activity, however, is prefaced by the long-standing excuse that "Hunter" has "drunk a lot of wine," and therefore he's "feeling fine." His drunkenness in turn forces him to pose the question, "Is there concrete all around or is it in my head?" But in almost split second timing, Hunter drops all his guards, accepts the fact that he wants "the cat," and he triumphantly proclaims "I'm a dude now," as if to acknowledge that his sexual proclivities are to be rewarded. By the end of the song, just before the final refrain, Hunter positions himself as a supreme sensualist—he wants to "hear," "see," and finally "kiss" *all* the "young dudes." In a gasp, he cries, "I've been wanting to do this for years!"

Even though the song seems to suggest rather progressive notions concerning gay sexuality, the theme is underlined with a sense of traditionalism as well. If we take a few steps back to the middle of the song, before Hunter loses his inhibitions, we find lyrics that present the glitter rocker protagonist, Billy, as one who is "feeling squeamy cause he dresses like a queen." "But," as the narrator suggests, "he can kick like a mule. It's a real mean team." In other words, as Bowie's lyrics and Hunter's vocals point out, glitter rockers may have *appeared* to be androgynous, but many of them, like their predecessors the Mods, may have also sported a sense of traditional machismo under the surface. Thus this premiere anthem managed to cross two intertwined paths: most likely, some gay and bisexual glitter fans heard it as a call to arms, the "intricacies" of Hunter's proclamations deftly ignored. But other listeners may have noted that glitter also posed the possibility that heterosexual fans could experiment with "homosexual drag" (Duncan 93). Glitter allowed them to "try on" the so-called gay lifestyle. Critic Robert Duncan takes a more egalitarian point of view:

> In fact, I would venture that the ambiguity of "dudes" here is precisely the point, that actually "All the Young Dudes" is a kind of generic anthem: one size fits all. Indeed, it's a song for the misfit (whoever or whatever he or she might be); a song of disengagement for the disengaged, of group solidarity for the ungrouped; an anarchists' anthem and a nihilists' hymn—and so, of course, yet another song of the times as well. (96)

On Mott's first Bowie-produced album, *All the Young Dudes,* many of the other songs merged the production and arrangement techniques used in "Dudes" with lyrics that suggested a less ambiguous image of the band. And even though Mott the Hoople was most widely known for the "Dudes" anthem, other songs suggested that glitter may have also provided a traditional space for adolescent heterosexual males—ones who may or may not have been concerned with gender bending. For example, on "One of the Boys," Hunter takes on the traditional role of the delinquent school boy; his main concern lies in rifling his teacher. In hard rock numbers such as "Ready for Love" and "Momma's Little Jewel," heterosexual relations are the focus. Also, "Sucker" ends with Hunter nonchalantly informing the listener that his sexual partner is a woman.

At the same time, Mott the Hoople did include a cover of Lou Reed's "Sweet Jane," and like "Dudes" this song suggested the band's somewhat awkward fit within the glitter genre. In the song, Jack and Jane are introduced by a rock and roll narrator (Reed, or in this case, Hunter) who observes that the couple engages in cross-dressing. The narrator, however, makes the somewhat coy notation that although Jack and Jane may be cross-dressers, they also live a traditional New York middle-class lifestyle: Jack works at a bank and Jane is a secretarial clerk. Together, they are saving their money with the hope that something drastic will change their lives. But what? Certainly, they have no upper-class aspirations, no clear-cut goals. By the end of the song, Jack and Jane realize that the only solace from their daily routine at work occurs not in planning for the future but in their mutual love and celebration of rock and roll style. Thus, given the "one size fits all" nature of "Dudes" and the liberating escapism posed by "Sweet Jane," it becomes clear that Mott the Hoople meshed a number of themes that could be easily incorporated into the glitter format.

Through subsequent albums, glittery costumes, and flashy stage productions—complete with mechanical objects and bombarding lights—Mott the Hoople rose from obscurity to become a dominant glitter rock band. But even though the band gained a following in 1972, it could never come to terms with the label glitter rock. In fact, by the time the band released its follow-up album, *Mott,* lead singer Ian Hunter had denied any connection to the genre; he had denied that he was yet another Bowiephile, and he had explicitly denied all speculations that he was gay. Still, for a brief period, Mott the Hoople did provide glitter rock fans with a celebratory image and a song that did achieve anthemlike status. And even though the band swiftly adopted traditional hard rock themes on subsequent albums, its overall impact on alternative rock and roll should not be ignored. Critic Peter Lubin points out that in the end, "the fruits of Mott the Hoople's labor" were not wasted. The seeds planted by Hunter and Mott bloomed and fed a whole generation of pre-punk power chorders and post-punk prophets hungry for inspiration. The bands' legacy continues, their debts have been repaid—"But also let it be known that a pretty large orchard has sprung from one simple apple cart."

Bowie's Influence Expands

During March 1972, through the aid of Tony DeFries, Iggy Pop secured a two-record contract with Columbia. As a result, Pop moved to London and reestablished his ties with former Stooges' members Ron and Scott Asheton and James Williamson. By the summer of 1972, the Stooges had begun work on a new album, with Mainman providing the funding for studio space. During the summer months, Bowie continued to be infatuated with Pop, who had decided to take on a glitter-inspired image. He had dyed his hair silver, and he often wore gold lamé pants, lipstick, and eye shadow. Bowie's impact became more direct in later months, as he acted as a partial producer on Pop's *Raw Power.*

During the month of August 1972, Bowie also engaged in studio production work with Lou Reed, acting both as a musician and as a technical producer. The result was *Transformer,* an album that directly referenced Reed's association with Warhol, the Factory, and the late 1960s underground scene. More specifically, the most famous cut, "Walk on the Wild Side," eventually became *the* definitive glitter rock anthem of 1973—a million-selling single that reached number 16 on the U.S. charts and number 10 in the United Kingdom. In Reed's terms, "This is it—the song that started it all" (Clapton 52).

Here, Reed overstates the case, yet his point is well taken when the implications of the song are considered. It was the first AM rock song to make explicit references to gay sexuality, prostitution, speed, hustling, and transvestitism. Second, when "Walk on the Wild Side" was considered alongside Reed's visual style of black nail polish, spangles, black attire, and makeup, the implication was "chic decadence," another defining feature of glitter rock. Third, the song provides listeners with a series of vignettes that focused on the Factory's most notorious characters. Thus it was a single that made clear the connections between glitter rock and Warhol's Factory[4] entourage.

When compared with "All the Young Dudes," "Walk on the Wild Side" presents a more candid approach to the themes that were by this point steadily defining the genre. But in each vignette of the song, the characters simply engage in practices that are to them quite natural—therefore, these characters find that "walking on the wild side" is just another way of describing everyday life. The song constructs no justification for the "walk"; it is simply something that one could and *should* do if one so chooses. As the song became a nationwide hit and a cult item among glitter fans, these general themes gained momentum. The result was that the continuum of glitter was stretched to include any number of outcasts: queens, speed freaks, cross-dressers, and male hustlers. Hence "Walk on the Wild Side" was much more than a glitter anthem. It signified that Warhol's Factory had really arrived at the forefront of popular culture.

The other cuts on *Transformer* include "Vicious," a song based on Warhol's observations of New York while on a stroll with Lou Reed during the late 1960s. Along similar lines, "Andy's Chest" is a song that obliquely refers to the assassination attempt made on Warhol by Valerie Solanis. "Makeup" carries the glitter theme one step further than "Walk on the Wild Side" with a line-by-line message as to how one might design one's face for the "new era."

Thus both *Transformer* and the hit single "Walk on the Wild Side" added texture to the themes already presented by the Ziggy repertoire. Most important, Reed had much to do with the increasing sense of *hipness* that glitter fans were ascribing to bisexuality. In the words of Chuckie Starr, a well-known regular at Rodney's glitter disco in LA,

> You have to understand that back then, when Rodney's club was going, everyone was jumping into bed with everyone else and it was no big deal. You'd turn on the radio and it was Lou Reed singing, "Hey babe, take a walk on the wild side." It was hip to be bisexual; if you weren't you just weren't cool. (Loud, "Los Angeles 1972-74" 79)

Certainly, this observation is quite important in terms of discerning the manner in which glitter came to connote fresh perspectives on gender relations. In turning to an examination of glitter offshoot bands from the period, we will examine in more detail the recurring themes of bisexuality and gender bending that, at times, found glitter rock treading a thin line between liberation and traditionalism. At the same time, we will note that the excessiveness of glitter rock often provided for a range of possibilities for fans. Glitter indeed developed a continuum that suggested that all were to be admitted. Thus, if Bowie, Reed, and Mott the Hoople defined the center of this continuum, I would like to consider two bands that revealed the outer limits of the genre. In so doing, I will address the ways that glitter came to define a range of perspectives regarding sexuality and gender bending.

Roxy Music and the New York Dolls: Glitter Offshoots

As the Bowie/Reed/Pop/Mott allegiance became noticeable, glitter rock had an impact on other bands as well. In turn, as a number of American and British musicians and performers attempted to enter the glitter arena, the genre became multidimensional and diversified. Here, we can examine this notion through identifying the spectrum created by Roxy Music and the New York Dolls, two bands noted for producing glitter rock in its extreme variations. And even though neither band explicitly set out to produce glitter rock, we will find that each maintained an allegiance to many of the themes that were common to the genre.

In giving consideration to Roxy Music, we can note that lead singer Brian Ferry teased upper-class pretensions by dressing in elegant high-fashion "retro" suits. Keyboardist Eno offset this image by wearing conventional glitter fare such as lamé, sequins, and makeup. These clothing styles were appealing to glitter fans, and because glitter was partially about style for the sake of style, Roxy Music's appearance fit the mold.

The band's music was based in an electronic wall-of-jazz sound that was effected by heavy-handed guitars and Ferry's warbling vocals. The result was music that often seemed spasmodic; at the same time, the instrumentation was brilliantly timed and highly professional. As Roxy Music expert Johnny Rogan claims, the music "Defied any monistic classification. Ferry was determined to juxtapose his 50s tinged vocals and lyrics with distinctive 60s rhythms and 70s electronics. It was a pot-pourri of musical styles, unlike anything heard in rock music up to that point" (18).

Here, we should note that Ferry's approach to rock and roll also had some relation to Warhol and to the themes that permeated pop art. In the late 1960s, Ferry studied fine art at the University of Newcastle-Upon-Tyne, where he was a student of Richard Hamilton's, Britain's most famous pop artist and a promoter and follower of Marcel Duchamp. Drawing on the pop ideas of Hamilton and Warhol, Ferry experimented with ways to employ pop techniques in his everyday life. In the late 1960s, as many of his fellow college students were growing long hair and donning dungarees, Ferry was styling his hair into a 1950s pompadour and wearing smartly tailored suits. He was also quite noticeable as he drove around his university campus in a bold red 1950s automobile, playing "the part of the rich, arty, dilettante" (Rogan 11).

In 1970, Ferry moved to London and befriended Brian Eno. For two years, they exchanged ideas and began work on a number of musical concepts. During the summer of 1972, Ferry and Eno, along with saxophonist Andy McKay and guitarist Phil Manzanera, surfaced as Roxy Music, opening for performers such as Alice Cooper. They also recorded their first single, "Virginia Plain," which became an instant hit in Britain. The song was written as a homage to Warhol; the Factory superstar Baby Jane Holtzer; and the pop landscape of billboards, freeways, and casinos. This single was followed by *Roxy Music* and a series of concert dates in Britain. As David Fricke claims, the image of the band, although not directly formatted in the style of Bowie, Pop, or Reed, was in fact very much in line with glitter rock: It was a package of deviant sexual elegance, oft-center camp, and art-deco flash—all wrapped up in feathers and leather and glitter and "hairstyles that looked like the fins" of a '57 Cadillac (44). England had already tumbled to its knees because of Bowie's sexual flamboyance, but the impact of this "freak chic and avant-pop" look developed by Anthony and Price, the Ferry and Laden fashion pioneer, was even more devastating because each flashy and elegant detail had been carefully planned before the assault. And no one knew Roxy music had a history because what they did had never been done before.

However, in the July 1972 issue of *Melody Maker,* critic Richard Williams provided a brief indication as to the *artists* who set the precedent for Brian Ferry:

> His official biography states: "He names Duchamp and Warhol as two significant musical influences." Bryan thinks that its too bold and sounds pseud [sic] and elaborates: "Someone like Picasso develops a style and then flogs it to death. Marcel Duchamp was a kind of will o' the wisp of art, lending his hand to all kinds of activity—which one would wish to emulate.
>
> Warhol's idea is to make art with as little effort as possible—he's an ideas man, really. And if you have faith in an idea, it is easy to make it happen." ("Roxy Music" 16)

In Ferry's view, then, Warhol's pop practices had suggested that the concepts that guide one's work were as important as the work itself. Thus Ferry set out to compose songs that were cluttered with jumbled words and images, ones that he had lifted from the popular landscape. In this manner, his "messages" were often intended as chaotic verbal onslaughts that didn't allow for simple translations. Roxy Music's compositional structure was equally as tangled—the production lacked a sense of clarity, and the blur of rock, jazz, soul, English dance hall, and other forms made for a somewhat discordant effect. Indeed, all of this was related again to Warhol, whom Ferry viewed as a conceptual auteur.

In addition to his pop approach to music, Ferry "created" himself as a cool, reserved lounge lizard, and he controlled every gesture as if he were being watched. In this way, Ferry represented the perfect adaptation of the Warholian ethos; he had superstar looks, a superstar persona, and he acted the part of a supreme stylist. In turn, glitter fans and critics acknowledged Ferry's self-conscious pretensions; Ferry made sense and Roxy Music's sound added another dimension to a genre that was more oriented toward spectacular visual style than it was toward instrumental coherence.

As Roxy Music gained a popular following in Europe and a cult following in the United States, another band, the New York Dolls, was inadvertently defining *and* confusing the lines of demarcation in glitter rock. From January 1972 and throughout the months of rehearsals that spring, the Dolls made it obvious that they were treading on entirely dubious territory in this the era of guitar rock virtuosos and introspective folk songwriters. Perhaps because of these prevailing forces in pop music, the Dolls reacted in their acclimated manner and played and behaved as they were: amateurs from Staten Island who wanted to produce music that resided on the far latitudes of rock minimalism.

By the summer of 1972, the Dolls had gained weekly billings at the Mercer Arts Center, a defunct Manhattan hotel that housed an art gallery, a clothing boutique, a theater, and a number of "performance rooms." Although the Mercer eventually suffered a literal collapse, in the Dolls' early days it was the center of a burgeoning scene, one that featured video artists (the Kitchen) and raucous rock and roll bands such as the Magic Tramps, Wayne County's Queen Elizabeth, Ruby and the Rednecks, and Teenage Lust. But none of these spoke to and of the Mercer scene as accurately, viciously, sympathetically, and comically as did the New York Dolls.

For a period of three months, the Dolls were virtually unknown outside of this venue, and then unexpectedly in July 1972, the band found a prominent yet transitory position on the international music map. Britain's Roy Hollingsworth, already a committed Bowie/Lou Reed fan, believed that in the New York Dolls he had discovered a group that was gloriously unrefined and much more mean-spirited than any contemporary glitter act. He announced in the July 22, 1972 edition of *Melody Maker,* "The Dolls just might be the best rock and roll band in the world" ("You Wanna Play House?" 17). He went on to explain that the Dolls and their fans were decidedly bored with "endless singer-songwriters" and the "switches and swatches of progressive music" (17). Instead the Dolls had "picked up on the remnants of things that are gone, things that have been misused. They sound like a cross between the Deviants, Pretty Things, and very early Rolling Stones" (17).

Whereas the general tone of the praise was well taken, the more specific comparisons were both condoned and rejected by the New York Dolls. In reference to "things that are gone," the band did acknowledge its most obvious derivations from the early 1960s girl group sound and mid-1960s British invasion pop. In addition, the Dolls were quick to claim that their musical inspirations included Sonny Boy Williamson, the Shangri-Las, Archie Bell, the Velvet Underground, and early 1960s Motown. In the views of band members, however, these somewhat discordant sources coalesced to form the group's musical inner core. In this sense, Hollingsworth's article only hinted at the Dolls' actual musical roots while simultaneously encouraging a comparison to the overtly commercial Rolling Stones. The resulting journalistic tendency was to compartmentalize the band as "Stones Clones,"[5] a label that particularly disturbed lead singer David Johansen, even though he couldn't disavow some of the more directly apparent visual and musical similarities. In reference to this association, Johansen stated sarcastically:

> That comparison bothered my mother. I don't know. I have a pretty shitty attitude towards [rock] journalism in general. Most journalists cop out a lot. They like to take short cuts. Rock journalism is just like a free ride. It's not a very dedicated profession. (qtd. in Cagle 17)

In the heady days of 1972, however, this "free ride" had much to offer for a beginning band with little equipment and virtually no professional musical skills. By the end of the summer, the New York Dolls had flown to London to open for the Faces, and as Pete Frame explains, "every record label in America got on their trail" (27). Undoubtedly, what confounded the A&R scouts the most was what they actually discovered in the process—a band whose music was more uncompromising than that of Iggy's Stooges and one whose visual demeanor proved to be just as extreme.

With David Johansen on lead vocals, Johnny Thunders on lead guitar, Sylvain Sylvain on guitar and piano, Arthur Kane on bass, and Billy Murcia on drums, the Dolls began their career amid a wave of public notice and subsequent controversy. After the London gig, drummer Murcia died due to a drug overdose, and as Frame states, "the band beetled home in disorder" (27). Nonetheless, as Sylvain explains in Jon Savage's *England's Dreaming,* "It got us a lot of publicity. We were living this movie: everybody wants to see it, and we were giving it to them" (61). Murcia's death immediately established the band as one that was dedicated to the principle of intemperance—whatever the form. And the incident, in fact, seemed to add evidence to the label Roy Hollingsworth had printed as an applicable reference to the Dolls: "subterranean sleezoid flash" ("You Wanna Play House?" 17). Subsequently, the band faced a number of complex creative decisions; yet during the summer and fall of 1972, the label seemed only to suggest a gloriously inexhaustible adventure.

"We're trisexual," David Johansen often claimed of the Dolls; "We'll try anything once" ("First Annual" 10). Although the statement was perceived by the rock press as being a frivolous reference to Bowie's bisexuality, the real implications of this claim were quite demonstrable. The band seemingly knew no aesthetic (or philosophical) limits. Thus, by the time Jerry Nolan had been acquired as the new drummer, the New York Dolls had already begun to squander conventional rock standards in America by swirling together past visual images and musical styles that seemed brilliantly reckless in those early days. Indeed, if Phil Spector's girl groups represented a glamorous sense of ocular vulgarity in 1962, by 1972 it was as if the Dolls had suddenly (re)discovered the male version of the lesson. In terms of fashion, they dressed (both on- and offstage) in all manner of tawdry, gender-bending attire: gold lamé capri pants; tacky polka-dot dresses; fishnets; bouffant wigs; shorty nightgowns; leopard print tights; jerseys; feather boas; open-neck shirts; multicolored, reveal-all spandex; off-the-shoulder T-shirts with "New York" emblazoned across the front; black, narrow-legged, "poured-on" jeans; Mod caps and bowlers; oversized plastic bracelets and chokers; bow ties; satin scarves; platform shoes; high heels; and thigh-riding stacked boots. The Dolls complemented such stylistic inventions with the cheapest brands of Woolworth's lipstick and eye shadow, which always maintained the appearance of slightly haphazard application. Adding to these images were the Dolls' "haircuts": mounds of choppy, teased locks that were often transformed into a number of preposterous styles. And in all public arenas, the Dolls not only *swaggered* as they walked; they reinvented the term—sluttishly wobbling in their high heels as if they'd literally thrown themselves together after a long night of drinking, smoking, and street tricks. In the process, the Dolls managed to look menacing, as if they might wield the filed end of a switchblade at the first sign of harassment. On the whole, it was an unyielding and intimidating appearance, one that on the surface seemed to defy reason. Then again, the milieu that had become their own was the Mercer and, by late 1972, Max's Kansas City, where all forms of misfits were held in high esteem. As Jon Savage points out, "The Dolls were sharing space with the tail end of the sixties Warhol scene which had been the venue for drag queens, speed freaks, every possible outcast" (60).

In this particular milieu, the New York Dolls represented a direct extension of the late 1960s Warholian underground, as opposed to a commercialized version of it (glitter rock). And initially, the band's oblique "opposition" to glitter was in fact demonstrated by its disdain for conceptualism (Bowie's Ziggy Stardust), the absurdity it accredited to the creation of stage personas (Alice Cooper), and a dislike in general for the seemingly orthodox classification schemes of the rock press.[6] The Dolls, instead, generated paradoxes that were analogous to those inscribed by Iggy Pop and the Stooges and Lou Reed and the Velvet Underground—only they weren't about to learn from past "mistakes," nor were they to admit to taking their cues from former bands. Hence the Dolls self-consciously became the living embodiment of their predecessors' aesthetic approach to form, yet in so doing, they concocted both musical and visual styles that were even more untamed and chancy. Ken Tucker claims that "[Lou] Reed's example was followed by virtually every street smart band in the city and nowhere was his influence more vividly felt than in that great protopunk band, the New York Dolls" (549). Yet, as Robert Christgau acknowledges,

> The Dolls carried to its illogical conclusion the egalitarian communalism that was once the logical response of fun filled affluence to alienation: they refused to pay their dues. So we had to pay instead. . . . And they wanted their music to sound like whatever it was. ("New York Dolls" in *Stranded* 134-35)

Drawing on Christgau's assessment, we arrive at a number of related assertions. In the New York club circuit, the Dolls became the epitome of instant rock celebrities. Such fame was acquired in part because the band's music was considered so abrasive that it was immediately labeled as *difficult,* even among those listeners who had managed to develop the requisite "acquired taste." Again, Robert Christgau claims, "The joy in the Doll's rock and roll was *literally* painful; it had to be *earned*" (emphasis added; "New York Dolls" in *Stranded* 134). In one sense, this "pain" was directly illustrated by the fact that the Dolls were self-taught and proud of maintaining their nonprofessional status. Indeed, their lack of proficiency often played into their justification for a sound that intentionally mimicked the fast pace of innermost Manhattan. And for those critics who increasingly detested contemporaneous rock, the Dolls' music seemed comparable to the commotion of subways and buses roaring past stops, sirens wailing nonstop, New York aural energy as if it had been laced with amphetamines.[7]

The band's inspired rush of musical energy, its technical amateurism, and its lackluster attitude toward contrived rock formats thereby worked in a coherent manner to define the group as one that was reconstructing rock primitivism for a new decade of listeners. Twenty years later, this musical assault is still relentless, as revealed by a close listening to both the *Mercer Tapes* and

New York Dolls: Thunders's guitar doesn't strum, it pounds and confuses the chords. Simultaneously, Kane's bass misses any notion of a prompt—because none is provided. Clashing intentionally are Sylvain's skillful but piercing rhythmic blasts, which set the whole force into motion, thus leaving Nolan's drums not ordering the beat but, instead, struggling just to maintain the pulsating momentum. Amid the chaos Johansen slurs his words and barks his vocals, thereby adding even more mayhem to the already maniacal pace. Yet as a musical barrage, this certainly was not rock and roll that was returning to its purist roots. And despite the claims of diverse inspiration, this grating musical conglomeration seemingly had no systematically traceable references. Consequently, by raising the decibel levels to extraordinary degrees and by playing so "sloppy" and so fast that the music furnished its own relentless antimelody, the Dolls managed to gain an atypical and extremely dedicated following. In so doing, however, the band did not espouse the long-held (typical) notion of "finding" fans; the fans had to both discover and come to terms with the Dolls' unsettling brand of music. In New York, this was the case, and the maxim of "paying your dues" became one applied to devotees, not to the band itself.

If such dues had to be paid, there was obviously a reason. The Dolls were, quite simply, like no other band in the city—or the nation—at that time. Their hard-edged simplicity and extraordinary visual style thus meant that devoting one's energy to the band called for an evident engagement with the chaotic format that it presented. Accordingly, faithful followers began to employ the mismatched "sleezoid" look in their own personal fashion designs: clothes and objects that were "cheap," plastic, gaudy, ribald, and (especially) rejected (thrift stores, dime stores, closeout sales) became the norm for female and male followers. In addition, cross-gendered fashion references to Frederick's of Hollywood and International Male coincided with insidious shades of makeup and nail polish. The effect was to make the streetwalkers on 42nd street appear tame by comparison; thus the most instantaneously gratuitous and revealing styles became those that were the most esteemed. As rock critic Emily Oakes noted, "The look of the moment for the sex of your choice was straight ahead billion dollar baby hooker" (6). The result was the self-appointed label, "smack and scandal," and an almost exhausting display of adoration from dedicated New York rock writers who found themselves habitually lured to the Dolls' sets not only to observe the onstage exhibition but also to note the audience's "performances" as well. In turn, the primary function of this polymorphous approach to fashion was the knowing complicity that unites all "insider's clubs"—the added bonus being that this particular club appeared too disheveled to appeal to even the most curious of uptown vogue adherents.

But the conspicuous fashions and the brutal, slanderous rock and roll came to a headway at precisely the most opportune and inopportune of moments. During the late months of 1972 and the early months of 1973, the Dolls were often perceived outside their inner circle as another glitter band, one that seemed to be following in the trails of a Bowie-inspired "camp-charged" project.[8] The truth was that this was the one band that didn't belong in the shadow of Bowie's highly methodical glitter spectrum, the one band that—at least in the beginning—was steadfast in defining its own terms. And in the initial stages of the band's development, the fans were following suit, complementing the unrefined spirit that drove the Dolls to their own particular stylistic extremes. Yet, as the Dolls began to tour outside of New York, thereby gaining more widespread national coverage, many untutored critics didn't grasp the contextual ramifications of their musical/visual demeanor. With some critics and reviewers basing their labels almost purely on visual style, both the Dolls and their fans thus became glitter rockers, a label that was both subtly suitable *and* broadly inappropriate. At the same time, however, music critics (Bangs, Christgau, Marsh, Robinson) who had insider's knowledge of the Dolls' insurgent themes were determined to situate the band within a new musical range; yet it was one that had no existing labels that could be appropriately applied aside from the ever convenient label of glitter rock.[9]

If not for the impact of David Bowie, these predicaments may have never unfolded. But it was in fact his technocracy that inspired the press as well as the small factions of U.S. followers to hope for something that was not simply the pure theatrical equivalent and/or replacement. Instead, factions of glitter-oriented fans whose alliances lay more with Bowie's influences (Iggy Pop and the Velvets) than with Bowie himself, craved a music form that was more hard-edged and thus grievously comforting. They also wanted to be a part of an insider's club. But as the Dolls attempted to extend their inbred premises outside of the New York, it was the band's very tie to contextuality that posed limitations in the end. As David Johansen stated, "The make-up thing was hard to comprehend. In New York the gangs wear make-up. It wasn't that big a deal" (Cagle 16). Notwithstanding, as glitter rock rose to brief prominence, the Dolls suddenly became a very big deal, precisely because so few seemed to really understand them. Such confusion is in fact documented by the infamous 1973 *Creem* readers' poll in which the band was voted both "best new group of the year" and "worst new group of the year" (Readers' poll). Along the way, as this dichotomy was in the process of forming, the Dolls managed to forward a number of episodic celebrations, ones that eventually resulted in the casualty of what remains to be the most alternative of all 1970s alternative bands.

Having given consideration to the two representations of glitter's splinter factions (Roxy Music/New York Dolls), I would like to return once again to David Bowie and his portrayal of Ziggy Stardust. In discerning the importance of this image in the United States during glitter's rise as a genre/style, we will eventually come back to the New York Dolls, this time noting the ways in which journalists were led to formulate additional assumptions about the Dolls and the entire glitter genre.

The Style: Bowie Meets American Audiences

During late summer of 1972, Bowie was planning a U.S. tour. At this time U.S. audiences had been treated to journalistic accounts of Bowie's performances, and many were intrigued by press reports on Roxy Music and the "revamped" Lou Reed. Yet, during the summer of 1972, glitter was still a London-based form of rock style, and none of the bands or solo artists that fell within its ranks (wittingly or unwittingly) had toured the United States. Thus Bowie's fall tour inspired much anticipation. The rock press had presented Bowie as the master, or, in some cases, the savior of rock and roll, and his music had created the impression that he was to be the leader of a new brigade. As a result, Bowie and "Ziggy" arrived in the minds of fans as identical personas, as parallel heroes.

On September 22, 1972, Bowie and his band performed their first American *Ziggy Stardust* "warm-up" date at the Cleveland Music Hall and then on September 24 the band performed at the Memphis Ellis Auditorium. It might seem odd that such cities were chosen for Bowie's U.S. premiere, but further observations suggest that these were excellent sites for Bowie's arrival in the States. For example, in Memphis at the Raincheck II—a predominately gay disco bar—Bowie's "anthems" were often staples on the weekends, thus drawing a mixed crowd of rock-oriented fans to the club. In addition, the Highland

Square area, known for its 1960s hippie image, had begun to change its face. Prior to Bowie's arrival, many of the most prominent clothing stores had begun to stock glitter rock clothes, glitter makeup, and platform boots. And by autumn, even the trendy and somewhat provincial Overton Square area welcomed the opening of Chelsea, whose owners flew to London once a month to purchase the latest glitter fashions. It was in Memphis as well that DeFries granted one of the only interviews of the tour to *Rolling Stone* correspondent Tony Parsons. Then, after the highly successful performance in this southern city, Bowie and company—heady with confidence—traveled to Carnegie Hall for one of the most publicized performances of the tour.

On the evening of the show (September 28, 1972), as Bowie fans trekked toward the hall, they noticed that a kleig light was rotating, as if to signal a Hollywood premiere. Audience members ranged from 13-year-old boys and girls in glitter outfits to Harvard students attired in tuxedos. Some fans wore glitter pants and glitter gowns, and a small group of New York Dolls fans could be found wearing fishnet hose, cutoff jeans, see-through blouses, and high heels. The rock press and the national news press were also present, as were Andy Warhol and his cohorts and numerous New York socialites. Hence the New York Ziggy show was the media event of the moment. In fact, it was a concert of such monumental importance that British rock critic Roy Hollingsworth claimed that a "new decade" had arrived. After the Carnegie Hall show, he noted:

> I've never seen quite such a strange gathering of people who resembled Christmas trees on legs. There was much glitter, and several men dressed as ladies. As somebody quite rightly said, "The 60s are over well and truly over." ("Can David Bowie Save?" 37)

In a more extended account, journalist Tim Jurgens related the importance of this concert and described Bowie's overall impact in the United States during the fall of 1972:

> David Bowie and the Spiders from Mars couldn't have picked a better time or place than the present in America to begin working their voodoo on an unsuspecting public. Rock and roll ain't dead but, with a few exceptions, it has lost its power to challenge and mystify. Records and concerts exist as durable commodities like TV, drugs, and booze for a generation beating it to Main Streets old and new, the quest necessarily forgotten. The Quest, sure we all remember The

> Quest, an imminent evolution/revolution that awaited us at the next bend of the Sixties road. So common sense tells us the dream's over now, even though we've woken up in a different place than where we were before we fell into that cracked reverie. There's a price on our heads: how to go about the business of self-preservation and still maintain credence in our yet brief history. Gross evidence to the contrary, there is something in the air. And what's been lacking in our day-to-day lives—very simply, some Rock and Roll Wizard who can function on the mass, extra-musical levels Dylan and the Beatles did during their heyday—may have possibly and probably arrived in the form of one David Bowie. (17)

Manager Tony DeFries took a more literal point of view in his proclamation that "Bowie is setting a standard in rock 'n' roll which other people are going to have to get to if they want to stay around in the seventies. I think he's very much a seventies artist" (Miles 58). In line with this assessment is the one forwarded by rock historian Dylan Jones who stated, "Even though Ziggy Stardust was a self-confessed 'plastic' pop star, next to him the others looked like they were made out of wood" (67).

In giving consideration to the dominant theatrical features of Bowie's stage act, such claims of rock and roll wizardry seem highly justified. By today's performance standards, the technological aspects of the act seem underplayed, but in 1972 such aspects had not yet been employed in the same style and manner by other rock performers. Perhaps the most noticeable feature of the stage set was a rotating mirrored ball that was beamed with intense strands of white light, thus causing the auditorium to achieve the ambience of a galaxy. In addition, colored lights were directed toward the backdrop of the stage, therefore providing visual representations of planets. On the center of the backdrop was the "Ziggy insignia" which was flashed during the entire performance. And, most important, all of these images were highlighted by orange, blue, and red lighting focused explicitly on Bowie as Ziggy.

Onstage, Bowie demonstrated a calculated approach to theatrical rock. Each song had been rehearsed so that Bowie's choreography and gestures would be brilliantly timed and executed. In fact, most commentators noted that throughout the performances there were no hints of improvisation; even Bowie's stage entrances and exits were planned so that he could swiftly change costumes and reappear as another aspect of the Ziggy personality. In addition, the band did not have the qualities typically ascribed to a unit. Band members were there to flatter Bowie, and in so doing, they downplayed the notion of equal access to the stage.

Perhaps the most astounding feature of the Ziggy performances was the costuming. Although the costumes varied somewhat as the tour progressed, three often remained dominant no matter the locale. The first to become a Ziggy trademark was a yellow silk "shirt/skirt" that reached thigh level and, due to splits on the sides of the garment, often revealed Bowie's underwear. This costume was also enhanced by matching shoes and knee-high leggings, both of which added to Ziggy's allure. During another portion of the performance, Bowie appeared in a suit that suggested both the androgynous and alienlike qualities of Ziggy: a tight, glimmering red- and blue-striped zippered shirt fitted over snug matching pants. The shoulders of the suit were extended on each side, and Bowie's boots were a gleaming tone of shocking glitter red. In yet another portion of the performance Bowie wore a one-piece fitted outfit that presented viewers with one bare shoulder. It was also designed so that the tops of the leggings were at crotch level. Often, this outfit was accompanied by a floor-length kimono, which was promptly discarded at a prime moment to reveal what appeared (from a distance) to be a peculiar form of "glitter underwear." And, of course, Bowie added a number of accessories to these outfits (earrings, bracelets) and his makeup was reapplied during each costume change. Consequently, the overall effect of the lighting, Bowie's precise movements, and the numerous changes in apparel was to provide audiences with visual images that aided in the overall creation of the bisexual/alien Ziggy character. Cherry Vanilla, Bowie's publicist at the time, has claimed, "When I think back to those early shows—the immense theatricality that no one had ever included in rock before David, that flamboyance—No wonder Lou (Reed) was enthralled by him! We all were" (Clapton 49-50). As fan David Currie observes,

> Throughout the show Bowie manipulated the audience with an authority that was likened only to people like Jagger and Dylan. There he was, a cosmic yob from Brixon, injecting his fantasies into hundreds of screaming American kids. This was the big time. ("Pow" 16)

Bowie Triumphs and Glitter Expands: 1972-73

By December of 1972, Bowie and his style of glitter rock had succeeded on many levels. His 13 U.S. tour dates bolstered his position as the king of glitter rock. In turn, this distinction fueled RCA's demands for new material. Thus, while touring the States, Bowie wrote the material for a new album, *Aladdin Sane.* Concurrently, he worked on developing ideas for projects with other musicians, and he influenced a host of bands. Most important, however, he helped to ignite a glaring and subversive youth style that had phenomenal consequences among his followers.

In concert halls around the country, fans began to rival Bowie's onstage theatrics by creating stylistic bedlam in aisles and lobbies. Some of the fans' outfits were designed so as to directly imitate the clothing worn by Ziggy. Other outfits ranged from sequined jumpsuits, dresses, and jackets to apparel that combined scarves (as neckwear or dresses), feather boas, silk jackets, secondhand mink coats, sleek retro suits, and platform shoes. Intermissions became visual showdowns as fans paraded up and down the aisles and stairwells, swapping comments and collecting stories about Bowie. And the common catchphrase among fans was that they were "simply being 'on,' " a comment that referred to the idea that they were also onstage. In these ways, Bowie's act inspired the art of "posing" and presenting one's self as a star. In the process, Warholian notions concerning instant fame and the importance of self-creation had finally found their way to a mass-mediated phenomenon. The construction of a performance-art-based persona off the stage was just as important to fans as the concert itself. In fact, the audiences composed the real living theater—the parallel extension of the staged event.

In the United States, where flamboyant public style was not a subcultural mainstay in the early 1970s, some brave fans began to use their glitter apparel/attitude as a way to confront the context of everyday life. Tricia Henry points out that "Bowie's fans began to emulate him, appearing at concerts and on city streets as Ziggy look-alikes" (35). Along these lines, we can take particular note of Los Angeles glitter rock fan Chuckie Starr, who was adept at introducing Bowie-inspired glitter fashions into the realm of pedestrian settings. Quite clearly, he also gained a great sense of self-esteem in doing so:

> Let's see . . . what did I wear back then? Silver lame hot pants, fourteen inch high "Li'l Abner" platform shoes, red garter belts with fishnet stockings, sequined halter tops . . . oh yes, and a Las Vegas showgirl type feather fan. Where did I go dressed like that? Honey, I went to the *market* dressed like that. (Lance Loud, "Los Angeles 1972-74" 77)

In a similar manner, Dasa Goode, winner of *Creem's* David Bowie look-alike contest explained:

> I'm not into Bowie drag, he's into my drag. I've looked this way for years. I got my eyebrows blown off in a stove accident. Looking like this gets me into some interesting places, and gets some unusual reactions. There was a kid sitting across from me on the bus the other day that I thought was gonna wet his pants. He sat down next to me and said, "You look just like Lou Reed." And then of course there are the ones like the guy who came running up to me in a crowd, yelled, "Faggit!" [sic] and ran away. (Williams, "Your Mother Wears Combat Boots" 30)

Beth Flinn—another contest winner—forwards a different, yet equally intriguing assessment of her Bowie-inspired style and attitude:

> All the kids at school think we're freaks because we like Bowie—all they care about is the Allman Brothers, and they call David a fag. I think it's pretty weird calling a girl a queer because she likes David Bowie. (Williams, "Your Mother Wears Combat Boots" 31)

As Bowie's legions became more widespread that fall, promotional logos and T-shirts claimed, "David Bowie Is Ziggy Stardust / Ziggy Stardust Is God." And throughout both the United States and Great Britain, as fans increasingly became obsessed with Bowie/Ziggy, some reporters made a connection between Bowie's rock and roll and fascist politics. At times, Bowie agreed with their impressions; yet, like Warhol, it was often difficult to determine the complete sincerity of his remarks:

> At first I just assumed the character on stage. Then everybody started to treat me as they treated Ziggy. As though he were the next big thing, as though I moved masses of people. . . . I became very convinced that I was The Messiah. Very scary . . . Almost Nazi rock. (qtd. in Fletcher 28)

In an interview with *Rolling Stone* journalist Cameron Crowe, Bowie made the claim that he

> got hopelessly lost in the fantasy. I could have been Hitler in England. Wouldn't have been hard. Concerts alone got so enormously frightening that even the papers were saying, "This ain't rock and roll, this is bloody Hitler! Something must be done!" And they were right. It was awesome. Actually, I wonder . . . I think I might have been a bloody good Hitler. I'd be an excellent dictator. Very eccentric and quite mad. (Crowe 90)

During January 1973, Bowie and the Spiders took on an even more hectic schedule. The band played four U.K. gigs and performed on a London weekend talk show. In addition, they laid down the tracks for *Aladdin Sane,* the title designed to imply "a lad insane." Finally, on January 25, 1973, Bowie and the Spiders set out on a 100-day world tour that began in New York. Of Bowie's opening performance, Kevin Cann states:

> New York, Radio City Music Hall, first night of the second U.S. tour. The Valentine's Day performance was a triumph and New York once again took to David in a big way. The shows were a complete sellout, and even Andy Warhol found getting tickets a problem. One music paper in New York called David the "Darling of New York." This was to be David's real breakthrough in the States. (104)

By the time of the second tour, the theatrical devices had also undergone several transformations. As the performance began, a spotlight focused on Bowie, who appeared inside a cage that had been hoisted 50 feet above the stage. As the cage slowly descended, bombarding lights flashed throughout the stage arena. The Spiders appeared as well—entering the stage through a trap door, as if they had been "zapped" to planet Earth. The performance also contained numerous costume changes, and it continued to replay many of the same themes already described.

After the U.S. tour ended on March 11 in Los Angeles, Bowie and the Spiders toured Japan, where rioting occurred at several performances. By May, they were back in the United Kingdom, where presentations combined songs from both *Ziggy* and the forthcoming *Aladdin Sane.*

RCA released *Aladdin Sane* on April 13, 1973, when advance orders had reached the 100,000 mark. RCA had not received orders of this magnitude since the mid-1960s when the Beatles had risen to fame. But even though the record was a commercial success, its compositional tone could not be compared to the conceptual *Ziggy Stardust.*

The material on *Aladdin Sane,* however, was not designed to present an overall thematic tone; the album did not present a general narrative. Instead, the songs revealed Bowie's spotty impressions of America, and they were written as a partial homage to Jack Kerouac and *On The Road.* From Bowie's point of view, America was a land of lonely people, a fragmented nation with very little cultural unity. Perhaps this brooding attitude accounts for the somewhat uneven arrangements. Nevertheless, the album further established Bowie's image as the king of glitter rock.

Most noticeable to glitter fans was the album's striking cover, which pictured Bowie sporting a longer version of his carrot-colored spiky haircut. In addition, his skin looked unnaturally pink and rose-colored makeup filtered across his eyes. But the most conspicuous aspect of this close-up shot was the red and blue lightning bolt that came down across his forehead, over one eye, and down his cheek. It was a visual style that Bowie fans adopted at concerts throughout the country.

Aside from the visual aspect of *Aladdin Sane,* the album also spoke to many of the other images associated with the glitter genre. Although the sound production on the title track is less than perfect, the message—if listened to carefully—is one of subtle warning: The "new" fun-loving glitter fans could find themselves in danger should yet another war (like Vietnam) break out. "Jean Genie," commonly thought to be a reference to Jean Genet, was actually a tribute to Iggy Pop. "Lady Grinning Soul" was inspired by soul singer Claudia Linnear, also the inspiration behind the Rolling Stones' "Brown Sugar" (Carr and Murray 55-56). "Panic in Detroit" focused on the city that spawned Iggy Pop and the MC5, and it contained references to John Sinclair who was, at the time, serving a prison sentence for marijuana possession (Carr and Murray 56). "Drive in Saturday" made clear the role of the media in the lives of the new breed. According to Bowie, glitter rockers attended drive-in movies not to "make out" but to watch films and *learn* how to make out. Other cuts included "Cracked Actor" (a tale of Hollywood dementia), "Time" (an attempt to apply Brecht to rock and roll), and a cover version of the Rolling Stones' "Let's Spend the Night Together."

As *Aladdin Sane* rose on the charts, other musicians released records that Bowie had either (in some combination) written or produced, thus providing his audience with an even wider array of glitter rock. In 1973, these musicians began touring and concerts provided additional visual images for fans to absorb. For example, Lou Reed's *Transformer* was released in December 1972, and during the early winter months of 1973 Reed appeared at a number of British venues. Then on February 1 he made his solo debut at Alice Tulley Hall in New York. But as his album rose to number 29 on the U.S. charts by April of that year, he did not choose, as Bowie did, to construct a media blitz across the states, and he waited until autumn of 1973 to conduct a full-scale tour. In the meantime, the anthem "Walk on the Wild Side" had much to do with Reed's rise in popularity in the States, and it certainly added texture to the themes present in the Ziggy repertoire.

In addition to Reed's success, Mott the Hoople gained momentum with their release *Mott the Hoople* on July 28, 1973. During the same time (June 1, 1973), Iggy Pop's comeback album *Raw Power* was released. As these artists toured, rock publications such as *Creem* and *Rock Scene* in the United States and *Melody Maker* in London were making much ado over the glitter rock phenomenon and its effect on the whole of rock and roll.

For example, the August 1973 edition of *Creem* featured as its cover story, "The Androgyny Hall of Fame," in which Bowie was placed dead center, with the following surrounding his photograph (in clockwise order): Elvis Presley, Alice Cooper, Mick Jagger, Iggy Pop, Rod Stewart, and Marc Bolan. The feature article on this topic included a historical account of musicians who had explicitly experimented with self-conscious forms of gender-bending style. In addition to articles of this nature, *Creem* provided readers with Lester Bang's maniacal writing style, and his interviews and record reviews were unprecedented in the field of rock journalism. Also *Creem* presented fans with an entourage of writers who were in the process of creating a new form of rock journalism. Reviews and feature articles were often written in stream-of-consciousness style; the intention was to provide readers with images rather than accuracy. Finally, *Creem* conducted yearly rock polls, it promoted Bowie look-alike contests, and its letters section furnished fans with a forum allowed for debates on the topic of glitter rock. Here, fans wrote high-spirited diatribes on the subject of glitter, and editors responded with scathing in-house jokes. *Creem* thus became one of the major U.S. sources on glitter rock, even though the writers did not wholeheartedly advocate a celebratory view of the genre. But the "attacks" often became central to the magazine's freewheeling form of self-indulgent rock journalism. As such, fans had to consume the details of all articles, especially the letters section, if they were to remain informed on current glitter trends during the early 1970s. The following letters serve as exemplars of the alternating themes and styles of fan responses that flowed through *Creem* during this period:

JEALOUS?

While reading your July issue, I realized what a bunch of crap this whole Rock and roll set up is. It's just as much a farce as anything else. Who CARES, for God's sakes, what Marc Bolan's philosophy of life is or what Lou Reed has to say about music or what Alice Cooper wore to some ego trip party? Don't you think it's kind of futile to try and base a whole magazine on this kind of stuff? Van Morrison and Taj Mahal are the only legitimate musicians in the field. So what's the need of messing around with all these other schmucks? One more thing—tell your hip readers to keep sending in those funny letters. They're really getting inventive with their fellatio jokes.

Extremely sincerely
The Creature From 20,000 Fanthoms
Texas ("JEALOUS?" 10)

Creem:

As we all know, Ravishing Reed is Mother Nature's Son just Takin' a Walk on the Wild Side. Oh, by the way, if Lou's a "mama's boy," momma is probably just as glad as me that ol' Lou baby is out of his closet—once and for all.

Debbi
Bayside, N.Y. (Letter 10)

Osmondo Bendo

I don't think this is fair!!! In *16* magazine *they* don't say anything bad about Alice Cooper, Black Sabbath or anything like that. But in *Creem* they say the Osmonds are fags! It's not TRUE!!!! I don't think that is FAIR!

Your enemy,
A.D.
P.S. It's not FAIR!!!
(*Look, if it was good enough for William Shakespeare . . . Ed.*)
("Osmondo Bendo" 10)

Creem Casualty

For over a year now I've been reading *Creem* regularly, buying lots of records and stuff because *Creem* said they were good and not buying stuff *Creem* said wasn't good, and making public my *Creem*-inspired feelings on certain bands and kinds of dope and things. Now because of that all my old friends that I used to fart around and listen to Jethro Tull with think I'm some kind of human retardo or something and avoid me. And I don't have any new friends. Also, I bought this book *Naked Lunch* by William Burroughs because Lester Bangs is always plugging him and before I had a chance to read it one of the nuns (teachers) at my school (Catholic) catches me with it (this was last spring when school was in session) and gives me this big uptight private lecture on how sick it is and tells me that "(my) lack of security in (my) existence is very sad." I don't know what she meant exactly either but you know how embarrassing that sort of thing is, and this was this young, pretty and uninhibited nun that I kind of like, and I'll probably have her next year too and she'll still hate me. You have really fucked up my life *Creem* magazine. I was much happier when I was just a punk and not a sophisto punk.

Binky Brown
Columbus, Ohio
(*Stand by us, we'll stand by you even after we've ruined your life. You just got a free subscription.* Ed.) ("Creem Casualty" 82)

E's Flat Ah's Flat

Lou Reed once told me he wanted to give everybody in the state of Nevada an electric guitar and an amp, teach them an "E" chord, and at noon on an appointed day have them all play it at once. A year later ('69) I asked him about the idea and he said, "There's no point in it . . . There's enough shitty white blues bands playing all their material in the key of 'E.' "

Peter Laughner

Cleveland Heights, Ohio

P.S. A good hangover is like taking a snort of cocaine when you've got the Hong Kong flu. ("E's Flat" 2)

The six wives of MXL SPLB

Earthlings:

Mxlp ge tong ke "April *Creem*" gyak klo "page 82" kl1% "Coprophagous Fellations": "B. Martin and B. Haynes" GELP TI LODSMBN!! L@@TV! "YESYESYESYESYES" btop la izp! Bwasa "Opera?" HTP LA HTP LA! Yaqw tolk bonm "Andy Williams" htp la, HTP LA! Khle lpsel kwang klito zworp "Baby and a Rattle" Htp la, "M%$H%&FK@RS," HTP LA! Cvklq plitz "Fragile and close to the edge" wshtlp mbop Pure Trash? Htp La! HTP LA!

Altechmy slubberdegullions: bumptious flabergudgioms cretionous beoetians and alphaberic imbeciles: I bemouth anyone who will begore, bebleed, beblister, beclaw, bemud and emaciate the fools who spewed the fallacious animadversions against one of your sub-species saving graces: YES.

Slowly dissapating
Count Clapperdegeonisky
The little, silver haired,
green being you saw in your
backyard last night.
(*Thought we killed all you guys in World War II.* Ed.)
("The Six Wives" 8).

Dear *Creem* Poll Roll

I enjoyed your 1973 Rock and Roll Poll immensely but a few categories should have been there that were not. Please don't forget these next year:

Dinosaur of the Year
Wimp of the Year
Robot of the Year
Ego of the Year
Queer of the Year
Schizoid of the Year
Jesus of the Year
Maurice
Queens, New York
(*Any nominees?* Ed.) ("Dear *Creem*" 7)

While *Creem* analyzed, celebrated, and satirized glitter rock, *Rock Scene* gave fans around the country an insider's look at New York's trendiest glitter night spots. *Rock Scene* was akin to a pictorial *People Magazine*; it provided photographs of concert performances, backstage parties, and get-togethers at Max's back room. The publication also contained an advice column by New York transvestite and glitter rock singer, Wayne County, who answered readers' questions concerning style and sexuality:

> Dear Wayne,
> I need your advice. I dig make-up, the kind people think are supposed to be for girls. Except that if I wear any, my parents, my girl, my friends will call me a fag. Should I go ahead and ignore what people say and wear makeup? I'm forming my own rock group during my senior year in high school. Should I start wearing it then?
> Sincerely,
> Art
> El Paso, Tx.
>
> Dear Art:
> Words can't do you any harm, just pray they don't start shooting at you!! Since you're going to be forming a rock band, people will be more receptive to your wearing makeup. But if you enjoy wearing makeup on the street, then I suggest you find other boys who like wearing makeup and start your own gang. (County 59)

In addition to the photographs and the advice column, *Rock Scene's* editor, guitarist Lenny Kaye (later a member of the avant-punk Patti Smith Group), covered topics relevant to the New York scene and to rock and roll in general. And although publications such as *Crawdaddy*, *Fusion*, and *Rolling Stone* gave occasional coverage to glitter rock performers, none provided fans with as much intensity and fervor as did *Rock Scene* and *Creem*.

With their own fan journals, their own coherent styles, and their own massively popular and cult-oriented musicians, glitter fans developed a sense of subcultural unity during the spring of 1973. Clearly, the networks that bonded them included the mass-mediated formats through which they enjoyed glitter rock (magazines, albums, concert arenas), the styles that made them recognizable to one another, and the particular urban locales where they began to gather (such as the Raincheck II, Rodney's, or Max's). And even though glitter was a genre geared toward commercialization, it provided fans with options typically ascribed to more traditional subcultures. At this point, then, we can begin to see clearly the links suggested in earlier chapters—glitter rock usurped bohemian ideals and made them palatable to a mass market. But it is likely that great portions of this market would have otherwise remained incognizant of the immediate subcultural premises promised by glitter had its stylistic assumptions not been exposed through (especially) the rock press, fashion boutiques, song lyrics, and performances. In this sense, glitter inverted the traditional subculture's role by starting with commercial assumptions that were laced with subversive premises that had been plucked from localized cultures (New York/Detroit). In the subsequent chapters, these claims will be examined in further detail in a considereration of glitter's additional relevance to various subgroups of artists and fans. In addition, the demise of glitter as a genre and the ways in which glitter rock ultimately influenced both alternative rock and mainstream rock during the late 1970s will be noted.

Notes

1. For examples, see the September 1972 and October 1972 issues of *Creem.*
2. Note especially, 1972-73 issues of *Creem* and *Melody Maker.* For summaries of articles and reviews see Fletcher; Miles; and Carr and Murray.
3. For example, see Simon Frith's "Letter from Britain" column in the September 1972 issue of *Creem* 33.
4. Even though I make this claim, I am aware of the fact that by this point the "old Factory" had been closed. Nonetheless, Warhol's "new Factory" and the scene at Max's provided another extension of the original Factory.
5. See Jack Hiemenz; see also Tricia Henry's chapter "Glitter Rock and the New York Dolls" in *Break All the Rules! Punk Rock and the Making of a Style* 40. Whereas neither author uses the colloquial label of Stones Clones, they do acknowledge and briefly describe the origins of the comparison.
6. For a similar description of these attitudes, see Robert Christgau's "New York Dolls" in *Stranded* 133.
7. Both Robert Christgau and Jon Savage have forwarded similar claims and descriptions. See Christgau's "New York Dolls: Luv 'Em or Leave 'Em" and Jon Savage's *England's Dreaming* 60.
8. See Robert Christgau's "New York Dolls" in *Stranded.*
9. *Punk* was not yet a term that was used to define particular genres of rock and roll.

Bowie "Retires"

THE FRAGMENTATION OF GLITTER

During the summer of 1973, glitter rock hit its peak in both the United States and the United Kingdom. Bowie had attained international superstar status. Glitter-oriented bands such as the Stooges and Roxy Music were touring. Rock magazines such as *Creem* and *Rock Scene* continued to focus on trends within the genre. Most urban areas witnessed the rise of local glitter bands. In cities such as New York, Los Angeles, Detroit, Chicago, and Memphis, dance clubs promoted "glitter nights." But just as glitter rock was gaining momentum as an "out-there" style, a particular incident in London interrupted its midsummer progression. On July 4, 1973, at the London Hammersmith, Odeon David Bowie announced that he was retiring:

> "Of all shows on the tour this one will remain with us the longest not only because it is the last show of the tour, but it's the last show we'll ever do." "No," screamed the audience as all hell broke loose in Odeon. There were even tears as the enormity of the statement broke the hearts of the three thousand in the auditorium . . . and the band broke into a slow emotional "Rock and Roll Suicide" and the audience clapped along to the beat. . . . "Oh no love you're not alone . . . sing along . . . you're wonderful . . . you're not alone . . . thank you, we love you . . . " and it was all over but the shouting and the tears. (Hoggart 42)

The mass confusion that followed Bowie's claim is perhaps understood only in retrospect. The truth of the matter was that Bowie was speaking through the character of Ziggy; thus he was actually implying that his persona was retiring from the stage. The announcement therefore represented one more attempt by Bowie to effectively manipulate the media in a Warholian manner. This tactic had extraordinary effects because journalists and fans had no clue as to the real implications of the retirement claim. As a result, many predicted the end of glitter rock. If Bowie was the leader, who would take his place and perpetuate the trend? Certainly, his protégés had the ability to present comparable performances, yet none had access to the kind of financial resources available to Bowie through Mainman.[1] In addition, even though the majority of glitter performers were overtly commercial in their approach to rock, none had been able to establish the kind of following that would ensure capacity crowds at stadiums. In one sense, then, Bowie's retirement from Ziggy posed the question, How could glitter rock proceed without him? In another sense, however, the retirement story bolstered the confidence of some rock critics and fans, as they speculated that Pop, Reed, or Ferry might succeed Bowie as the king of glitter rock. But as we will see, several dominant glitter performers had no interest in the kind of media-made image that Bowie had been so adept at constructing. In other cases, certain performers began to pursue artistic endeavors that suggested *their* retirement from glitter rock.

Consider, for example, Lou Reed, who released *Berlin* in October 1973. Although redeemed as a classic 20 years later, at the time the album seemed a bewildering follow-up to *Transformer. Berlin* presented listeners with a morbid, slow-moving story line that focused on two amphetamine addicts and the self-destructive tendencies that prompted the breakup of their relationship. The music on the album was designed to parallel this general theme; it was moody, and the songs often shifted abruptly from one tempo to another. The album was panned by critics and glitter fans, which is understandable when we consider that Reed was intending to create "an album for adults" (Clapton 56).

The record may have been more highly regarded had Reed not already veered into glitter rock territory with the AM chart breaker "Walk on the Wild Side." But unlike many artists, Reed self-consciously attempted to avoid the commercial niche that could have been exploited as a result of the hit single. Also, Reed did not want to stifle his own artistic development by remaining too closely aligned with David Bowie.[2] He could have easily made the aesthetic decision to continue his reign as "Bowie's protégé," but instead, he chose to reinvestigate many of the musical and lyrical ideas that had fueled the Velvet Underground. Of course, most glitter fans were too young to have followed this band; consequently, *Berlin* seemed an awkward addition to the more pop-oriented *Transformer.*

During this time, other musicians also withdrew from the center of the glitter spectrum, sometimes intentionally, and at other times as a result of circumstantial events. For example, after their first U.S. tour, Mott the Hoople recorded an album that contained explicit heterosexual overtones, thereby accentuating their apprehension in regard to glitter rock. In another case, Roxy music was able to establish a popular following in Britain, but in the United States, they were often viewed as being too eclectic and avant-garde (especially when compared to Bowie/Ziggy). In the case of Iggy Pop and the Stooges, they were able to maintain a steady touring schedule, but by summer 1973, it was evident that the band would never gain more than a cult following. At the same time, Pop had always attempted to negate the kind of commercial image that had been constructed by Bowie. For example, Glenn O'Brien provides a description of a Welcome Back to Detroit performance that occurred in March 1973:

> The highlight of the show is when he enters the audience. It's the theatre of cruelty come alive. Iggy jumps off the stage. He grabs a girl in the first row and kisses her hard. He holds her and grinds into her while he sings. When he's finished he pushes her down to the floor. Then he goes chasing after a boy. The boy doesn't want any of what Iggy might be offering, but he gets grabbed anyway by the silver-haired black-lipsticked singer. But Iggy doesn't kiss him this time, he shakes. Some kids run, afraid they're next. Others watch in awe. (Nilsen and Sherman 57)

At the time of Bowie's "retirement" and during the fall of 1973, Pop continued to produce similar performances across the United States. In so doing, he helped to solidify the precept that glitter rock was a somewhat anomalous musical category. In other words, Pop's visual image was coherent with that of other Mainman performers, whereas the Stooges' stage demeanor and music remained high-strung and abrasive. Thus Pop became linked with glitter mainly as a result of his clothing and makeup. At times, he also hinted that he might be bisexual, which came as no surprise to fans or rock journalists.[3] In these ways, Pop could be viewed as a glitter rock performer, even though his stage shows and music were hardly synonymous to the kind of music and performances produced by Bowie. Consequently, Pop could never be accused of succumbing against his will to the overarching demands of high commercialism. As Mike West claims, "Inevitably *Raw Power* by Ig and the Stooges did not follow *Aladdin Sane* and *Transformer* into the charts. Iggy had got his way" (13).

In regard to Iggy Pop's 1973 New Year's Eve performance at the Academy of Music in New York, longtime friend and associate Anne Wehrer provides a description that reveals the main reason Pop continued to remain on the fringes of the glitter phenomenon during the months following Bowie's retirement:

> Andy Warhol called me, "I hear Iggy's going to commit suicide on stage. You have to stop him." The last act—designing his own death—could I interfere? I went as a *Penthouse* reporter with a bodyguard-photographer, Bob "White Eagle" Hendrickson. Iggy sang with demonic energy, in his hot pink pants and high top black boots. But his body control was off: backbends collapsed, and then he missed the ramp, falling into the audience. He pleaded to be touched. He asked to be destroyed, but with NO intention of destroying himself. Backstage he was flat out on the red concrete floor, rolling in spilled beer, dead cigarettes, and broken dreams. (Pop and Wehrer 120-21)

In reference to a performance at Rodney's some weeks later, record producer Tom Ayres states:

> Just before the show, it was rumored that he was planning to kill himself onstage at the end of the act. Sure enough, when the set was coming to a close, Iggy got out a butcher knife and went wild, man, all across his chest. The security guards had to jump onstage and literally carry him off. (Loud, "Los Angeles 1972-74" 79)

In no uncertain terms, then, what separated Pop from other glitter rockers was his performance aesthetic as well as the "punk" music that he was producing. Obviously, Alice Cooper and David Bowie drew on the shock rock theatrics that Pop had initiated, yet neither had actually taken the concept of annihilation to its limits. Furthermore, these artists constructed personas on stage, whereas Pop's theater was frighteningly realistic. In fact, as 1973 came to a close, Pop increasingly became so sporadic in his stage antics that club owners were afraid of the consequences should they book his act.

By February 1974, Pop had temporarily retired from the music business, having proven that a truly maniacal theater of cruelty could rarely be sustained by both audiences and performers without some casualties on both ends. In a world that was for a moment dominated by Ziggy and his compatriots, Pop damned his career, his audience, and his own body. He proposed that even though his image was grounded in glitter rock, his music and theatricality could not be easily sold to a mass public. Unlike most glitter performers, Pop was content to remain a cult artist, and in this sense, he never veered from the fringes of glitter rock style.

If Pop and the others treated earlier were not willing or able to take Bowie's place as the king of glitter rock, then I would offer an analysis of one U.S. band that inadvertently incorporated a number of glitter themes while maintaining an uneasy balance between a commercial image and one that was associated with the New York underground. As we will see, the New York Dolls provide us with an interesting case in regard to the questions fans were asking at the time. For if musical discordance, stylistic outrageousness, and the overturning of dominant sexual proscriptions were elements that cohered through glitter, then it seemed as if the New York Dolls might be the band to follow Bowie's lead. However, I propose that the band (and its fans) self-consciously attempted to remain on the margins of glitter style while still striving to attain some of the benefits promised by commercialism. First, this position was somewhat schismatic given the already radical precepts demonstrated by glitter during the early 1970s. To remain on the margins of a style that was by its very nature both commercial and marginalized, the Dolls and their fans had to "cut-up" glitter's significatory fractions even further by juxtaposing and playing with many of the tensions already apparent in the genre/style. Second, the key features of this process demonstrate that even though the band reacted against the critical label of glitter rock, it also amplified many of glitter's stylistic modes and themes. Third, this unique position was underscored by a number of interconnected paradoxes, ones that were neatly summarized in the Dolls' first promotional logo: "A band you're gonna like; whether you like it or not."

In giving further consideration to these claims, I believe that to understand the way in which the Dolls constructed a marginal position, we must keep in mind the kind of orchestrated, proficient, and conceptual rock and roll that was being produced by Bowie.[4] In fact, as the Dolls began to gain critical recognition, rock journalists were focusing most of their attention on Bowie.[5] And quite well aware that Bowie represented the center of glitter's commercial spectrum, the Dolls engaged in an opposite approach and played the only way they knew how—as nonprofessionals.

Accordingly, whereas Bowie presented a self-conscious form of space-age androgyny complete with extraordinary fashion ensembles, the Dolls opted to step onto the stage in their habitual manner, thereby introducing a highly contextualized statement that resulted in the label "sleezoid flash" (Hollingsworth, "You Wanna Play House?" 17). At the same time that the Dolls attempted to both undermine *and* accentuate such differences on all levels, they also managed to acquire a number of critically coveted titles, ones that could have ostensibly launched the band into the musical landscape that it both parodied and resisted. But even though "the best rock and roll band in the world" ("You Wanna Play House?" 17) sought some of the provisions that were typically associated with critical recognition, it ultimately maintained an uncompromising stance. I will analyze the nature of this stance through investigating the musical tensions that the New York Dolls generated during their first tour and subsequent performances (1972-74).

The Case of the New York Dolls: Camp as "Camp"

Having given attention to both the musical and visual features of the New York Dolls, I will consider the somewhat odd manner in which the band decided to construct a commercial image via glitter rock. Even though the Dolls often charged that glitter rock constituted commercial hype, the band presented audiences with a number of double entendres that suggested that they were to be understood as a camp caricature of glitter style. As will be demonstrated, however, even caricatures can be interpreted quite seriously by fans. Thus, in 1974, when the Dolls attempted to break from their camp-laden mold and enter into a more mainstream rock format, former techniques did indeed enforce particular demonstrative restrictions. Hence, in reconsidering the Dolls' initial axioms (as presented in Chapter 9), I will explain how these finally hampered the band's accessibility, irrefutably positioning it as so alternative that it stood little chance of actually becoming the "answer" to David Bowie. In discussing these claims, it becomes possible to discern how the band was (re)interpreted by original fans who, in this particular case, had the definitive last word.

In the early stages of glitter rock, the New York Dolls emerged from the Mercer scene with manager Marty Thau in search of a record deal. Thau, believing that the Dolls' music could at least find a marketable cult following in the United States, met with 20 executives from major labels during the late fall of 1972 and the winter and spring of 1973. His asking price for the Dolls was $250,000, a figure that astounded most executives who turned up at Mercer shows only to find the band's music and clothing style reprehensible. In fact, CBS Records president and reigning "liberal" Clive Davis maintained " 'that if you wanted to work in the music business you didn't go around admitting that you saw the New York Dolls. That was like admitting that you had friends who were homosexual' " (as told to Bob Gruen, Savage 61). Likewise, the band's unswerving contempt for the executives in attendance at their gigs didn't assist in the progress toward a contract. As David Johansen stated, "Ahmet Ertegun and Mick Taylor decided we were the worst high school band they'd ever heard. Mick Taylor told us, 'you guys got just six months to go polish up.' I told him to go screw" (Edmunds 41).

Although the Dolls held strong in their contempt for "old relics with polished heads," one younger representative, Mercury A&R head Paul Nelson, did find some favor with the band (Edmunds 41). Repeatedly returning to Dolls' performances a total of *80 times,* he engaged in a one-man crusade to get the band signed to the label. By late spring 1973, his persistence won through, and the band was contracted to Mercury, the head executives still reticent but willing to tolerate a risk. After all, Mercury was trailing in the market, and after losing David Bowie to RCA, the label's executives felt that even though they despised the Dolls, the band might at least help to update the company's image. With the project in the works by summer 1973, both the band and its manager agreed on Todd Rundgren as producer. Rundgren explained:

> The main reason that I did the Dolls album was because it was a *New York City Record.* There was no reason to get David Bowie or some other weirdo to produce it; the only person who can logically produce a New York City record is someone who lives in New York. I live here, and I recognize all the things about New York that the Dolls recognize in their music. It doesn't necessarily mean that I testify to that stuff; it doesn't even mean that the Dolls' music testifies to that stuff. The only thing it testifies to is that they're punks! But it doesn't say "take drugs" or "hump" or "go to outer space." It's more like scenario music. (qtd. in Edmunds 42)

By August 1973, the *New York Dolls* was completed, and by the end of the month, it had been placed in record stores across the United States. By appearance, and thus by comparison, the cover presented the most direct exertion of gender bending since Bowie's *The Man Who Sold the World.* And like many of Andy Warhol's films, the jacket design sparked a tremendous amount of controversy, whether one ever heard the music inside the sleeve or not.

On the album's cover a stark black and white photograph was highlighted at the top by the band's name, which was presented as having been inscribed with a tube of hot pink lipstick. Below the bullet-shaped tube sat the Dolls, who were crammed on a sofa in all their sleezoid grandeur. Center frame was Johansen, who sported a highly teased hairstyle, white face makeup, lipstick, eye shadow, bracelets, an unbuttoned striped shirt, skintight satin pants, and clog-style glitter platforms. Most noticeably, in his left hand an open powder compact allowed for a rather blatant display of narcissistic infatuation. To Johansen's left sat Sylvain Sylvain, who had applied glaring circular rouge marks to his cheeks. Looking sullen and removed from the ensemble, Sylvain reclined on the sofa, presenting the viewer with his mismatched wardrobe, which consisted of a cowboy shirt, a polka-dot scarf, tight black jeans, and roller skates. His right arm was nonchalantly resting on the bare shoulder of Arthur Kane, whose "high vamp" makeup was accented by a single strand of gaudy pearls. Of all the Dolls, Kane appeared to be the most obliterated, as he stared toward the floor, ignoring his smoking cigarette and his half-filled champagne glass. To Johansen's right was Johnny Thunders, complete with a bouffant hairstyle, heavily applied makeup, tight black pants, and white platforms with leather anklets. In slight contrast to Johansen's self-obsessed gaze, Thunders' hard glance toward the camera implied the sexual provocation of a drunken harlot, his legs spread wide to further the invitation. On the edge of the sofa sat Jerry Nolan, who stared neatly ahead at the camera, a long spit curl falling down his forehead. Nolan presented the only dissimilar image, in that he was positioned in a prim manner, pulling his embroidered jacket together at the lapels, with his heeled ankles tucked to one side.

Overall, this coherent/incoherent image was much more flamboyant than any of those presented on the covers of *Love It to Death* (Cooper), *Raw Power* (Pop), *Transformer* (Reed), or *Ziggy Stardust*.[6] The Dolls were not only flagrantly toying with transvestitism; they were portraying for a national public an image that presumably could not be comprehended outside its inner ranks at the Mercer and Max's. Subterranean sleezoid flash was thus on the verge of announcing itself to a larger audience. And to *that* audience it seemed that in the context of summer 1973, the only immediately comparable frame of reference might have been media-induced images of hardened street prostitutes.[7] Curious about the Dolls' intentions, Danny Sugerman asked of Johansen, "But what about the midwest where the kid comes in looking for the new Allman Brothers album and he sees five guys in drag on this cover with their name drawn in lipstick?" (20). David Johansen responded:

> That album cover, we wanted to do a high camp kinda thing on pop, you know what I mean? A camp on pop, that's one of our favorite hobbies. Take pop to its logical extension. That's pretty much what pop is about anyway. If you're gonna be a pop artist and really understand what pop is, then you *have* to camp on it, I mean that's cause that's part of what pop is. So what we do is camp on all the elements of rock and roll and things like that. We designed the cover as kind of a joke. I think when the kid comes in and sees that picture, he's gonna forget about the Allman Bros. and he's gonna have to buy it. You know he's gonna have to wonder what the hells inside that! . . . Decadence means a lot of different things to me on a lot of different levels. . . . I think the Dolls are part of a decadent time in a sense, especially in New York. New York is really an anarchy, you know? I mean there's not any rule . . . New York is kinda like there's no standard of rules, no morals. A cop isn't really a cop in New York. It's when they call us the "decadent band of New York." I guess they mean we represent the kids who grew up in this age. (qtd. in Sugerman 21)

Once the album was opened and actually heard, the "kid" of David Johansen's description was presented with a record that was certainly indicative of early punk.[0] Indeed, the album was a major source of inspiration for John Lydon (aka Johnny Rotten), the future members of the Ramones, and a broad spectrum of young musicians who considered it to be of immediate significance in the early 1970s. In fact, by 1977 *Punk* editor John Holmstrom claimed that the New York Dolls "were the most influential group in punk rock. They proved to the world that anybody could do it." [9] And as Tony Parsons states,

> Until the *New York Dolls* a hangover from the sixties had permeated the music scene. That album was where a new decade began, where a contemporary version of the original essence of rock 'n' roll emerged to kick out the tired old men and clear the way for the New Order. (Liner Notes)

In summing up both the album's musical content and the Dolls' overall impact on glitter rock, Robert Duncan asserts:

> Where Alice Cooper and David Bowie at the start of glitter were third generation, the New York Dolls at glitter's high water mark were fourth—post-Bowie. Where Bowie, no less than Alice, played the rock star as much as the rock 'n' roll, the Dolls seemed prepared to dispense with the rock 'n' roll altogether. They seemed prepared even to dispense with the rock stardom, playing instead "rock stars" from yet another distance, "*glitter* rock stars." But not unlike the double negative movie-within-a-movie of *Gimme Shelter,* finally it worked. The quotes-

> in-quotes, all that self-consciousness laid on self-consciousness, somehow served to make the Dolls about as genuine a rock 'n' roll band as turned up in the last decade. (98)

It was, in fact, this sense of genuineness that caused rock critics to herald the band as *the* avant-rock (glitter-styled) group of the moment. Certainly, Iggy Pop, Bowie, and Lou Reed were the instigators of the glitter genre. But the Dolls added a sense of mayhem to glitter and inadvertently transformed it in ways the former couldn't. The Dolls, for one, were not even 20 years old when their first album was released.[10] Second, their youthful, angst-ridden approach to rock and roll made them appear to be both unrefined and honest. In addition, the band's streetwise, working-class stage demeanor drastically contrasted with the more elevated class pretenses subscribed to by performers such as Bowie and Brian Ferry. And amid the implementation of catchy hooks and standard pop items, such as whistles, sighs, and glaring riffs, the Dolls still forwarded the notion that they were producing difficult music.

In sensing the album's glaring chaotic textures, dedicated critics wondered if the band's music would be decipherable to listeners who were not involved in New York's Max's Kansas City scene. In pondering the very notion of contextuality, however, most critics agreed that the Dolls unrefined image could actually be used as a springboard for creating effective publicity. In other words, this New York band was distinguished as qualifying the essence of rock and roll energy and teenage rebellion, which could be interpreted similarly no matter the particular local context. Thus, in defending the band's contextual limitations, critics also forced the argument that in this case authenticity could and should coincide with commercial appeal. For example, rock critic Ben Edmunds claims:

> The question exists as to whether something so totally tied to New York can possibly mean anything to somebody in Kansas; the kind of culture gap that cost the Kinks much of their American audience with "Waterloo Sunset." The answer is *yes*. In the first place the Dolls' music talks to rock and roll kids about things common to all of them; New York just makes those things more obvious and immediate. And the Dolls, in turn, help New York transcend its ugliness and become again the city of myth and mystery it once was. Many observers contend that the Dolls define New York in the same way as the Velvet Underground, but the way the Dolls define New York is actually much closer to *West Side Story*. The difference is that between success and failure. (42)

The following month *Creem* writer Robert Christgau began his review of the Dolls' album by first discussing the inconsistencies posed by contextuality even in the city that had spawned the band. Christgau briefly explained that if you claimed to be a Dolls' fan in New York, heterosexuals assumed you were gay. Likewise, in a tongue-in-cheek manner, Christgau claimed that gay people assumed Dolls' fans to be straight.[11] After all, the Dolls were not representative of the music played in gay nightclubs. Finally, Christgau contended that *any* claim of allegiance to the band would result in the "hip people" baiting you for being too trendy; thus for the Dolls such "abuse" had become "more or less the natural thing" ("New York Dolls: Luv 'Em" 62). After spending four paragraphs pondering the "dynamite riffs" and the "careening screech of their music," Christgau concluded:

> Most adults really hate it, which of course is heartening. But the Dolls are so fine that even the adults will catch on if the Dolls can break out of New York, and the Dolls can. All good music—all good art, if you'll pardon my French—is rooted in particulars and moves out from there. This is the most exciting hard rock band in the country and maybe the world right now, and it has room to get two or three times as good as it is. I know you don't believe me yet, but listen to "Trash" and "Personality Crisis" and "Looking for a Kiss" two times and tell me I'm wrong. I fucking dare you, kid. (63)

In essence, each of these critics (Christgau, Duncan, and Edmund) *and* Johansen was concerned with a similar type of question: Would the band's camp approach somehow conceal its attempt to produce earnest, primal rock and roll? In addition, all of these commentators were cognizant as to the confusion that might arise in regard to the band's doubly ironic stance of "camping on pop" (which, in the Dolls' case, actually suggested "camping on 'glitter.'"). Johansen seemed to straightforwardly defend the double ironies of camp when explaining the band's album cover, and the critics were implicitly aware of these qualities in their attempts to determine the record's "translatability."

To further clarify these kinds of concerns, we might briefly note the differences between the New York Dolls and the Velvet Underground (as mentioned by Edmunds 42). In so doing, I believe that the Velvets were *explicitly* serious in their endeavors, never mocking the world that they were describing but, instead, exposing its dichotomies through a series of juxtaposed vocal, lyrical, and stage-produced arrangements. The Velvets were certainly, as Ellen Willis has pointed out, "punk aesthetes," and thus when willing to transcend their world and reach the possibilities of another, they engaged in more directly philosophical pursuits. Indeed, the classic "Jesus"/"Heroin" dichotomy provides the clearest case (Willis). Conversely, the Dolls were to be taken seriously, but they were working on the pop terrain of avant-rock, not the darker and more brooding avant-garde format subscribed to by the Velvets. In reaching this more pop-oriented plateau, the Dolls employed what gay historian Michael Bronski cites as "camouflage" by not expressing the world as it is but, instead, "imagining it as it could be" (43). This, the very nature of camp, seems highly analogous to the inordinate penchant that the Dolls had for maintaining a sense of humor throughout their music and stage act. As Bronski has claimed:

> Camp is the re-imagining of the material world into ways and forms which transform and comment upon the original. It changes the "natural" and "normal" into style and artifice. . . . Ultimately camp changes the real, hostile world into a new one which is controllable and safe. (42)

In attacking Sontag's suggestion that camp is apolitical, Bronski retorts, "Because it contains the possibility of structuring and encouraging limitless imagination—to literally create a new reality—it is not only political but progressive" (43). But what are we to make of a camp aesthetic that was designed to be self-referential to *its own* transformation of the natural? In attempting to answer to such a question Robert Duncan provides insight by suggesting that in the case of the New York Dolls,

> it was that they were not capable of taking [any of] it seriously—not rock 'n' roll, not rock stardom, and especially not the back room [of Max's]. Nihilism on nihilism, and before it inevitably imploded, it served to keep them honest—and us too. By which I mean it kept us all laughing. (103)

In comparing the Dolls' ironic stance to the more serious one implied by the Velvets, Duncan explains:

> Johansen and the boys climb a fence to paint a mocking smirk on Lou Reed's "Heroin" in their own "Looking for a Kiss" ("not a fix," they add), mocking the "beautiful" trendy junkies who are regrettably, "so obsessed with gloom." Always laughing—in particular at the scene around them—always with an edge. Indeed sometimes it wasn't really laughing at all—and so just the kind of laughing, I, for one, could dig. (103-04)

Based on Duncan's assessment, we can begin to ascertain the impact of presenting glitter as "glitter," for whereas the Dolls may not have claimed to have subscribed to the concept at all, it is quite certain that they implemented it in principle. And it was perhaps this tenet of camping on an already camp-laden genre that resulted in confusion among those who were not explicitly aware of the insider premises that guided the band. After all, double negative "films within films" are never quite perceived as such unless the audience is explicitly made aware of the director's intentions. The trouble began for the Dolls when they assumed that the "kid buying the Allman Bros." (i.e., the mass audience) would be able to listen to their music and watch their performances, and in so doing, delineate between quotes, and, "quotes layered on top of quotes." The band in fact assumed too much about their foreseeable "kids in Kansas," which ultimately led them to exclaim of both their fans and their excessive lifestyle, *Too Much Too Soon.*[12] But in the process of comprehending the impact of double citations, the Dolls encountered what seemed to be a set of endless possibilities—well-intentioned or well-perceived, it mattered not. By the fall of 1973, they had begun a 13-gig tour, with stops across the East Coast, the Midwest, the South, and the West Coast. Banking on the possibilities of Mercury's promotional banner ("A band you're gonna like, whether you like it or not") the Dolls found that their image *had* struck a chord among an unexpectedly large group of fans.[13] Such fans composed a cult audience, and the Dolls were booked mostly in small concert venues, but nonetheless, the capacity crowds suggested that, yes, even the kids in Kansas were perhaps capable of comprehending the band's camp approach to rock and roll.

Of all the stops on the tour, Los Angeles and Memphis were the most significant, due to the fanatical responses of fans in these cities. In Los Angeles, the Dolls had been booked to play two nights at the infamous Whiskey a Go-Go, where, on the afternoon of their first performance, fans had already begun to line up in anticipation. Lisa Robinson, native to the New York Max's/Mercer scene, was sent by *Creem* to investigate both the fans and the L.A. rock circuit. In so doing she made the assessment that "kids in L.A. *live* for rock concerts," because unlike the scene makers in New York who are "up all night anyway," the L.A. kids are starved for *any* addition to their "mundane lives" ("New York Dolls" 44). Robinson's snobbery was also supported by local resident David Robinson of the Modern Lovers: " 'This is the dullest town. This is absolutely the biggest thing to hit this town. . . . little kids have been waiting all their lives to see the New York Dolls' " (Robinson, "New York

Dolls" 44). After setting out on her journey, one of Robinson's first encounters with fans occurred outside the Whiskey:

> Kids who can't be more than twelve years old, boys with lipstick smeared on their faces, girls with all those kitschy, clutzy shoes, hot pants and feathers. Like some kind of fungus, it's slowly creeping across the country, but it's at its best in L.A. I'm talking about *sleeeeeze.* (44)

On the evening of the Dolls' debut she observed:

> It's showtime and the Whiskey is packed with kids, glitzy glitter fans, and of course the Bon Bons[14]. . . . The music biz folk are really the most interesting though. The same kind of people who came down to the Mercer Arts to dislike in advance what they saw are in evidence. ("I guess they expected us to come out in our mother's clothing!" David laughed later when talking about how some people didn't think they were "outrageous" enough). (44-45)

In describing the second evening's performance, Robinson presented the following summation:

> David's having this *problem* with onstage raps. His humor doesn't get through to them. I mean, he's introducing a song like "Give Me a Great Big Kiss" and announcing that he's from the neighborhood where Kitty *Genovese* grew up and no one is laughing. Kitty Genovese: the one who was stabbed thirty-seven times or something in Queens and all the neighbors heard the screams and did nothing. In New York do you *know* what kind of reaction that would get?
>
> "At the celebrity table over in the corner there," David screams, "LINDA KASABIAN!" A few muttered snickers. "Your enthusiasm is overwhelming," he sneers. "I don't know how you L.A. queens get it up." (45)

But whereas the L.A. "queens" may *not* have understood Johansen's shticks, they at least had the inordinate ability to understand the Dolls' musical and visual allusions. Indeed, after the second performance Johansen excitedly described the fans' sense of style and humor as "low camp," and gazed in bewilderment at the crowd:

> It was amazing. I didn't think they let children like that out at night. If you could have seen it from where I was standing, little kids grabbing at me; literally they couldn't have been more than twelve years old. Little boys with lipstick—thirteen year olds, and they would touch my legs and hands. I *loved* it. Those kids just want to be part of the pandemonium. (Robinson, "New York Dolls" 76)

Robinson concluded her journey to L.A. with a stroll down Hollywood Boulevard. Wearing high heels and tight jeans, Johansen and Thunders accompanied her. At one point the two performers stopped to pose beside a show window at Frederick's of Hollywood. Robinson then arrived at an appraisal concerning the two-day experience: "New York Trash had met L.A. Sleaze and the confrontation was formidable" (78). Elektra promoter Danny Fields, also along for the trip, summed up the Dolls' impact in a more direct manner. When questioned as to the reason that the Dolls had inspired a cult following in Los Angeles, Fields provided a concise and satiric answer: " 'Don't talk to me about [the Dolls'] music. . . . It's too absurd. Anyone connected with this industry who talks about *music,* well that's just astonishing. Play music indeed—thank god they don't have to' " (Robinson, "New York Dolls" 78).

On September 21, 1973, roughly one month and five stops later, the Dolls set their sights on Memphis, Tennessee, a city with officials who did not prefer to let the band perform without facing some local harassment. On the day of the concert, the Memphis Board of Review announced that opening performer Iggy Pop would be arrested for any number of offenses if he dared to engage in his routine antics. As for the Dolls, the board assumed that they were a troupe of female impersonators, and because this kind of presentation was outlawed in the city, the band was informed in no uncertain terms that it could not portray women on stage.

By 8:00 p.m. that evening, the Memphis police force had been doubled for the concert, with the uniformed officers surrounding the stage and the boundaries of the auditorium. The Dolls played all of the numbers from their impudent repertoire, while facing what David Johansen described as "Red Square on May Day" ("Random Notes" 26). Leading the brigade was a collection of teenage males who were visibly noticeable due to their military haircuts and sequin-covered faces. After the Dolls had completed a grueling 90-minute set, these young men guided the crowd through chants that emphatically demanded that the band provide an encore. In giving concession to the outbursts, the Dolls returned to the stage, therefore exciting one young man to the point that he ignored the police and pushed straight over the orchestra pit. In so doing, he managed to embrace Johansen and kiss him on the mouth. Johansen responded positively by lurching out toward the crowd in an attempt to endorse more participation. By this point, however, the police force was in action. The "intruder" had been captured and was visibly being beaten; thus causing Johansen to stop "Jet-Boy" in midsentence and scream,

"Are we going to take this?" Collectively, the crowd resounded with negative remarks as Johansen led a series of obscene taunts. Amid the concerted mayhem, audience members pushed further toward the stage and cheered wildly as Johansen grabbed Thunders's guitar, broke the neck on center stage, and then threw the pieces directly into the crowd. But during these proceedings, the police had encircled the band, causing Johansen to react by lifting his fists in anger, while presenting a casual, pouting pose. The officers responded by jerking Johansen from the stage and hustling him out the side door. Still, not wishing to be upstaged while exiting the concert hall, Johansen managed to momentarily disengage a wrist and blow kisses to his fans. Taking Johansen's arrest none too lightly, the fans became so unruly that they were forcibly pushed (by the police) into the downtown streets, where many were then arrested on a number of "riot" charges.

On the way to the police station, handcuffs intact, Johansen asked, "Would you do this to Elvis?" The arresting officer responded, "I'd *love* to get Elvis" ("Random Notes" 26). After spending a night in jail for disorderly conduct, Johansen appeared on the courthouse steps and announced to a shocked and eager local press: "They *loved* me in the cellblock!!" [15]

It was a night that seemed to bring together all that the band had come to epitomize during the past year. For the New York Dolls, camp as "camp" certainly *did* have serious ramifications. And these were ones that Dolls fans in Memphis understood all too well. Within a week, the band had become local heroes, and the stories of arrests and court proceedings provided fans with evidence that they (like their New York compatriots) were also an insider's club. And quite obviously, this was a club that was willing to risk a great deal to find refuge in the Dolls' campy style.

1974: The Dolls Attempt to Redefine Their Stance

As 1973 drew to a close, the New York Dolls had begun a tour of Europe, starting in London, where they played Biba's Rainbow Room. While in Britain, the Dolls were perused by fashion designer and situationist Malcom McLaren, who had met the band earlier that year in New York and found their music "so awful that it crashed through into the other side, into magnificence" (Savage 62). Accompanying the Dolls on every stop and noting their outrageous clothing and cynical attitudes, McLaren was careful to absorb all he could, especially from David Johansen. But by this point, the band had taken a number of subtle turns, and it was simply not the same as it had been in its inception.

For one, the extremity of the Dolls' transvestite image had caused journalists to draw comparisons to a number of glitter acts in Britain. Thus sensing what were to them obvious differences, the Dolls toned down the more overt gender-bending exhibitions.[16] In doing so, the group began to toy with other visual images of shock. Most notably, Thunders began to wear a swastika arm band while on stage. The British press, however, did not consider the Dolls to be extremely interesting or humorous on any account; thus the focus centered on the band's "malicious reasoning" and "awe-inspiring" public behavior.[17] But even though the Dolls were provoking reporters in London, they were continuing to achieve an inordinate amount of critical acclaim in the States, especially at *Rock Scene* and *Creem,* where Dave Marsh, Lester Bangs, and Lisa Robinson were delivering reverent accolades on the band. Such attention thereby encouraged the Dolls to realize a steadfast desire: they desperately wanted to move from the level of cult appeal into a broader arena, one where they would still be accepted on their own terms yet one that would also provide them with the benefits of well-deserved fame. Because the critics were so unwavering in their claims, perhaps the Dolls could in turn *become* the very band that was being described.

After their return to the United States in the spring of 1974, however, the Dolls did not become "America's answer to David Bowie," nor did they achieve the kind of compensation that might seemingly coincide with impassioned critical labels and an excessive amount of enthusiastic press releases. Although continuing to tour, they found that, at most, only small factions of fans around the country seemed to grasp their hard-edged sense of camp style and their musical nihilism. Hiring Shadow Morton as the producer of their second album didn't improve matters, even though critics such as Dave Marsh claimed that the band's effort represented "the best hard rock in America" ("Too Much" 79). Nonetheless, the band's attempt to really break out of New York on a massive scale failed, and too many among the broader audience simply viewed the Dolls as yet another version of the "it's so bad it's good" approach to rock and roll. But as Robert Christgau recounts:

> Camp or no camp, theirs was not a cause of a "seriousness that fails," of this-is-so-bad-it's good. On the contrary, the Dolls were the ultimate instance of the miracle of pop, using their honest passion, sharp wits, and attention to form to transmute the ordinary into the extraordinary. ("New York Dolls" in *Stranded* 146)

Given this assertion, I believe that the Dolls' inability to actually achieve the extraordinary in the manner established by David Bowie was, in part, due to the kinds of premises (trisexualism, "anyone can do it") they had so forcefully advanced during the Mercer days and, subsequently, during their first U.S. tour. For even though the Dolls sought the widespread appeal that often follows enormous amounts of conclusive acclamation and the formation of cult followings, they could never cross the hurdle of being perceived as a play on camp—the very theme that had been self-consciously constructed during the band's early days, the very theme that in some senses seemed dated by 1974. After all, it was difficult to tease the image of glitter rock stars when the actual stars had by this point abandoned the genre and in so doing moved on to other formats. Thus, if glitter could no longer be played out as glitter, then the task for the Dolls was to break somewhat from this self-referential mold and attempt to find favor with a larger audience (*Too Much Too Soon*). Yet, as the Dolls disposed their feminine clothes and repeatedly reinforced the fact that they weren't glitter (though they may have been hard rock), such tactics seemed to align them with the creation of a new image. At the same time, this new image was ill defined; more was said about what it did *not* represent as opposed to what it was actually capable of revealing.

Here, we might consider that these loosely defined stratagems would probably be more readily acceptable in contemporary times,[18] but in 1974, these only worked toward discrediting the band's original stance. For one, the much hoped for broader audience actually had very little frame of reference for "ordering" or locating the Dolls within the sphere of a preordained hard rock genre. Punk—the most applicable reference in the late 1970s—was not a coherent or even overtly apparent genre during these earlier years (even though rock critics such as Lester Bangs frequently employed the term in reference to the Dolls). Likewise, *Too Much Too Soon,* although admittedly more pop oriented, was a long distance from any genre where it might have found an easy fit. The album certainly wasn't similar to Bowie's *Ziggy Stardust*; it was too sophisticated for the listeners of Grand Funk; and it was not "heavy" enough for fans of Led Zeppelin or Black Sabbath. Thus the Dolls, having no conceptual framework except their original one, could do little except assume that a few subtle musical shifts and verbal disclaimers would aid in the acquisition of mass appeal. This assumption, however, did not pan out, and by the end of summer 1974, as Pete Frame stated, "the Dolls were back where they started in small New York clubs. . . . 'A wrecked monument to pill-popping, booze swilling, multisexual, wasted teenage America' " (27).

But what was *ultimate* reason for this kind of conclusion? In part, the New York Dolls ignored the negatively inspired premises that had guided the band's initial cult following.[19] In the process, the Dolls attempted to construct a new image, and more important, they attempted to construct a new audience. In this sense, the Dolls were like any other commercial act, but in another sense this was not a band that could hope to envision the possibilities of commercialism through process of the ready reckoner. Thus, as the Dolls proceeded to enter into the hard rock genre, they ignored the fact that their audience (as a base group) had never claimed to want more than dissonant pleasure. Indeed, the Dolls had always required that fandom arise through the development of "acquired" tastes, and in the end the dismissal of this premise resulted in the band's failure as an act with broad commercial appeal. Yet, although this procedure did not result in disavowal by the insider's club, it did position the band as one that seemed to be wavering between authenticity and blatant dishonesty.

Not Paying the Price: The Fans' Last Word

Confusion among original followers during this time resulted from the fact that the Dolls actually attempted to give credence to the critical labels ("greatest," "best") that seemed inherently oppositional to their lawless infrastructure. Such credence was observable in interviews with the press during the winter of 1974 in which the Dolls, in a very urbane and defensive manner, continued to play down the notion that they were a glitter band or that they were still attempting to "play a joke on glitter." [20] What seemed shortsighted about these ongoing, and thus wearisome, claims was that in the few short months in which the band *had* gained a following, it was admired for having an honest and veritable stance, even though it attempted at times to slightly shift the reigns of contextuality that regulated its initial appeal. In fact, it was the Dolls themselves who established the premise of camping on camp, and an attempt to disavow this premise in an extremely serious manner seemed contrary to the band's well-established chaotic and humorous patterns. To extend this premise would have perhaps been admirable. To disparage its existence altogether, however, seemed fake. For we must remember that the Dolls, unlike Bowie, had not adopted personas, nor had they attempted to become professional musicians. Thus, during 1974, as Bowie created new personas and experimented with sophisticated musical styles, the Dolls could not have endured such freedoms. By way of further comparison, consider that Simon Frith has claimed of David Bowie that he is the only star who cannot "sell out" because his emphasis has always been on the invention of self. Thus, as Frith suggests,

> To appreciate Bowie was not just to like his music or shows or his looks, but also to enjoy the way he set himself up as a commercial image. How he was packaged was as much an aspect of his art as what the package contained. ("Only Dancing" 132)

Unlike Bowie, the Dolls presented an image that was not constructed per se but one that, instead, forwarded the premise that they were to be held in high esteem simply because they were "outcasts." [21] At the time of the Dolls' first tour, they appealed to a small following that felt empowered by the band's inordinate ability to relate a sense of disempowerment: what it meant to be a part of "wasted teenage America." The population that actually embraced the Dolls' possibilities was small, disenfranchised, and very much of the belief that it understood the Dolls' ironic premises, as well as the more straightforward notions apparent in Johansen's claim regarding the band's *tri*sexualism.

Certainly, this particular notion of sexual freedom provided some fans with a method for trying on a lifestyle, but more potent, Dolls followers found the sexual claims (and images) of the band to be within the realm of pure approachability and thus complementary to their own sense of sexual libertarianism. In fact, David Johansen assessed the attitudes of his most dedicated fans in the following manner:

> Kids are finding out that there isn't that much difference between them sexually. They're finding out that the sexual terms, homosexual, bisexual, heterosexual, all those are just words in front of sexual. . . . You can go to England where they have homosexuals, heterosexuals, and bisexuals but it doesn't make any difference because *nobody* gets laid. That's just an analogy. I mean, people are just sexual, man. (qtd. in Sugerman 29)

Along similar lines, Christgau claims:

> What made them different was that their sweetness and toughness and alienation knew no inhibitions, so that where love was concerned they were ready for anything. By their camping they announced to the world that hippie mindblowing was a lot more conventional than it pretended to be, that human possibility was infinite. Of course between Arthur's instinctive awkwardness and Syl's clowning

> and David's pursuit of the funny move, they suggested that human possibility was hilarious. And the band's overall air of droogy desperation implied as well that human possibility was doomed. ("New York Dolls" in *Stranded* 133-34)

In part, the demise of the Dolls was inevitable, because they had originally addressed the broadest scope of human desire. In this sense, Bowie's claim of "I'm bisexual" was to the right of radical when compared to Johansen's assertion that "We're trisexual . . . we'll try anything." In addition, Bowie's presentation of the Ziggy alien could be located within the realm of fantasy, whereas the Dolls brilliantly confused fantasy through combining cross-dressing (as a camp on pop) with a very *real* image of the frustrated (and joyous) rock and roll teenager. But the disengaged possibilities set forth by such try-anything premises were in fact too open-ended to appeal to more than a cult audience. Such premises were, oddly enough, *generic,* and perhaps, given the context of 1972-73, a little too all-assuming. In fact the Dolls' "one size *should* fit all" principle was so impartial that it simply did not translate beyond particular insider locales and contexts.

The pockets of fans that appreciated the Dolls did not comprehensively dismiss the band due to its attempt to reach outside the sect; nor were the Dolls rejected due to their shift toward a more toned-down gender-bending style, because even at their most commercial level the Dolls were a far cry from Bachman Turner Overdrive or Grand Funk. Instead, it was the Dolls themselves who—through a crude and egalitarian form of musical and visual mayhem—actually hoped to envision a broader spectrum, one where they would still be accepted on their own terms. But what they seemed to forget in the interim was the message that their original fans had related all along: Dolls' fandom didn't require the hard sell; it had to be earned. The fans were content to pay their own dues, and this often carried with it an implicit understanding that the Dolls were not meant to be comprehended beyond the progressive, ironic, and disruptive structures of meaning that they had so cleverly forwarded. But as the Dolls attempted to reverse the premise of fans developing *with* them, original followers simply could not conceive or attempt to claim the same set of possibilities—because the open approbation of the Dolls' generic yet indigenous premises when matched with their grievously comforting form of rock and roll was indeed the point of it all, the reason for grasping the exhilaration that was so often misunderstood. All things considered, the Dolls' music did translate outside of New York, but in doing so, it reached another insider's club, one that was unwilling to admit those who wanted the pleasure without paying the price.

Having given treatment to the New York Dolls as a band that remained on the fringes of glitter style, I now turn to a description of Bowie's "comeback" performance in 1974. Here, we will note that Bowie's new act did present a number of glitter-oriented themes, whereas his visual style made clear the notion that he had moved in a new artistic direction. At the same time, *Diamond Dogs* signaled the perfect closure on the glitter phenomenon.

Bowie: The Comeback Tour

During the spring of 1974, Bowie returned to the stage as a new character, Halloween Jack, a man caught up in the bedlam of Earth's dying days, a man faced with the annihilation of the human race. In *Diamond Dogs,* Jack is an astute observer of "alienated humanoids," people who have been forced into submission by dogs that have reached human consciousness. As the dogs wreak havoc, the humanoids band together in packs, awaiting rescue by "Big Brother." In some ways, then, *Diamond Dogs* represented a twist on the Ziggy theme, while demonstrating Bowie's infatuation with George Orwell's *1984.*

In May 1974, the *Diamond Dogs* album was released, and by summer it had reached the prestigious status of "gold" (i.e., 1 million copies were sold). That summer as well, Bowie brought the stage show to the United States, playing a total of 62 dates from June 11 through December 2. It was Bowie's most triumphant tour to date, and rock fans responded enthusiastically, while the rock press provided further acclamation concerning his musical talents.

The set for *Diamond Dogs* was designed to emulate the scenery in Fritz Lang's classic science fiction film *Metropolis.* Thus the stage gave the appearance of a huge, decaying cityscape. The many stage props included a tall, phallic-shaped tower that dripped "blood," a long catwalk that rose and fell above the stage, and light towers that sent out radiant beams. The scenery was cleverly constructed to suggest that *Diamond Dogs* was—for the most part—Bowie's performance, as the band was situated behind the props.

When Bowie appeared on stage for the opening number, "1984," fans were astounded, first by the theatrical set, and second, by Bowie's noticeable change in appearance. Much to the shock of the makeup-adorned glitter fans, Bowie was wearing flat-heeled shoes, a pleated and tapered double-breasted suit, and his hair was neatly parted on the side. Despite the new look, fans were enamored with Bowie's lavish production, and the tour grossed 5 million dollars.

The *Diamond Dog's* stage performance featured elaborate choreography, multiple costume changes, and meticulous lyrical pieces. The performance contained all the songs from the album as well as Bowie's own favorites from past records/performances. Most notable was his rendition of "Sweet Thing" in which he appeared on a catwalk, surrounded by smoke and dim lights. As the song began, a single yellow spotlight focused on Bowie, who was dressed in a Humphrey Bogart styled trench coat. If the image seemed confusing in light of the Ziggy performances, it is because this was one of Bowie's first attempts to emulate musically what William S. Burroughs had created with "cut-up" literature. That is, the song contained "splices" of meaning, none necessarily relating to the other.

The notion of cut-up was applied to other portions of the show as well. For example, during "Cracked Actor," Bowie donned a red cape and sunglasses and sang the song to a skull that was held at arms length. In "Space Oddity," he was hoisted above the stage by a space vehicle and the vocals were then sung through a telephone. In the title number, "Diamond Dogs," he was tied to a pair of leashes, then released into a boxing ring, where he sang the song of alienated humanoids while punching the air with red glitter boxing gloves. Other numbers presented morbid themes concerning alienation, radiation, decay, and death. To offset these serious numbers, however, Bowie included "Rebel-Rebel," the only song that spoke purely of the glitter era, which was, for the most part, coming to an end.

In "Rebel-Rebel," the lead character is an androgynous young man whose parents are outraged by his transvestitism. Bowie celebrates this confusion in the song and announces that the gender-bending rebel should attempt to further exaggerate his shocking styles. In the refrain, Bowie admits his own lust for the person and claims that he wants the individual to ignore parental authority. In the end, Bowie states that he loves the rebel, and he provides reassurance as a way of boosting the young man's self-esteem. It was a fitting anthem for a genre and style that was indeed on the wane. And even though Bowie no longer wore glitter clothes and makeup, "Rebel-Rebel" made it clear that he still held gender bending in high regard. At the same time, Bowie's wardrobe in *Diamond Dogs* certainly provided fans with the notion that glitter had most assuredly come to an end.

In reference to these performances *Melody Maker* critic Chris Charlesworth noted:

> The one and a half hour long show is a completely rehearsed and choreographed routine where every step and nuance has been perfected down to the last detail. There isn't one iota of spontaneity about the whole show.
>
> It's straight off a musical stage—a piece of theater complete with extravagant mechanical sets, dancers and a band that stands reservedly to stage right and never even receives a cursory acknowledgement, like an orchestra in a theatre pit.
>
> The show belongs on Broadway. . . . But David Bowie circa 1974 is not rock anymore. He can only be described as an entertainer who looks further ahead than any other in rock and roll. His far reaching image has created a combination of contemporary music and theatre that is several years ahead of its time. (*David Bowie Profile* 39-43)

Glitter: The Effect Splinters

Although Bowie's act perpetuated theatricality in rock and roll, it also aided in the splintering of glitter rock as a performance style. By 1974, a number of musicians and performers began to incorporate Bowie-inspired theatrics into their stage shows, and in so doing, they attempted to pass themselves off as glitter rock acts. For example, Kiss took glitter rock "theater" to its comic book extremes, as the band became known for fire spitting, madcap makeup, and its use of explosives on stage.[22] In an even more incongruous manner, LaBelle implemented glitter's science fiction motif, but the members had very little in common with glitter rock aside from their large, cumbersome outfits. In a similar vein, the camp New York bathhouse singer, Bette Midler, attempted to appeal to glitter audiences with her humorous versions of classic rock songs, her brazen wit, and her Broadway-styled theatrics. On the other end of the spectrum, some groups (Queen, Aerosmith, White Witch) achieved mass popularity by playing hard rock amid a spectacle of flashing lights and special effects. Also during this time, established "mega-rock" performers relied more heavily on theatrical sets and androgynous appearances. Mick Jagger, no stranger to gender bending, increasingly wore sequined jumpsuits and heavy eyeliner. Likewise, Rod Stewart usurped the visual style of performers such as Bowie and Brian Ferry by appearing in shiny tiger print suits. On occasion, he also used a traveling "rock and roll circus" as an opening act. Among others, Elton John also reaped benefits from the glitter trend, incorporating into his act elaborate costumes and a dazzling array of theatrical devices.

In other sectors more closely aligned with the genre, drastic changes were also occurring. As I have noted, the New York Dolls recorded a second album, but sales did not warrant their widespread success during 1974. Mott the Hoople abandoned glitter, Ian Hunter still denying at every step that he was gay. Concurrently, the first Roxy Music tour fared so poorly in the United States that it had to be canceled, and Brian Ferry set his sights on Europe. Finally, during the fall of 1974, Lou Reed released *Sally Can't Dance*, the most commercially successful album of his career. But what seemed odd about the album was Reed's reemergence as a pop-oriented performer. This time, it seemed as if he was actually playing a joke on glitter—the album's crassly commercial sound was combined with lyrics that seemed contrived in their depiction of sexually ambiguous characters.

Thus, with all of these changes, by late 1974 it seemed as if glitter as a musical genre and as a youth style had slowly dwindled to an end. Evidence was provided by *Creem* journalist Richard Cromelin, who titled his January 1975 piece, "Kiss It Goodbye." Here he described a Hollywood "trash dance" that was held at the Palladium one evening in October 1974. The dance was organized with the specific intention of defining the "end" of glitter rock:

> But the question all along has been "when," not "if" it will pass on. Almost by definition the scene was an inbred, cloistered, elitist system, which immediately limited its spread and guaranteed an inexorable downward spiral. It's the proletariat bands—Allmans, BTO, et al. that are defining today's rock dream for American kids. Smart ones like Bowie and Mott knew that the outrage wouldn't last and deftly scampered to the *outre* [sic] edge. The less astute are doomed to live out dead fantasies.
>
> The Trash Dance was as convenient and visible a "when" as any, and was headlined by one of the latter—judging by their four L.A. appearances, anyway, all of which have been progressively less promising duds—the New York Dolls. They were a fitting climax to an evening and an era, thrashing violently, strangely admirably, totally in vain against the inevitable. (41)

Speaking in reference to the trash dance, Chuckie Starr explained to commentator Lance Loud:

> All over Hollywood that night it was glitter! Glitter! The line to get into the Palladium was incredible—everyone in L.A. knew that it was going to be their last chance to wear platform shoes and eyeshadow! This was *it*! ("Los Angeles 1972-74" 79)

As the Dolls concluded their set, a glitter coffin was placed on the stage. As part of the eulogy, Starr climbed inside the coffin and glitter fans carried him around the dance hall. He states:

> There was a drum roll, and I up shot my legs! I had on black fishnet stockings and my hugest platform shoes. People threw lipstick and roses and glitter into the coffin as we went. At the door I lifted myself up and grabbed a lipstick—hot pink. I started smearing it all over my lips. Then I threw a kiss out into the crowd and they carried me out. That was the last time I wore those platforms. It was the end of it all. (Loud, "Los Angeles 1972-74" 78)

Michael Des Barres, also a prominent player in the L.A. glitter rock scene, explained, "By this time the sequins were just lying in the gutter. It was October of '74 and it had all come and gone so fast, everybody was burned out" (Loud, "Los Angeles 1972-74" 78).

A few months later, during the spring of 1975, the New York chapter of the National Association of Recording Arts and Sciences (NARAS) took a more serious approach to the death of glitter rock. NARAS held a panel discussion that included rock critics, journalists, and former glitter musicians, as well as members of the New York rock scene and Warhol associates. The panel was titled Superstar or Superstud? and it focused on the fact that glitter was "shimmering on the edge of extinction" (Loud, "Rock Autopsy" 16). In reference to the discussion, Lance Loud commented, "The post mortem was finally called to an end. The cause of death was determined as an overdose of phony dazzle causing irritation and finally boredom. R.I.P." ("Rock Autopsy" 16).

That same year, Alice Cooper produced an extravagant one-man rock and roll show, and he appeared on *The Hollywood Squares.* In addition, he performed at Lake Tahoe, and he played golf with the likes of Bing Crosby. Longtime fan Lester Bangs stated:

> You tended to ignore the fact that even the rag tag teen audience who embraced him when those who considered themselves more sophisticated graduated to David Bowie was now somewhat contemptuous of Alice's yearning for acceptance in the world of legitimate showbiz. . . . It's as easy as popping another beer to forget that Alice once seemed to stand for something genuinely outrageous. ("Alice Cooper All American" 52)

These observations provide us with an intriguing premise. Glitter rock was the first genre of rock and roll to actually construct and celebrate its own death. At the same time, as would be demonstrated throughout the 1970s and 1980s, glitter rock had a monumental impact on many rock genres and styles, the most notable being punk, new romantic music, heavy metal, and 1980s androgyny rock. Thus the genre did not end on a note of complete finality in 1974-75. Glitter rock influenced a number of additional styles as its main premises took on new meanings within new contexts.

During the first half of 1975, such transformations were beginning to occur in New York as London fashion designer and entrepreneur Malcom McLaren attempted to change the New York Dolls' visual image into one that was more directly shocking. He dressed the band in red patent leather, draped a communist flag onstage behind them, and dubbed the new group the "Red Patent Leather Party." But in essence, this was simply the New York Dolls in new outfits—and the fact that they seemingly had communist overtones only forced them into yet another musical bind. Nonetheless, as Pete Frame has suggested, "McLaren crystallized his observations of the New York scene during the first half of 1975 and returned to London with the blueprint for a band that would change the world: the Sex Pistols" (27).[23]

After his return to London, McLaren was particularly taken with a scruffy, spiky-haired young man who went by the name of Johnny Rotten. By the end of 1975, McLaren had put together the Sex Pistols, with Rotten, Glen Matlock (later replaced by Sid Vicious), Paul Cook, and Steve Jones.[24] By 1976, the Sex Pistols had helped to initiate a new trend in rock and roll as hoards of "punk rockers" gathered in U.K. nightclubs to "pogo" amid such highly political rock anthems as "God Save the Queen" and "Anarchy in the U.K." By the end of that year, a host of punk musicians emerged, both in London and New York, each paying homage to Bowie, Warhol, and the Factory. As Carr and Murray suggest, "In 1972, Bowie applied Warhol's Revelation; in 1976, kids started taking the lesson seriously. Johnny Rotten, Sid Vicious, Siouxsie, Joe Strummer, Poly Styrene, Elvis Costello, Billy Idol: all children of Ziggy Stardust" (9).

Of central interest here is not only the pervasiveness of Bowie but also the pervasiveness of Warhol in yet another rock and roll genre. And if glitter rock was considered an outrage, then punk by comparison was an explosion of outrages that threatened on all fronts.

Punk rock, like glitter, did not exist in an isolated situation but within a complex and multidimensional context. So we need to ask, How was punk influenced by Warhol and by glitter rock? First, like glitter, punk was obsessed with self-conscious style. At least initially, if one sported a punk haircut and punk attire, it was to create a method whereby style would guarantee shocking results. This premise was, of course, based on something Bowie learned early on from Warhol and his entourage. Second, punk's androgynous style opened a space for women singers and musicians to perform on an equal footing with men. Additionally, punk took Warhol's artistic maxim concerning "all is art" to its extreme in that anyone capable of picking up a guitar could be considered a rock and roll musician. Like Iggy and the Stooges and the New York Dolls, punks did not have to be adept musicians, which accounts for the genre's wide variance in style. Finally, punk revalidated many of the performers who had been influenced by Warhol, and by the late 1970s, Iggy Pop, John Cale, Lou Reed, Bryan Ferry, and David Johansen were once again at the forefront of another rock genre/subculture, this time dubbed as the "godfathers of punk" by both the press and rock fans.

And if it seems curious that Andy Warhol maintained such a strong influence on rock and roll, consider Robert Duncan's insightful summation:

> It wasn't Warhol's art that attracted rockers to him. It was something much more elusive, much more intangible, mysterious, uncommon, and ultimately perhaps dangerous. It was him. And the arty, pan-sexual, decadent, demimondain, infantile, ultrahip hurricane of which he was the invisible placid eye. Andy Warhol was a perfect adaptation in a self-conscious age: everything he touched was effortlessly subsumed into an Andy Warhol movie—including Andy Warhol. He was the film. (Which may be a couple of steps down from Christopher Isherwood's being the camera, but then neither was this Berlin). In other words, not even "Andy Warhol" existed. There was only " ." (99-100)

In contemplating Duncan's assessment of Warhol, we are left to ponder a necessary "blankness" or void in relation to the artist's influence on rock and roll style. Duncan's suggestion (i.e., " ") that Warhol was inauthentically authentic provides an interesting point concerning the artist's impact on styles such as glitter and punk. Duncan's summation, in fact, implicitly pronounces the very nature of style itself: its power/lack of power, its presence/nonpresence, its contradictory qualifiers. Certainly, such contradictions and dichotomies lay at the very heart of the styles that emerged both at the Factory and through glitter rock. But as I have noted, the contradictions posed by these styles were what made them so interesting, so potent, so abrasive.

Thus, as rock and roll style is about the nature of "floating" surfaces and contradictions, it is also about the foundations of artistic and musical genres. It is my hope that we will be inclined not to treat Warhol and his influence on style merely as a set of lived experiences and contradictory signifiers that were ultimately usurped and regurgitated in the form of "incorporated blankness." The styles and attitudes created by the Factory and glitter rock were always evolving, shifting, and giving way to new forms of experimentation, which suggested that "surface style" was not always a dismal, failed attempt at revolt. For those involved in the Factory and for glitter rock fans, style was empowering; it was endowed with blatant significatory praxis—it demanded attention in the world of everyday life. Glitter rock opened up possibilities for fans; its style gave them a key into another world. Thus, if we treat this study simply as Duncan treats Warhol (" "), we will never uncover the important idea that some forms of incorporation do indeed have liberating results. In the end, we will be left not unraveling the power of myths but, instead, only describing and elaborating on the nature of mystification.

Notes

1. Even though Lou Reed and Iggy Pop were associated with Mainman, DeFries did not provide them with the kind of financial resources accorded to Bowie.

2. Ironically, the *Berlin* album did bear a direct relation to some of the themes of glitter. Consider that the film *Cabaret* (1972) was also released during glitter's early days, and the themes of this film (decadence in pre-World War II Germany, bisexuality, fetishism) were central to many of those presented by Reed in this album. Although *Berlin* was morbid in many respects, it also paid homage to the city and to the themes found in a film such as *Cabaret*. (Also, along more specific lines, the main character of this film, Sally Bowles, first came to life in Christopher Isherwood's *Berlin Stories*, a source that Bowie acknowledged as an important reference for much of his work in the 1970s). But, all in all, the composition of Lou Reed's *Berlin* and the dark images were too sublime for fans who were in search of a more upbeat musical approach. Perhaps, however, the complexities that figured into this record also played a part in its eventual acclaim as a masterpiece.

3. Here, it should be pointed out that Pop merely hinted that he "might be" bisexual. For example, in an interview with *Creem* that spring, Pop alluded to the fact that he and his band "were all straight," yet laughed uproariously upon making this claim. Also, among rock circles, a number of rumors circulated, some of which linked Bowie and Iggy. There is no documentation, however, to give credence to such rumors, yet the point is that many fans simply assumed that Iggy Pop was bisexual. His coauthored autobiography, *I Need More*, never deals with his sexuality except in heterosexual terms.

4. This claim is made in reference to Ziggy Stardust.

5. Here, I am referring specifically to rock journalists who were supportive of glitter rock (Lisa Robinson, Dave Edmunds, Simon Frith, et al.).

6. Here, I am referring specifically to *visual* images, especially as presented on the album covers of these musicians.

7. Audiences were no doubt familiar with Bowie and his androgynous Ziggy, yet this particular image was fostered by a "play" at gender confusion. Bowie never appeared as a woman

during this period. So fans who were already predisposed to glitter found in the Dolls a more directly confrontational presentation of sexual ambiguity. The aforementioned Rolling Stones record sleeve of the 1960s and Bowie's "man dress" thus seemed quite mild by comparison.

8. I am using the term as a reference to the music that would arise two years after the Dolls demise: New York punk rock.

9. The original source for this reference is to be found in a spring 1977 edition of *Punk,* ed. John Holmstrom. *Punk* was a fanzine that didn't always adhere to copyright standards—thus the journal contains no other information. The edition does not indicate a specific release date. The quotation can also be found in a New York Dolls promotion package that included this particular quotation among many others.

10. Bowie was not much older, yet his music seemed extremely sophisticated. Conversely, the Dolls presented an unrefined, garage-anthem-style rock that was more in line with the early Detroit sound than with Bowie's highly structured conceptual approach.

11. It should be noted that although Christgau's claims were perhaps intended to be humorous, he does use the term *fags* in reference to gay men. Given the negative connotations of the term, I refuse to quote him directly in this particular case. The content of the article is, however, directly described.

12. The album's title reflected the overall ambience imposed on the band during its first U.S. tour and its subsequent trip to Europe. The title referenced personal as well as more audience-based concerns.

13. In other words, their music was translatable outside of New York, yet as David Johansen will later point out, the "kids" didn't often comprehend the "camp on camp" punch line.

14. The Bon Bons were two male performance artists/glitter rock fans who often appeared in drag.

15. I attended this performance, and many notes come from a "fan journal" that I kept at the time. For a direct reference to the quotations, see "Rolling Stone" October 25, 1993, p. 26.

16. Of course, at this particular point, glitter rock was also a dying (if not dead) trend/style. The Dolls also had grown tired of explaining their fashions, and at the same time they felt that a less obvious approach might gain them more fans.

17. See Jon Savage's *England's Dreaming* 62-63. This is not to say that the Dolls did not receive positive reviews in Britain. I am suggesting, however, that their language, and streetwise attitudes were not appreciated by an eager British press, one that was accustomed to a more reverent demeanor.

18. Consider, for example, a band such as Nirvana (circa 1991-93). It was able to effectively cross between a number of musical genres and visual styles.

19. I am referring to the notion of fans paying their dues.

20. See Sugerman 20-21.

21. I have no direct information that suggests the sexual orientation of band members. At the same time, the social construction of "sexual otherness" positioned the band as outcasts. And, indeed, while onstage, Johansen and other band members often appeared to be more attracted to males than to females.

22. Kiss had been performing prior to 1974, but it was during this year that the band gained widespread popularity.

23. For an extensive account, see Jon Savage's *England's Dreaming.*

24. Here, it should be pointed out that Jones and Cook were directly inspired by the New York Dolls and Mott the Hoople. Rotten also liked early Alice Cooper but found the lyrics somewhat simplistic. One drawing force, however, was David Bowie's "Diamond Dogs"; both the album and single cut were repeatedly blared from McLaren's shop during this period.

Pop Practices/Subcultural Articulations

The case studies presented in this book are linked by an effort to trace Warhol's impact on glitter rock through an examination of the ways in which his pop theories were interpreted and used by David Bowie, Lou Reed, Iggy Pop, Brian Ferry, and other glitter performers. In a congruent manner, I have noted particular cases in which the Factory subculture—as an extension of Warhol's pop ethos—provided glitter with many of its most pertinent themes and motifs. As I have demonstrated, the interchange between Warhol/the Factory and glitter rock was sometimes direct, as in the case of David Bowie, who had personal connections to Warhol's aesthetic/social world. In other cases, the impact was indirect, as in the case of Brian Ferry, who was inspired by the notion of a Warholian underground. Taking both kinds of instances into consideration, the case studies were intended to provide thematic unity through an emphasis on the aesthetic principles that guided those who produced the art and rock genres under consideration.

Although my strategy is not too surprising, I have stressed the aesthetic and social networks of artistic and musical production because even though scholars of popular music have provided analyses of the Warhol/Factory/glitter connection, none have provided explicit details regarding the chronological development of a rock version of pop art. For example, Frith and Horne (*Art into Pop)* argue that glitter celebrated many of pop's tenets, and they provide an intriguing account of Warhol's impact on the Velvets, Bowie, Brian Ferry, and Brian Eno. At the same time, in *Art into Pop,* the analysis of glitter rock's connection to pop art is related to a larger contextual problem: how to account for a 35-year span in which British art schools[1] played a significant role in the development of rock and roll. Thus, although Frith and Horne argue that pop art and glitter rock represented devious plays on commercialism, they do not offer an extended account of the interactional networks that provided the foundation for glitter rock's emergence as an "out-there" subcultural form.

In the case studies presented in *Subculture,* Dick Hebdige also locates glitter rock within a broad cultural matrix: glitter is analyzed as one of many rock and roll genres that can be situated within the context of British class relationships. In Hebdige's terms, glitter was particularly significant because it *did not* attempt to deal explicitly with class issues, but instead, it attempted to subvert sexuality and gender typing (62). Again, like Frith and Horne, Hebdige deals only briefly with the artists and musicians who were responsible for developing the guiding premises of glitter; yet, unlike these authors, he shows that glitter rock was a powerful subcultural tool that contained seditious premises regarding gender bending.

Iain Chambers[2] (*Urban Rhythms*), also coming out of the tradition of British cultural studies, stresses the aesthetic connections between Warhol, the Velvets, and glitter rock performers. Like the previously mentioned authors, Chambers recognizes the centrality of the interrelationship between pop art and glitter rock. But his analysis of this relationship is also framed by a larger issue: how to account for the dominant genres of British pop music that arose between 1956 and the early 1980s. His overriding assumption is that "contemporary popular culture [in particular, pop music] is experienced directly on the immediate surfaces of everyday life: coming out of the radio, the record grooves, the headphones; off the adverts, the television screen" (211). In a particularly insightful summary that concerns Bowie's chameleon-like "poses," Chambers argues, "Such characters underlined the continual sign production of the mass media, that possibility foreseen by Warhol in which everyone would be a 'star' for fifteen minutes, a 'hero just for one day' " (136).

Each of these writers proposes to analyze a specific aspect of glitter's relation to pop art (as part of an art school tradition, as signification, as a particular kind of genre within the tradition of British rock). At the same time, none have traced the lineage of glitter rock through an explanation of the numerous, complex interactions that took place among artists, rock and roll musicians, rock critics, music industry executives and employees, and rock and roll fans. Therefore, my aim has been to underscore the multifarious strategies that gave rise to glitter rock. It is my argument that an analysis of glitter's subcultural dimensions requires an examination of the chronological development of glitter as genre. For this reason, I have focused on the networks of social and aesthetic production, while reserving an analysis of reception to Chapters 2, 9, and 11. This approach allows readers to determine how and why a particular audience was drawn to certain pop art themes that were presented through the medium of glitter.

In Chapter 2, and in this chapter, I am attempting to provide a method for understanding the relationship between glitter's development as a musical genre and the ways in which fans used this genre. How did the fans handle the "materials" presented to them by the rock media? How did they attempt to "mark" themselves and insert themselves within the lineage of glitter rock? To answer these questions and to offer an expansion of the preceding points, I will briefly return to the main premises of subculture theory. In so doing, I will reexamine the notion of "in-there"/"out-there" subcultures. I will then offer an argument concerning the relationship between subcultural forms (in-there/out-there), subcultural style, and the process of incorporation.

Employing British Subculture Theory: A Comparative Analysis

As I suggested in Chapter 2, British subculture theorists did not intend to provide a theoretical framework that would allow for the analysis of youth subcultures across contexts. Both Hebdige and Clarke et al. treat subcultures within the larger framework of British postwar culture; subcultural style is viewed as representing a response to the class conditions of postwar British society. Taking the contextualism of cultural studies into account, I am concerned with constructing a comparison that allows us to determine the similarities and differences between British youth subcultures and in-there/out-there subcultural forms. In the course of my comparison, it will become apparent as to the reasons that subculture theory is both appropriate and inappropriate when applied to an analysis of the Factory and glitter rock. It is my hope, then, that the reader will supply his or her own critique of my appropriation of subculture theory, noting in particular the places where I have attempted to extend the premises provided by Hebdige and Clarke et al.

Although I have dealt with the major premises of subculture theory in Chapter 2, Hebdige's claims concerning subcultural style provide a useful starting point for the final analysis. As we will recall, Hebdige proposes that "the challenge to hegemony which subcultures represent is not issued directly by them. Rather, it is expressed obliquely, in style" (*Subculture* 7). In Hebdige's terms, the relationship between subordinate youth subcultures and the dominant culture can be analyzed through an examination of the "surfaces of subcultures"—in the styles "which have a double meaning" (2). According to Hebdige, these double meanings symbolically pronounce the subculture's resistance to the order that guarantees its subordination (18). Seen in this manner, subcultural style represents a struggle with signification (17). And as Hebdige points out, this is a struggle that "extends to even the most mundane areas of everyday life" (17).

Given these premises and the claims presented in Chapter 2, we can note that subculture theory provides important ideas that can be extended to an analysis of Warhol's Factory. On the one hand, I would like to propose that the Factory qualifies as a subculture whose tactics are comparable to those of postwar British youth subcultures. On the other hand, as I have pointed out in Chapter 2, the Factory was an in-there subculture: it had many of the qualities typically ascribed to British youth subcultures, but it was dissimilar due to the manner in which it handled class relationships. In a correlative manner, members of the Factory subculture produced individualized methods for symbolically organizing the objects that were used to express a collective sense of "otherness."

As I have previously suggested, the individuals and subcultures at the Factory assimilated into their everyday lives many of the aesthetic principles that were associated with Warhol's pop practices. This particular process of assimilation resulted in the formation of a subcultural unit that consisted of a network of matched as well as mismatched groups. Included within this network were young, wealthy socialites, working-class gay men, Harvard students, street people, Village artists, rock and roll musicians, transvestites, and numerous other social types. As this network-as-subcultural unit evolved, a "shared sense of refusal"[3] united these groups and individuals. In turn, those known as Factory regulars collectively defined the Factory as a subculture.

One of the central features of this self-defined subculture was that it could not be traced to a particular class. Even so, an analysis of class is warranted, especially because the Factory subculture consisted of young people whose parent cultures ranged from working class to upper class. In giving consideration to this wide range, we can draw a comparison between the Factory's parent cultures and the parent (class) culture of British youth subcultures. The underlying reason for drawing this comparison is, oddly enough, somewhat obvious: the Factory did not represent a unified class-based subculture. Hence it did not propose a symbolic solution to the dominant/subordinate relations of one particular class. At the same time, however, the Factory subculture did propose a collective solution to some of the more general problems posed by the American class system. And this solution was common to many bohemian subcultures: the dominant notion of "fitting in" was replaced with the subcultural possibility of "opting out." This meant that art students, street people, sexual and drug subcultures, and former socialites could form an in-there subculture that contradicted the model of normal social relations that typically operated between classes in American culture. Thus the Factory ignored the guiding social concepts that positioned social classes in a dichotomous relation to one another. And an egalitarian social system replaced the class-based society that was all too familiar to those who had gained membership in the Factory subculture. In this sense, the problematic notion of class as a marker of identity was denounced and resolved.

This general solution had several important implications. At the Factory, acquiring status did not mean working one's way up the ranks, so to speak, but instead the acclamation was, "Transform yourself into a 'superstar.' " In a corresponding manner, education was not to be acquired in prestigious colleges but under the tutelage of Andy Warhol (the master of "blank minds"). In addition, the open avowal of one's sexual orientation (gay, straight, bisexual) was reason for celebration, not cause for consternation. As Factory regular Steven Koch puts it,

> The Factory begins to seem the Great Good Place for children of an ideology dominated by petit bourgeois sexual repression, a hypocritical contemptus mundi, and a preoccupation with the miracles of grace. The Factory was a region of resolution for those dilemmas, another world. (11)

In considering Koch's claim, as well as the preceding points, I believe that the Factory subculture developed its own particular kind of imaginary response to class. Whereas the subculture did not symbolically address the problems posed by the structuring experiences of a subordinate class,[4] it did reveal that relations between different class fractions could be reversed, cut apart, and reworked in a coherent and harmonious manner. Thus, to move from parent culture to subculture was to move into a world that promised the bohemian ideal of a classless society. Broadly speaking, then, at the Factory the "hidden and unresolved contradictions" of each parent class were collectively "expressed" and "magically resolved" (Cohen 23).

If style is the most significant aspect of the subcultural response to class relations, then the notion of style as resistant practice is particularly applicable to the Factory subculture. Here, we can consider that subcultural members engaged in individual acts of bricolage that (oddly enough)[5] revealed an "organized group identity in the form and shape of a coherent and distinctive way of 'being-in-the-world' " (Clarke et al. 54). These individual acts of recontextualization—although not affirming a uniform stylistic alliance—did allow for the operation of "semiotic guerrilla warfare" (Eco, qtd. in Hebdige, *Subculture* 105). In other words, at the Factory, there were no standard haircuts uniforms, or accessories, but one feature permeated the styles developed by individual members: they clothed themselves in chaotic "gear," which had "*already* been arranged, according to social use, into cultural codes of meaning" (Clarke et al. 55). In each particular case, subcultural members thereby transformed and subverted the naturalized meanings that were commonly associated with objects and fashions. In turn, the activity of stylization—although individual in practice—provided a method whereby subcultural members could formulate a collective self-image.

We can begin to consider the significance of individual bricolage through an examination of the way in which Warhol resignified his own naturalized appearance. In an attempt to juxtapose his pale complexion and meek bodily features with a contradictory image, Warhol "complemented" his pallid skin tone with garments lifted from the military. In addition, he added to his attire fashion accessories that were associated with the New York leather subculture. As Victor Bockris points out,

> As the sixties developed, so did Andy's new look. He now dressed like an SS guard in a B-movie about the Second World War, with a few embellishments of his own: black leather jacket, tight black jeans (under which he wore panty hose), T-shirts, high-heeled boots, dark glasses, and a silver wig (to match his Silver Factory). Sometimes he emphasized his pallor and Slavonic features with make-up and wore nail polish. He was now very thin and the general "look" he was after was clean, hard, and arrogant. He hardly ever laughed and rarely spoke in public. (Bockris 148)

In an analogous manner, other Factory members acted as bricoleurs. Most notorious in this regard was Edie Sedgwick, the "poor little rich girl," who arrived at the Factory direct from Cambridge, where, in the tradition of her old-line monied family, she had been attending college. In a deliberate attempt to denounce her class lineage, Sedgwick developed a style that consisted of cheap knee-length men's T-shirts, black tights, and gaudy, oversized jewelry. Gerard Malanga adds, "She [also] applied a great deal of make-up before going out. When she spoke she made sense. She could not be the fool or be made to look foolish" (qtd. in Bockris 164).

Likewise, other subcultural members can be noted for their individual constructions of stylistic bricolage: Nico clothed herself in medieval capes accented by white rocker boots. International Velvet was known for her elaborate false eyelashes and for her makeup, which seemed as if it had been poured onto her face. These individuals were complemented by the Factory's most glamorous drag queens, who "pulled off" their roles so well that they were viewed as modelesque (for example, Candy Darling). Also, we might consider a drag queen such as Holly Woodlawn (aka Harold Ajzenberg) whose "trashy" appearance gained her immediate recognition as a Warhol superstar. In relating the details of her first encounter with the pop master, Woodlawn states, "You can bet I was a sight to behold in my white vinyl go-go boots, backless minidress, untamed hair and a face boasting more paint than the . . . Mona Lisa!" (Woodlawn, with Copeland 4).

In addition to these individuals, we can consider others who also transformed and thereby subverted the meanings commonly associated with the appropriate attire worn by women and men: Factory "A-men" (such as Silver George) dyed their hair in shocking pink colors and they often wore feather boas, scarves, snake bracelets, and sequined outfits. In a different manner, the overtly "butch" hustlers also commented on masculinity as they appropriated fashions that were typically associated with working-class straight culture (construction workers, bricklayers). Finally, we can consider other Factory regulars, such as Lou Reed, who often wore clothing that was associated with New York's urban Afro-American subculture.

In giving consideration to all of these individuals and groups, I am not suggesting that bricolage operated at the Factory in precisely the same manner as it did among the subcultures studied by the British scholars. Nonetheless, the collective notion of adopting a persona—as reflected through style(s)—was one of the most consistent features of the Factory's in-there subculture. In this sense, then, the individualized activity of stylization that consumed the Factory subculture allows for a comparison to the collective activity of stylization that was operative in subcultures such as the Mods. In varying ways, both groups functioned as bricoleurs in that they recontextualized and reordered objects and fashions so as to subvert the naturalized meanings that were associated with them.[6] In explaining the implications of this process, John Clarke points out that the subcultural use of commodities is "posited on the existence of other groups . . . who would originally have bought, used, and expressed their own lifestyle through these object signs" ("Style" 178). Given this premise, we can come to a clearer understanding as to the manner in which stylistic subversion was evident at the Factory. There, the process of recontextualization meant that one could create an identity that would subvert socially prescribed standards of sexuality and class.

This notion of recontextualization can also be extended to an examination of the general behaviors and attitudes of Factory participants. Here, we are reminded of the numerous media events that were staged by Warhol and the Factory subculture. One of the most significant of these was the Factory's assault on the New York Society for Clinical Psychiatry. In addition to such group efforts, individual Factory participants often constructed outrageous media personas, which disrupted the "calmly orchestrated crisis of everyday life" (Hebdige, *Subculture* 114). For example,

> Brigid Polk shocked the nation on September 11, 1967 on [the] Merv [Griffin Show]. She would not deign to speak to Merv, infrequently or nastily answering questions, and offering insults on fellow celebrities, much to his chagrin. Griffin expected Hollywood protocol to extend to superstars, anticipating obsequiousness and flowery flattery, as was the norm. (Berlin and Bryan 57)

In an equally systematic manner that spoke of the Factory's cohesiveness through outlandish and ironic media gesturing, Allen Midgette spent four months during 1967 acting as Warhol. Booked to give numerous college lectures across the country, Warhol had decided at the last minute that he didn't want to go. So he asked Midgette to stand in for him. Midgette sprayed his hair silver, doused his face with pale white powder, and set out on the tour. The plan worked beautifully until a college official compared a photograph of Midgette to one of Warhol. When the story leaked out to the national press that Midgette was not Warhol, many colleges either demanded that their money be returned or that the *real* Warhol do the lectures. Warhol responded:

> Allen made a much better Andy Warhol than I did—he had high cheekbones and a full mouth and sharp, arched eyebrows, and he was a raving beauty and fifteen/ twenty years younger. . . . Who wants the truth? That's what show busi-

> ness is for—to prove that it's not what you are that counts, it's what they *think* you are. (Warhol and Hackett 248)

These examples point to the explicit playfulness of the Factory subculture and to the way in which it contextualized a relation between pop art as an aesthetic and pop as a lifestyle. In presenting all of the preceding examples, I have attempted to demonstrate how the Factory subculture used both stylistic bricolage and media manipulation as methods for subverting the meaning systems associated with the normalized world. In addition, I have implied that the Factory's stylistic activities were homologous with its media gestures, its focal concerns, and its collective self-image.[7] In these ways, the Factory's in-there subculture can be compared to postwar British youth subcultures in that there was a sense of group cohesion and order at the Factory—even though the subculture seemed to represent a somewhat disorderly group of individuals. Thus Clarke et al.'s explanation of subcultural orderliness provides us with a key insight concerning the Factory's homological social system: "It is this reciprocal effect, between the things a group uses and the *outlooks* and *activities* which structure and define their use, which is the generative principle of stylistic creation in subcultures" (emphasis added, Resistance 56).

If we assume that the Factory's subcultural methods were ones that cohered, then what can we say about the incorporation process? Here, we are reminded that incorporation refers to the manner in which commercial and ideological forms ensure the defusion and diffusion of the subculture. Thus, typically, incorporation disrupts the homological system of subcultures. Given these claims, however, we must consider that the Factory represented a rather atypical example. The process of incorporation had little effect on the order that had been established within the subculture. As Koch points out,

> With its hierarchies, its stars and leaders and followers, with the aggressive enthralling secret knowledge that outcasts share with one another and the sense of an awful isolation somehow redeemed within those walls, the Factory inverted the traditional subculture's role. While the little world mocked and mimicked the big one, the big world looked on fascinated, making the Factory shine under the spotlight of its attention. (6)

This description in mind, I would redirect our attention to Hebdige's notion that the process of incorporation takes two characteristic forms: (a) the conversion of subcultural signs (dress, music, etc.) into mass-produced objects (i.e., the commodity form) and (b) the labeling and redefinition of deviant behavior by dominant groups—the police, the media, the judiciary (i.e., the ideological form) (*Subculture* 94). Each of these forms was applied to the Factory, although it did not always encounter them in the manner described in *Subculture* (90-99). First, the Factory was never a large enough subculture to warrant any law and order campaigns. Second, there was little concern over the possibility that "our young men and women" would become directly involved in the Factory's local lifestyle. At the same time, an attempt to exploit the Factory's sense of otherness was apparent in a number of significant ways. Members of the press often went to the Factory to uncover the "sex-drug subculture" that resided there. But during interviews with Factory regulars, reporters often became confused. The responses to questions were usually so incoherent that reporters walked out of the Factory with little basis for the kinds of stories that might appeal to tabloid readers.

In another more important manner, however, the press often located the Factory within the tradition of pop art. Thus, if pop art represented a non-serious, commercialized view of the world, then Factory participants were often made over so as to correspond with such impressions. Indeed, Edie Sedgwick was victim to such accounts in that her self-created style was proclaimed by fashion editors to be "new and exciting." In addition, a number of glossy magazines often presented Sedgwick as "this year's girl" and the "princess of pop." In a particularly telling example, a November 1965 issue of *Life* featured four photographs of Sedgwick that were "announced" by the headline "The Girl with Black Tights" and carried an accompanying description that mentioned her connection with Warhol and her socialite status, but focused on her legs and her sense of style (see Stein and Plimpton 248). The significance of such a description is the fact that—from the perspective of the Factory subculture—its trivialization seemed unimportant. After all, the Factory had embraced Warhol's premise concerning fifteen minutes of fame. Indeed, this premise was celebrated by many of the Factory's subcultural members, who found that to acquire fame, they actually had to do very little, except pose in front of Warhol's static camera. As Holly Woodlawn explains,

> All you had to do was hang out, look fabulous, and with the bat of a false eyelash, you were a star. I felt just like Lana Turner. . . . I had never taken an acting lesson. Who had the time for vocal coaches, dance lessons, or rehearsals? Who had the money? We didn't go to school to be fabulous; we *were* fabulous. . . . No discipline. No struggle. No nothing. And there I was, wallowing in the bliss of having

> landed my first film role, a role that guaranteed an unforgettable ride on the Warhol gravy train. And I was on board for the run! Overnight I became a curious phenomenon. A celebrity. A media star. But not your typical Hollywood star mind you. I was a Warhol Superstar, a vixen of the underground. Finally, little Harold Ajzenberg was somebody. (7-8)

In giving consideration to this perspective on stardom, I believe that the Factory maintained an ironical attitude toward media incorporation. Subcultural members didn't avoid the possibility of misrepresentation in the press; they didn't particularly care if assessments of the Factory's lifestyle proved to be inaccurate. According to those at the Factory, *any* press was good press! Indeed, this attitude was so central that even though the styles and behaviors of Factory participants were often trivialized, the process did not result in the defusion or diffusion of subculture. It was simply difficult to incorporate a subculture that seemed to embrace any form of attention given to it by the media.

In another more general manner, however, the incorporation process can be seen as operating through the medium of glitter rock. As I argue, glitter rock represented an incorporated version of Warhol's pop ethos and the Factory's style and attitude. And although this version of incorporation did not manifest itself in a direct manner, its characteristics allow for an understanding of the ways in which mass media often attempt to resituate the themes of subcultures.

In the case under investigation, many of the premises of glitter can be traced back to the Factory's local lifestyle. In this sense, the Factory advocated 15 minutes of fame; glitter rock championed its audience members as stars. The Factory rebuked traditional class-oriented values; glitter rock denounced notions of class altogether. The Factory provided sexual autonomy; glitter rock provided performative ways to glorify bisexuality, homosexuality, and androgyny. Consequently, if we turn to an analysis of glitter-as-rock incorporation we will find that many of the principles that typically guide the commodity and ideological forms seem appropriate. The point of difference, however, is that glitter rock did not represent "the exploitation of subcultural style by the *dominant* culture" (John Clarke, "Style" 185). At the same time, in an ironic manner, glitter rock did represent "a heavy investment in the youth world of fashion trends" (John Clarke, "Style" 185). In addition, glitter rock made persistent use of "style-characterizations as convenient stereotypes to identify and hopefully, isolate groups dominantly regarded as 'anti-social' "

(John Clarke, "Style" 185). In the process, glitter provided an illustration of Hebdige's argument concerning the (negative) impact of commodity incorporation:

> Once [subcultural styles are] removed from their private contexts by the small entrepreneurs and big fashion interests who produce them on a mass scale, they become codified, made comprehensible, rendered at once public property and profitable merchandise. (*Subculture* 96)

Yet, even though glitter rock did provide a commercial interpretation of the Factory's style and attitude, it did not subscribe to Hebdige's parallel premise that "as soon as the original innovations which signify 'subculture' are translated into commodities and made generally available, they become 'frozen' " (*Subculture* 96). In other words, glitter rock represented a rather ambiguous form of incorporation as it engaged in many of the tactics that are often associated with both the commodity and ideological processes. Nonetheless, although glitter rock may have *appeared* to be just another manipulative media trend, its lived effects suggested something else altogether. Glitter ushered in a subversive out-there style, and in so doing, it meticulously (re)defined the qualities that Hebdige attributes to all youth subcultures: "secrecy, Masonic oaths, an Underworld" (*Subculture* 4).

The Subcultural Impact of Glitter Rock

If glitter rock did not represent a process whereby otherworldly styles and attitudes were plucked from their origin points and forced unwillingly into the realm of "mass style," then what kinds of promises were granted by commercial assimilation? I believe that the incorporation of the Factory's Warholian premises via glitter rock resulted in a liberating genre of out-there subcultural rock and roll, one that represented an authentic widespread transfusion of pure (in-there) subcultural innovations. This process occurred as the major practitioners (Bowie, Lou Reed, Iggy Pop) applied aesthetic principles learned from Warhol and the Factory subculture while embodying (onstage, in song, and in interviews) the sexual themes that had permeated the Factory's lifestyle. In turn, the rock press played an enormous role in the incorporation process, as it initially transmitted glitter's incorporated propositions to potential fans. In all of these cases, however, the Factory's styles and attitudes were translated intact, even though the method of commercialization seemed to suggest that effective translation was always impossible. In this manner, glitter rock implied that styles and attitudes that were once subversive could be introduced into a broader context; and in this context, commercialism was realized as a method for unlocking the possibilities of subcultural practice on a wider scale.

As I have pointed out, glitter rock suggested a collapse of the original style/co-opted style dichotomy. Consequently, the guiding maxim of rock criticism—"if its commercial, it isn't authentic"—became problematic. In fact, in the pop world being described, authenticity was never an issue that had to be resolved. In addressing a similar point, Frith and Horne have argued that among British pop art musicians, questions concerning individual expression were never at stake because pop art rhetoric referred to "commercial music-making, to issues of packaging, selling and publicizing, to the problems of popularity and stardom" (101). In discerning the impact of pop art on British art school musicians Frith and Horne claim:

> For them pop was, in Dick Hebdige's words, "a discourse on fashion, consumption, and fine art"; a response to what Lawrence Alloway had called in 1959, the "drama of possessions."
>
> The first consequence of this was the increasing use of music along the lines of Alloway's definitions of Pop, as "art about signs and sign systems." Musicians . . . began to make music as bricolage, quoting from other work, incorporating "real" sounds, recontextualizing familiar sonic symbols. . . . For the more theoretically minded Townshend it meant making records about mass communication, about the media disruption of commonsense distinctions between the real and the false. (107)

Along similar lines, I suggest that glitter rock both celebrated and critiqued the commercial rock process by demonstrating that to effectively transmit oppositional ideas, one had to be at the center of popular culture. Thus David Bowie played the commercial game, yet he did so under the guise of a character (Ziggy) who transmitted artful ideas about sexuality and gender coding. In this sense, Bowie and other glitter rockers challenged the very system that they used as a lever for transmitting their ideas.

Accordingly, if glitter rock can be used to explain a unique form of incorporation, then I propose that as a musical/artistic/sexual genre it also represented a special case for the way incorporation proceeds once its forms are in place. Here, we can consider that glitter rock was strategic in that a few individual musicians lifted innovative subcultural premises and subtly rearranged them for a mass audience. However, if glitter rock musicians ignited out-there subcultural sensibilities, then the question becomes, In what manner did fans absorb these sensibilities? In an attempt to answer this question, we can consider Hebdige's argument that subcultural style "goes 'against nature' "; it interrupts "the process of 'normalization' ":

> [Thereby] our task becomes, like Barthes' to discern the hidden messages inscribed in code on the glossy surfaces of style, to trace them out as "maps of meaning" which obscurely re-present the very contradictions they are designed to resolve or conceal. (*Subculture* 18)

In giving consideration to this point, I maintain that glitter rock fans represented a "culture of conspicuous consumption" (*Subculture* 103), and through style, they were able to reveal "a secret identity" that contained "forbidden meanings" (103). But although glitter rockers may have functioned as bricoleurs, their inspirational sources were not directly analogous to those that had activated postwar British youth subcultures. Glitter stylists represented an out-there subculture whose look was originally located in the "texts" of concert performances and magazine layouts. In this sense, the true innovators of subcultural style were glitter performers and rock journalists; both groups presented the audience with materials that were then doubly recontextualized. In the process, glitter rockers therefore appropriated messages from these texts and went about the activity of developing their own parallel versions of glitter style. In so doing, they borrowed conventional objects and fashions from homes, thrift stores, and dime stores and combined these with other forms of apparel that were purchased in commercial boutiques.

Through these combined methods, glitter rockers rearranged taken for granted objects (commercial/homemade) into a series of "totalizing compositions." The most essential (and thus common) object within these compositions was the sequin, the defining trademark of glitter rock. With its obvious connotations of gaudiness and its traditional association with Las Vegas lounge singers and musicians such as Little Richard and Liberace, the sequin was borrowed and recontextualized within a complete ensemble that immediately signified one's alliance with glitter rock. Consequently, bags of multicolored sequins were purchased so that "dots" could be glued onto faces with Vaseline. In addition, sequins were sewn onto shirts and jackets; they lined the seams of pants; they were sprinkled onto the hair. In the process, the sequin—already loaded with connotations of excess—was "made over" to signify a sense of subcultural difference. Along similar lines, the clothing material of choice was typically satin, which was *always* designated by ribald dyes such as hot pink and lipstick red. The most flamboyant stylists also chose garment extras, which included feather boas (suggesting both strippers' accessories and evening wear), secondhand mink coats (usually tattered around the edges), glitter socks, shiny gold belts, and platform shoes. And the most inventive fans transformed their shoes into "glitter blocks," using "backwards" masking tape on the platform soles and applying "ribbons" of glitter sparkles.

Some fans wore the conventional Sunday corduroy sport jacket, which they "symbolically defiled" (Hebdige, *Subculture* 107) by attaching flashy rhinestone stick pins to the lapels. In a corresponding manner, tuxedo jackets were "stolen" from their traditional domains and worn with tattered hot pants, glitter hosiery, and 7-inch knee-high boots. In some cases, men wore the makeup traditionally worn by women, using diagrams in *Creem* magazine as guides. Women wore makeup in an innovative manner as well, applying the most "glamorous" and glaring shades of pop art—green, yellow, purple, and gold. And during any night of the Ziggy Stardust tour, one could have observed numerous stylists who had "seized" objects from the most discordant of contexts: Christmas tree lights were wired to batteries and artfully placed within hairstyles; silver canes were used to display arrogance; long neck scarves were tied around thighs and arms; gaudy pendants were used to signify coolness; buttons were removed from shirts so as to expose flesh; jeans were shrunk to the point of absurdity; women wore underwear as outerwear; men wore lounging pajamas and silk bathrobes; hair was cropped close and dyed a mirage of bright reds and oranges. In congruent manner, the looks of streetwalkers, strippers, hustlers, and pimps were often appropriated to suggest an alignment with the sexual underground. As a result, Frederick's of Hollywood became the couture fashion house, and clothing that was designed for the boudoir was worn openly on the street. In essence, all of these styles cohered in such a unique manner because the bearers worked toward reversing the traditional performer-audience dichotomy. Important to glitter rockers was the notion that they were the stars, and often, the offstage displays rivaled the onstage antics of performers.

Stylistic bricolage was also linked, at least philosophically, to the posturing of difference so apparent at Warhol's Factory studio, where the notion of a new kind of self-invented celebrity became the mainstay. In a highly analogous manner, glitter rock provided fans with the premise that they could instantaneously transform themselves into stars. In fact, "getting up" and concert posing became regimented forms of behavior, with fans dressing as much for themselves as they did for each other. In this sense, the premise that anyone could be famous was lifted from the Factory—and brought to the fans via glitter performers. In the process, glitter fans took the premise and made it their own.

At the same time, the "secret code" that underscored glitter style was sexual androgyny, an inscription that begged the question, Is the stylist female or male? To imagine the attention gained by such a question is also to envision one of the most empowering features of glitter style. Androgynous style did not simply recontextualize dominant modes of fashion in 1972, it also crossed cultural margins, where traditional and comparable references were nonexistent. As Tricia Henry observed, "What was considered strange enough in the context of theatrical performance was even stranger in a pedestrian context" (35-36). In a more direct manner, glitter rock fan Llana Lloyd claims:

> For the first time in our lives we didn't care what people thought and we didn't need authority, and we didn't need validation. The fact is we were capable of loving ourselves, glamorizing ourselves, so we could accept ourselves for who we were inside. (qtd. in Miller 102)

In light of these claims, I want to examine how glitter rock fans were empowered as they self-consciously constructed androgynous—and thereby "unnatural"— sexual images. In other words, if androgyny was the key to glitter's stylistic differentiation, then what exactly did glitter rock—as an example of mass-mediated transfusion—offer its fans?

Most important, glitter proposed to open up active inquiries concerning adolescent sexuality, and its themes reflected new sensibilities toward conventional formations and representations of gender. In this sense, whereas race and class were seen as the determining levels of British youth subcultures, compulsory heterosexuality is seen as the determining level of glitter rock. The difference, however, is that the former determinations intersected with specific subordinate populations that were resolving many of the tensions associated with postwar British class culture. Glitter rockers did not find themselves structured explicitly by the same kinds of determinations; after all, they were too dispersed (out-there) across the United States to be determined in a coherent manner by specific local conditions (as in Cohen's model of the

East Enders).[8] In this sense, the tensions they resolved are not to be viewed as subforms of parental negotiation, adaptation, and resistance. At the same time, the "shock of glitter" would have never been possible without the parental determination of heterosexual "harmony." As David Bowie's former wife Angela claims of the Ziggy Stardust years, "Gay people came to thank us personally for the exposure we gave to the subject. They were no longer afraid, they said, although unfortunately I wish that had been true in more cases" (74). Likewise, as Hebdige has suggested of glitter rockers, "they artfully confounded the images of men and women through which the passage from childhood to maturity is traditionally accomplished" (*Subculture* 62). Given these assertions, it becomes understandable as to the forces that were being resisted in 1972-73. And although I am not claiming that all those who aligned themselves with glitter were necessarily gay or bisexual, nor am I claiming that glitter was pure or uniformly radical, I am suggesting that it depicted possibilities outside of those determined by heterosexual (straight) culture.

Given the context in which glitter was operating, these possibilities were not to be taken lightly. In an "in-between" era that was both on the wing of Stonewall liberation efforts and on the verge of the sexually abandoned late-1970s disco culture, glitter rock provided gay and bisexual youth with their first-ever role models, and it suggested to others that they might try on the roles of sexual subordinates through experimenting with androgynous style. Along these lines, glitter can be interpreted as either the opaque but still seditious pronouncement of a style that had sexual undercurrents or, more directly, as a method whereby fans used visual style to directly announce sexual preference(s) or orientation(s). Where glitter rock is concerned, each assessment is valid in that the genre operated both at the surface level of style and at the more affective level, where it allowed fans an outlet for displaying their sexual feelings.

Although these issues do not allow for intensive elaboration in a retrospective sense, I want to argue that glitter rock did not deconstruct in any simple way the total framework that encompassed dominant gender myths of the early 1970s. To be sure, glitter style was also used by a number of musicians and fans who simply reproduced traditional gender relations through the construction of sexually subversive identities.[9] At the same time, the androgynous fashions and the matter-of-fact messages of glitter "anthems" actually operated in such a manner so as to initiate dynamic inquiries into the ways that sexual subordinates were often framed in the real world.[10] In addition, as I have implied, glitter rock exposed the gaps in the heterosexual hegemony, and in so doing, it provided for the empowerment of those fans who discovered that their sexual identities were not lodged within the framework of the dominant heterosexual milieu.

Now that I have given attention to some of the more exhilarating principles of glitter, I want to conclude by explaining the main procedure that this genre employed as it attempted to work against its own commercial incorporation. Here, we can consider the ways in which glitter rock's musical texts were distinguished from other forms of popular rock and roll at the time. Most important, glitter as music was incoherent in form, ranging from the sophisticated, art-styled rock of David Bowie to the protopunk shock rock of Iggy Pop. Add to these musical styles the pop-metal sounds of Mott the Hoople and the antimelodic vocals of Lou Reed. In addition, there was Roxy Music, a band that exhibited lush and ornamental musical bricolages. And on the far end of the spectrum, the New York Dolls terrorized the music world with their anarchistic guitar riffs and mock decadent vocals. Thus, unlike any prior form of rock and roll, glitter rock was an antigenre; its musicians always coalescing around one defining element: androgynous style. Appropriately, then, to an outsider glitter rock (as a genre) made no sense because its musical textures vehemently suggested that its (anti)form did not follow its function.

Yet, even though glitter rock attempted to remain incoherent, this quality did not provide complete insurance against commercial incorporation. By 1973, Kiss had managed to lift glitter rock's notions concerning costuming and theatricality, subsequently creating a comic book spectacle complete with fire spitting and bombarding lights.[11] In an even more incongruous manner, groups such as LaBelle and singers such as Suzi Quatro simply employed the camp appeal of glitter while ignoring the underlying premises of glitter style. In addition, by the end of 1973, Aerosmith had incorporated into its stage productions a number of glitter-oriented theatrical techniques while suppressing the gender-bending mannerisms associated with David Bowie. Such cases prove that certain aspects of glitter rock could indeed be translated into new contexts. Yet, as this process took full force, David Bowie had announced Ziggy Stardust's retirement from the stage. By October 1974, glitter fans and musicians took heed, and in turn, they staged a number of "goodbye-to-glitter" balls, "trash dances," and "conferences." And all of these activities were explicitly designed to signal the end of an era. Thus glitter rock was frantically determined not to let others to wrest it from context, and in an attempt to circumvent the incorporation process, glitter both constructed and celebrated its own demise.

In the interim between its arrival and its final days, the most significant aspect of glitter was its ability to articulate a method for denouncing traditional notions of sexuality and gender. And in the United States, the articulation of this method was realized thorough the process of co-optation. Only when glitter rock became a mass phenomenon did it suggest the age-old stereotype: "they" really *are* everywhere. By taking gay/bi imagery to an extreme, American glitter rockers thus staked a claim initiated by Warhol's Factory studio: "Announce yourself!" Along similar lines, glitter fans ultimately absorbed the same anti-middle-ground attitude that had dominated the Factory. If the adult straight world ruled the day, glitter rockers certainly proposed the frightening notion that youth could "rule the night." Therefore, glitter fans emulated the very facets of urban existence that adults probably feared the most. Finally, by taking Warhols' cannibalizing of popular culture one step further, glitter rock (as a musical genre and as a form of youth style) became its own subject. Completely celebratory and wildly self-conscious of its own surfaces, glitter rock endowed rock and roll with the possibility of having a theory of itself, one that challenged time-honored notions of authenticity while creating a falseness that could be read only in its own terms.

Notes

1. This analysis is also equally concerned with the ways that particular art theories had an impact on certain rock musicians.

2. Chambers and Hebdige studied at the Centre for Contemporary Cultural Studies during the 1970s. Frith, although often included in cultural studies anthologies, did not study at the center. Frith's work derives from the field of sociology.

3. See Koch 5.

4. See Clarke et al. 47.

5. I point out that this activity was "odd," because I am quoting from *Resistance through Rituals* (Clark et al.). The analysis of stylization therein has a great deal of relevancy for an analysis of the Factory.

6. See John Clarke, "Style" 177, and Hebdige *Subculture* 104.

7. See Clarke et al. 56.

8. I am not denying the impact of class, race, and other determinations in the lives of glitter fans. At the same time, glitter rock could not be located within the specific sites of reception that had previously determined British youth subcultures.

9. At the same time, I am not proposing that this is a text on gender issues. Yet questions raised by glitter's gender-bending style are pertinent to my analysis.

10. Many glitter fans for the first time experienced what it was like to be perceived as a "sexual other."

11. Kiss was also empowering to its audience. But in the early days of the band, it often intentionally aligned itself with glitter rock, and in that capacity, the band was simply imprecise.

Works Cited

Alice Cooper Prime Cuts: The Alice Cooper Story. Dir. Neal Preston. Prod. Charles Murdoch. Summer Place Productions, 1991. Dist. Polygram Video.

Alloway, Lawrence. "The Development of British Pop." *Pop Art.* Lucy R. Lippard. London: Thames & Hudson, 1966.

———. *Topics in American Art Since 1945.* New York: Norton, 1975.

Althusser, Louis. "Ideology and the Ideological State Apparatus." *A Critical and Cultural Reader.* Ed. Antony Easthope and Kate McGowan. Toronto: University of Toronto Press, 1992. 50-58.

"A Man Called Alice." *Melody Maker* 22 May 1971: 29.

Amaya, Mario. *Pop Art and After.* New York: Viking, 1966.

Artaud, Antonin. *The Theater and Its Double.* New York: Grove, 1958.

Bangs, Lester. "Alice Cooper: All American." *Creem* Jan. 1972: 18+.

———. "Alice Cooper: Punch and Judy Play the Toilets." *Creem* Jan. 1972: 18+.

———. "Dead Lie the Velvets Underground." *Creem* May 1971: 44+.

Barker, Martin and Anne Beezer, eds. *Reading into Cultural Studies.* London: Routledge, 1992.

Barthes, Roland. *Mythologies.* London: Paladin, 1973.

Beezer, Anne. "Dick Hebdige: Subculture: The Meaning of Style." *Reading into Cultural Studies.* Ed. Martin Barker and Anne Beezer. London: Routledge, 1992. 101-18.

Berlin, Gloria and Bryan, Bruce. "The Superstar Story." *Cine-Action!* (Winter 1986-87): 52-63.

Bockris, Victor. *The Life and Death of Andy Warhol.* New York: Bantam, 1990.

Bockris, Victor and Gerard Malanga. *Up-Tight: The Velvet Underground.* New York: Omnibus, 1983.

Boultenhouse, Charles. "The Camera as a God." *Film Culture Reader.* Ed. P. Adams Sitney. New York: Praeger, 1970. 136-39.

Bourdon, David. *Warhol.* New York: Harry N. Abrams, 1989.

Bowie, Angela. *Free Spirit.* London: Mushroom, 1981.

Bratlinger, Patrick. *Crusoe's Footprints: Cultural Studies in Britain and America.* London: Routledge, 1990.

Bronski, Michael. *Culture Clash: The Making of Gay Sensibility.* Boston: South End Press, 1984.
Cagle, Van. "David Johansen." *Punk* May-June 1979: 14-17.
Cann, Kevin. *Bowie: A Chronology.* New York: Simon & Schuster, 1983.
Carr, Roy and Charles Shaar Murray. *David Bowie: The Illustrated Record.* New York: Avon, 1981.
Carson, Tom. "David Bowie." *Rolling Stone Illustrated History of Rock and Roll.* Ed. Jim Miller. New York: Random House, 1980. 386-89.
Chambers, Iain. *Urban Rhythms: Pop Music and Popular Culture.* New York: St. Martin's, 1985.
Charlesworth, Chris. *David Bowie Profile.* New York: Proteus Books, 1981.
———. "Caught in the Act." *Melody Maker* 17 July 1971: 22.
Christgau, Robert. "Alice Cooper." *Alice Cooper Scrapbook* [collection of articles from *Rolling Stone*]. New York: Straight Arrow Publishers, n.d. 7.
———. "New York Dolls." *Stranded.* Ed. Griel Marcus. New York: Knopf, 1979. 132-47.
———. "The New York Dolls: Luv 'Em or Leave 'Em." *Creem* Nov. 1973: 62-63.
Clapton, Diana. *Lou Reed and the Velvet Underground.* New York: Proteus, 1982.
Clarke, Gary. "Defending Ski-Jumpers: A Critique of Theories of Youth Subcultures." *On Record: Rock, Pop, and the Written Word.* Ed. Simon Frith and Andrew Goodwin. New York: Pantheon, 1990. 81-96.
Clarke, John. *New Times and Old Enemies: Essays on Cultural Studies in America.* London: HarperCollins, 1991.
———. "Style." *Resistance through Rituals: Youth Subcultures in Post-War Britain.* Ed. Stuart Hall and Tony Jefferson. London: HarperCollins, 1976. 175-91.
Clarke, John et al. "Subcultures, Cultures and Class." *Resistance through Rituals: Youth Subcultures in Post-War Britain.* Ed. Stuart Hall and Tony Jefferson. London: HarperCollins, 1976. 9-79.
Cohen, Phil. "Sub-Cultural Conflict and Working Class Community." *Working Papers in Cultural Studies,* No. 2 (Spring). Birmingham, UK: Centre for Contemporary Cultural Studies, 1972.
Cooper, Alice and Steve Gaines. *Me, Alice.* Toronto: Longman, 1976.
Coplans, John. *Andy Warhol.* New York: New York Graphic Society, 1970.
County, Wayne. "Dear Wayne." *Rock Scene* March 1975: 59.
Creem August 1973: cover.
"Creem Casualty." *Creem* Dec. 1973: 82.
Cromelin, Richard. "Kiss It Goodbye" *Creem* Jan. 1975: 41.
Crone, Rainer. *Andy Warhol.* London: Thames & Hudson, 1970.
Crowe, Cameron. "Ground Control to Davy Jones." *Rolling Stone* 12 Feb. 1976: 78+.
Currie, David. "Pow It's Bowie" *Starzone* No. 2. n.d.: 16.
Currie, David and Gina Coyle. *Starzone* Summer 1987: 8.
Dalton, David and Lenny Kaye. *Rock 100.* New York: Grossett & Dunlap, 1977.
"Dear *Creem* Poll Roll." *Creem* July 1974: 7.
D'Emilio, John. *Sexual Politics, Sexual Communities: The Making of a Homosexual Minority in the United States, 1940-1970.* Chicago: University of Chicago Press, 1983.
Denisoff, R. Serge. *Solid Gold.* New Brunswick, NJ: Transaction, 1975. 283-322.
Doggett, Peter. *Lou Reed: Growing up in Public.* London: Omnibus, 1992.
Duncan, Robert. *The Noise: Notes from Rock and Roll Era.* New York: Ticknor & Fields, 1984.
Eco, Umberto. "Towards a Semiotic Enquiry Into the Television Message." *Working Papers in Cultural Studies.* Birmingham, England: Centre for Contemporary Cultural Studies, 1972.
Edmunds, Ben. "The Dolls Greatest Hits Vol. I." *Creem* Oct. 1973: 38-42.
"E's Flat Ah's Flat." *Creem* Dec. 1973: 2.
"First Annual New York Dolls Trivia Quiz." *Zoo World* 3 Jan. 1973: 10-11.

Fletcher, David Jeffrey. *David Bowie: Discography of a Generalist.* Chicago: F. Fergeson, 1979.
Frame, Pete. "Out in the Streets." *The Complete Rock Family Trees.* London: Omnibus, 1979.
Fricke, David. "Brian Ferry." *Musician Player and Listener* Nov. 1980: 42+.
Frith, Simon. "Letter from Britain." *Creem* Sept. 1972: 33.
———. "What's the Ugliest Part of Your Body?" *Creem* May 1974: 49+.
———. "Get Down and Get With It—Or the White Meanies Will Get You." *Creem* March 1973: 45+.
———. "Only Dancing: David Bowie Flirts with the Issues." *Zoot Suits and Second Hand Dresses.* Ed. Angela McRobbie. Boston: Unwin Hyman, 1989. 132-40.
———. *Sound Effects: Youth Leisure, and the Politics of Rock 'n' Roll.* New York: Pantheon, 1981.
Frith, Simon and Howard Horne. *Art into Pop.* London: Methuen, 1987.
Fuller, Peter. *Beyond the Crisis in Art.* London: Writers and Readers, 1980.
Geldzahler, Henry. "Some Notes on Sleep." *Film Culture Reader.* Ed. P. Adams Sidney. New York: Praeger, 1970. 300-301.
Gidal, Peter. *Andy Warhol: Films and Paintings.* New York: E. P. Dutton, 1969.
Goldberg, Roselee. *Performance: Live Art 1909 to the Present.* New York: Harry N. Abrams, 1979.
Gramsci, Antonio. *Selections from the Prison Notebooks.* Trans. and Ed. Q. Hoare and G. N. Smith. London: Lawrence & Wishart, 1971.
Gross, Elaine. "Where Are the Chickens, Alice?" *Rolling Stone* 15 Oct. 1970: 13.
Grossberg, Lawrence. "The Politics of Music and Youth: American Images and British Articulations." *Canadian Journal of Political and Social Theory* 11.1-3 (1987): 144-51.
———. *We Gotta Get Out of This Place: Popular Conservativism and Postmodern Culture.* New York: Routledge, Chapman & Hall, 1992.
Grossberg, Lawrence, Cary Nelson, and Paula A. Treichler, eds. *Cultural Studies.* New York: Routledge, 1992.
Hadleigh, Boze. "The Vinyl Closet." *Christopher Street* June 1991. Reprinted from Boze Hadleigh, *The Vinyl Closet: Gays in the Music Industry.* San Diego, CA: Los Hombres, 1991.
Hall, Stuart. "Cultural Studies and Its Theoretical Legacies." *Cultural Studies.* Ed. Lawrence Grossberg, Cary Nelson, and Paula A. Treichler. New York: Routledge, 1992. 277-94.
———. "Cultural Studies and the Centre: Some Problematics and Problems." *Culture, Media, and Language.* Ed. Stuart Hall, Dorothy Hobson, Andrew Lowe, and Paul Willis. London: Hutchinson, 1980. 15-47.
———. "Culture, Media, and the Ideological Effect." *Mass Communication and Society.* Ed. J. Curran et al. London: Arnold Press, 1977.
———. "Encoding/Decoding." *Culture, Media, Language.* Ed. Stuart Hall, Dorothy Hobson, Andrew Lowe, and Paul Willis. London: Hutchinson, 1980. 128-38.
Hall, Stuart and Tony Jefferson, eds. *Resistance through Rituals: Youth Subcultures in Post-War Britain.* London: HarperCollins, 1976.
Hebdige, Dick. *Hiding in the Light.* New York: Routledge, 1988.
———. *Subculture: The Meaning of Style.* London: Methuen, 1979.
———. "The Meaning of Mod." *Resistance Through Rituals.* Ed. Stuart Holland and Tony Jefferson. London: HarperCollins.
———. "Posing Threats, Striking Poses: Youth Surveillance and Display." *Substance* 1983.
Henry, Tricia. *Break All the Rules! Punk Rock and the Making of a Style.* London: Ann Arbor, 1989.
Herman, Gary. "Rebels Without a Cause." *Rock and Roll Babylon.* New York: G. P. Putnam, 1982: 65-79.
Hiemenz, Jack. "New York Dolls: From Welfare to the Waldorf." *Zoo World* 20 Dec. 1973: 26-27.
Hoggart, Richard. *The Uses of Literacy.* London: Penguin, 1958.
Hoggart, Stuart. *David Bowie: An Illustrated Discography.* London: Omnibus, 1980.

Holden, Stephen. "Lou Reed." *Rolling Stone* 25 May 1972: 68.
"Horizon." *Melody Maker* 7 Aug. 1971:10.
Holdenfield, Chris. *Rock '70.* New York: Pyramid, 1970.
Hollingsworth, Roy. "Can David Bowie Save New York from Boredom?" *Melody Maker* 7 Oct. 1972: 37-38.
———. "The Pop Establishment." *Melody Maker* 5 June 1971: 25.
———. "You Wanna Play House with the Dolls?" *Melody Maker* 22 July 1972: 17.
———. "American Music." *Melody Maker* 21 Oct. 1972: 50.
Hughes, Robert. "The Rise of Andy Warhol." *Art After Modernism.* New York: The New Museum of Contemporary Art and David R. Godine, 1984: 45-57.
"JEALOUS?" *Creem* Oct. 1973: 10.
Jefferson, Tony. "Cultural Responses of the Teds: The defense of space and status." *Resistance through Rituals: Youth Subcultures in Post-War Britain.* Ed. Stuart Hall and Tony Jefferson. London: HarperCollins, 1976: 81-96.
Jones, Dylan. *Haircults: Fifty Years of Styles and Cuts.* London: Thames & Hudson, 1990.
Jurgens, Tim. "David Bowie Gimme Your Hands." *Fusion* Jan. 1973: 17-21.
Koch, Stephen. *Stargazer.* New York: Praeger, 1973.
Letter. *Creem* Oct. 1973: 10.
Leyland, Winston. *Gay Sunshine Interviews.* Vol. 1. San Francisco: Gay Sunsine Press, 1978. 2 vols.
Lippard, Lucy R. *Pop Art.* London: Thames & Hudson, 1966.
Loud, Lance. "Los Angeles 1972-74: Glam Rock Loses Its Virginity." *Details* July 1992: 76-79.
———. "Rock Autopsy." *Rock Scene* March 1975: 16+.
Lubin, Peter. *Shades of Ian Hunter.* London: Ganton House, 1979.
MacDonald, Dwight. "A Theory of Mass Culture." *Mass Culture.* Ed. Bernard Rosenberg and David Manning White. Glencoe, IL: Falcon Wing's Press, 1957. 59-73.
Marchetti, Gina. "Documenting Punk: A Subcultural Investigation." *Film Reader 5.* Chicago: Northwestern, 1982: 269-284.
Marcus, Greil. Lecture. "Elvis Experience: 1982," sponsored by Memphis University, Memphis Tennessee, 7 Aug. 1982.
Marsh, David. "Introduction." *Alice Cooper Scrapbook* [collection of articles from *Rolling Stone*]. New York: Straight Arrow Publishers, n.d. 5.
———. "The MC5: Back on Shakin' Street." *Fortunate Son.* New York: Random House, 1985. 204-20.
———. "Too Much Too Soon." *Rolling Stone* 20 Jan. 1974: 79.
———. "Iggy in Exile: Love in the Fire Zone." *Creem* March 1973: 56-57.
Marx, Karl. "The Eighteenth Brumaire." *Marx and Engels Selected Works.* Vol. 1. London: Lawrence & Wishart, 1951.
McGuigan, Jim. *Cultural Populism.* London: Routledge, 1992.
McRobbie, Angela. "Settling Accounts with Subcultures: A Feminist Critique." *On Record.* Ed. Simon Frith and Andrew Goodwin. New York: Pantheon, 1990. 66-80.
Mekas, Jonas. "Notes after Reseeing the Movies of Andy Warhol." *Andy Warhol.* John Coplans. New York: New York Graphic Society, 1970. 139-45.
Melody Maker 22 Jan. 1972: 1.
Miles, Barry. *David Bowie Black Book.* London: Omnibus, 1980.
Miller, Fran. "Glitter Goddess of the Sunset Strip." *Fiz* March/April 1993: 100-102.
Nelson, Cary, Lawrence Grossberg, and Paula A. Treichler. "Cultural Studies: An Introduction." *Cultural Studies.* Ed. Lawrence Grossberg, Cary Nelson, and Paula A. Treichler. New York: Routledge, 1992. 1-16.

Nilsen, Per with Dorothy Sherman. *The Wild One: The True Story of Iggy Pop.* London: Omnibus, 1988.
"1969 . . . the Stooges." *Creem* 28 July 1969: 9.
Oakes, Emily. "The Advent of the Obnoxiods." *Rock* 10 Sept. 1973: 6.
"Osmondo Bendo." *Creem* Oct. 1973: 10.
Parsons, Tony. Liner Notes. *The New York Dolls Double Reissue.* Cat. #6641631CF. London: Mercury/Polygram, n.d.
Perew, Dave. "All That Glitters Is Not Gold." *Rock* May 1974: 13+.
Polhemus, Ted and Lynn Proctor. *Pop Styles.* London: Vermilian, 1984.
Pop, Iggy and Anne Wehrer. *I Need More.* New York: Karz Cohl, 1980.
"Purging the Zombatized Void with Alice Cooper." *Creem* 19 July 1970: 22.
"Random Notes." *Rolling Stone* 25 Oct. 1973: 26.
Ratcliff, Carter. "Andy Warhol: Inflation Artist." *Artforum* March 1985: 69-75.
Readers poll. *Creem* May 1974: 46-48.
Robbins, Wayne. "Berlin." *Zoo World* 3 Jan. 1994: 34.
Robinson, Lisa. "Alice Cooper Did Not Invent Glitter." *Creem* Nov. 1973: 50+.
———. "The New York Dolls in L.A." *Creem* Dec. 1973: 43+.
Rockwell, John. "Art Rock." *The Rolling Stone Illustrated History of Rock and Roll.* Ed. Jim Miller. New York: Random House, 1980. 317-52.
Rogan, Johnny. *Roxy Music.* London: W. H. Allen, 1982.
Rosenberg, Bernard. "Mass Culture in America." *Mass Culture.* Ed. Bernard Rosenberg and David Manning White. Glencoe, IL: Falcon's Wing Press, 1957. 3-12.
Rosenberg, Bernard and David Manning White, eds. *Mass Culture.* Glencoe IL: Falcon's Wing Press, 1957.
Ross, Andrew. *No Respect: Intellectuals and Popular Culture.* New York: Routledge, Chapman & Hall, 1989.
Roxon, Lillian. *Rock Encyclopedia.* New York: Grosset & Dunlap, 1978.
Rudis, Al. "A Man Called Alice." *Melody Maker* 22 May 1971: 29.
Russell, John et al. "Interview with G. R. Swenson." *Pop Art Redefined.* Ed. John Russell and Suzi Gablik. New York: Praeger, 1969. 116-19.
Savage, Jon. *England's Dreaming.* New York: St. Martin's, 1991.
Shaw, Arnold. *Dictionary of American Pop/Rock.* New York: Collier Macmillan, 1982.
Sinclair, John. "The MC5 Is a Whole Thing." *Countdown 1.* Ed. Editors of *Countdown Magazine.* New York: New American Library, 1970. 48-49.
Sitney, P. Adams. "Structural Film." *Film Culture Reader.* New York: Praeger, 1978: 326-349.
"The Six Wives of MXL SPLB." *Creem* July 1974: 8.
Smith, Patrick. *Warhol: Conversations about the Artist.* Ann Arbor, MI: UMI Research Press, 1988.
"A Star Is Born." *Melody Maker* 15 July 1972: 43.
Stein, Jean and George Plimpton. *Edie: An American Biography.* New York: Knopf, 1982.
Sugerman, Danny. "They Walk, They Talk, They Eat and Excrete! They're the New York Dolls." *Rock* 25 Mar. 1974. 20+.
Swift, Harry. "Inside Alice." *Alice Cooper Scrapbook* [collection of articles from *Rolling Stone*]. New York: Straight Arrow Publishers, n.d.
Taylor, I. and Wall, D. "Beyond the Skinheads." *Working Class Youth Culture.* Ed. G. Mungham. London: Routledge and Kegan Paul, 1976: 41-55.
Thompson, E. P. *The Making of the English Working Class.* London: Penguin, 1963.
Tomkins, Calvin. "Raggedy Andy." *Andy Warhol.* John Coplans. New York: New York Graphic Society, 1970. 8-14.
Tremlett, George. *The David Bowie Story.* New York: Warner, 1975.

Tucker, Ken. "All Shook Up: The Punk Explosion." *Rock of Ages.* Ed. Ed Ward et al. Englewood Cliffs, NJ: Prentice Hall, 1986. 547-60.
Turner, Graeme. *British Cultural Studies: An Introduction.* London: Unwin Hyman, 1990.
Tyler, Parker. *Underground Film: A Critical History.* New York: Grove, 1969.
Village Voice 31 Mar. 1966: n.p.
Warhol: Portrait of an Artist. Dir. and prod. Kim Evans. Home Vision Video, 1987.
Warhol, Andy and Pat Hackett. *Popism: The Warhol '60s.* New York: Harcourt Brace Jovanovich, 1980.
Watts, Michael. "Meet Rodney Bingenheimer, Friend of the Stars." *Melody Maker* 14 Aug. 1971: 22.
———. "Oh You Pretty Thing." *Melody Maker* 22 Jan. 1972: 19+.
Welch, Chris. "Alice's Moving Performance." *Melody Maker* 13 Nov. 1971: 16.
West, Mike. *The Life and Crimes of Iggy Pop.* Essex, UK: Babylon, 1987.
Wilcox, John. *The Autobiography and Sex Life of Andy Warhol.* New York: Other Scenes, 1971.
Williams, Raymond. *Culture and Society 1780-1950.* London: Penguin, 1958.
———. *The Long Revolution.* London: Penguin, 1961.
Williams, Richard. "Horizon." *Melody Maker* 7 Aug. 1971: 10.
———. "Roxy Music: Sound of Surprise." *Melody* Maker July 1972: 16.
———. "Your Mother Wears Combat Boots." *Creem* Aug. 1973: 30-31.
Willis, Ellen. "Velvet Underground: Golden Archive Series." *Stranded: Rock and Roll for a Desert Island.* Ed. Griel Marcus. New York: Knopf, 1979. 71-83.
———. *Lou Reed Rock and Roll Diary, 1967-1980.* New York: Arista, 1980.
Woodlawn, Holly with Jeff Copeland. *A Low Life in High Heels.* New York: HarperCollins, 1992.

Index

About the Author

Van Cagle is Associate Professor and Director of Audio Services at Doane College in Crete, Nebraska. He has published articles on subculture theory, youth culture, mass culture, and film. He has also worked as a music publicist, concert promoter, and band manager. In addition, he has served has an adviser to WTUL in New Orleans and KNDE in Crete.